Irish Folk Lore: Traditions And Superstitions Of The Country, With Humorous Tales

Lageniensis

In the interest of creating a more extensive selection of rare historical book reprints, we have chosen to reproduce this title even though it may possibly have occasional imperfections such as missing and blurred pages, missing text, poor pictures, markings, dark backgrounds and other reproduction issues beyond our control. Because this work is culturally important, we have made it available as a part of our commitment to protecting, preserving and promoting the world's literature. Thank you for your understanding.

IRISH FOLK LORE:

TRADITIONS AND SUPERSTITIONS OF THE COUNTRY;

WITH

HUMOROUS TALES.

BY

"LAGENIENSIS."

> "Tread where we may on Irish ground,
>   From Antrim's coast to wild Cape Clear,
> From East to West, no view is found
>   Without some ruin, rath, or mound,
>   To tell of times that were;
> Some lone round tower, yet strong and tall,
>   Though swept by many a wasting age;
> Some wayside cross, or abbey wall,
>   With marks of man's unholy rage;
> Some graven slab, or giant stone,
>   Notched with old signs and legends dim,
> Some hallowed nook, with green o'ergrown,
>   Or mouldering castle, bare and grim,
> Initial letters, all and each,
>   Of many a wild and curious story,
> Mute tongues, that, silent, ever preach
>   On Ireland's past of grief and glory."
>
> T. D. SULLIVAN.

GLASGOW: CAMERON & FERGUSON,
88 WEST NILE STREET.
LONDON: 12 AVE MARIA LANE.

DEDICATION.

TO

Denis Florence MacCarthy, Esq., M.R.I.A.

Deem it not wholly vain, though rude the verse,
    Which fain would hymn a true-born poet's praise;
Could thought unfold, or measured line rehearse,
    Flow'rs ought we wreathe like thine to grace thy bays.
If faint the heart its inner warmth reveal,
    Or friendship touch with hand unskill'd the lyre,
    Though glow or light ascend not from the fire,
Its essence lives, as depths of earth conceal
Most latent heat. To thee, so generous, kind,
    So nobly gifted, might just tones convey
This tribute offering of a grateful mind,
    Our willing zeal should tune a worthier lay,
    By friends so lov'd, by country prized, yet long
May Erin's themes abound in thy sweet strains of song.

                                        LAGENIENSIS.

PREFACE.

To attract and merit the Irish reader's attention, a book should not only enlighten his mind, but exalt and refine his intellect and feelings. The writer must clearly understand his own object, and cater somewhat discriminatingly for that class of patrons whose suffrages he seeks to woo and win. He must neither injuriously nor uselessly encroach on his reader's or on his own time. Hence an appropriate moral tone ought to pervade any work he produces. Again, the moralist who will instruct and enlighten, without contriving to present his theories and teaching in some pleasing guise, knows as small a part of his true aim, as the rhetorician, who might seek to convince by the use of sound and logical arguments, yet couched in a disarrayed, an unconnected, a spiritless, and an uninviting manner. In the following chapters, a variety of subjects has been introduced, with a desire to instruct and amuse the reader. Not alone the author's countrymen, but even others, who have entertained incorrect or prejudiced notions regarding our historic, traditional, literary, or speculative lore, may find something of interest to invite further research, and to remove previously-formed misconceptions.

Various causes have operated, in our time, to limit, or partially to remove, several features of national idiosyncrasy. Disuse of the Irish language, and with it a declining knowledge of old legendary poems and romances, conveyed through its medium—an extension of utilitarian and scientific education among our rising generations—a transition-state from old usages and from a primitive condition of society—the migrating and industrial tendency of this age—a gradual intermixture of the Celtic race with distant and distinctive populations: these, and many other obvious reasons, might be assigned for the gradual disappearance of many almost forgotten social customs, traditions, and popular superstitions. Those days seem to have departed, when

"tales pleased the hamlet, and news cheered the hall,
And the tune of old times was still welcome to all,"

as a native poet * has so appropriately recorded his reminiscences of the past, in one of his most beautiful minor poems. Few things are so evanescent in their

* The Rev. James Wills.

nature as folk lore remembrances and theories; but their generic peculiarities have been fairly preserved in our ancient and modern literature. Of this source for information the writer has availed himself. Thousands of interesting local legends have been totally forgotten, however, because unrecorded; and yet many of these were essentially important for a perfect solution of historic problems, while they characteristically illustrated a people's moral and intellectual organization or culture, and speculative opinions. In the following collection, only a few Irish legends, mostly acquired from tradition, have been produced by the writer. They are introduced, in a simple garb and shape, adopted without much literary pretension, and as an experiment on public indulgence. If unnoticed in some form, such as that now presented, it is probable those legends and traditions must have been consigned altogether to oblivion. Should they afford any amount of recreation or information to the reader, the result will amply suffice for the writer's object.

Under one shape or other, certain familiar and romantic fables, with some possible variations of detail, have found expression in nearly every country of the world. These myths, having once made an impression on the popular mind, assume developments more or less accommodated to existing natural customs and habits of thought. For centuries, they pass current from sire to son, surviving even the more important but prosaic facts of authentic history. They grow from shadows into forms, and then become the folk lore of myriad retailers, through every phase of song or story.

Dublin, *April, 1870.*

CONTENTS.

CHAP.		PAGE
I.	The Living Ghost; or, Fallacies from over-hasty Conclusions,	3
II.	Lackeen Castle, O'Kennedy, and the Phooka,	20
III.	Fairy Mythology of the Irish,	30
IV.	Apparitions and Fetches,	39
V.	Changelings, Fairy-Men, and Fairy-Women,	43
VI.	Buried Treasures,	53
VII.	The Merrow-Maiden and Merrow-Man,	56
VIII.	The Lianhaun Shee,	60
IX.	O'Carroll's Banshee and Terryglass Castle,	64
X.	The Three Wishes; or, All is not Gold that Glitters,	69
XI.	Fairy Haunts and Fairy Celebrities,	74
XII.	Lake Habitations and Spirits,	83
XIII.	Monument Bushes and Road-side Cairns,	86
XIV.	Mr. Patrick O'Byrne in the Devil's Glen; or, Folly has a Fall,	89
XV.	Hy-Breasail; or, the Blessed Island,	114
XVI.	The Féar Gortha; or, Hungry Grass: a Tale of the Irish Famine,	126
XVII.	Various Popular Fancies,	135
XVIII.	Traces of Druidism in Ireland,	139
XIX.	The Wizard Earl of Kildare,	155
XX.	The Realms of Fairydom,	159

CONTENTS.

CHAP.	PAGE
XXI.—The Water-Sheerrie; or, Bog-Sprite,	166
XXII.—The Fomorian Warrior, Balor of the Evil Eye,	172
XXIII.—Ancient Planetary, Elementary, and Idolatrous Worship of the Pagan Irish,	182
XXIV.—Ancient Festival Celebrations in Ireland,	198
XXV.—All-Hallows' Eve, with its various Divinations and Festive Customs,	212
XXVI.—Memorials of Redwood Castle,	220
XXVII.—Irish Marriage Customs,	234
XXVIII.—The Solitary Fairies,	237
XXIX.—Divinations, Enchantments, Astrology, and Nostrums,	242
XXX.—Dungal the Recluse, a Learned Irishman of the Ninth Century,	253
XXXI.—Popular Notions concerning Good and Ill Luck,	285
XXXII.—Tir-Na-n-Og,	290
XXXIII.—Saint Legends,	295
XXXIV.—Sprite Frolics and Peculiarities,	303
XXXV.—Irish Fortune-Tellers, and Predictions,	308

IRISH FOLK LORE.

CHAPTER I.

THE LIVING GHOST; OR, FALLACIES FROM OVER-HASTY CONCLUSIONS.

> "Men left their beds, and night-capp'd heads
> Popp'd out from every casement;
> The cats ran frightened on the leads;
> Dijon was all amazement."
>
> CAMPBELL.

THE town and parish of A——, in the county of K——, were placed under the zealous ministrations of Father Gerald D——, during a rather lengthened residence of Friar Cummings in this same vicinage. Both of these clerical personages were on terms of friendly intimacy. A station dinner rarely came off without a social gathering being contrived by the delighted host, who almost invariably invited the parish priest and friar. Father Gerald well knew the chords he might touch to best advantage, whilst evoking the play of Friar Cummings's fantastic and droll reminiscences, during an after-dinner conversation. His parishioners loved their accomplished P. P. for his good-humoured jokes; and his capital stories, told with rare effect, rendered the portly friar no less popular amongst them. Interruptions of this social intercourse, however, occasionally occurred. A month's sojourn at the salt water might sometimes leave the parish widowed for a time, when the pastor had finished his round of Easter stations; and a questing excursion or a distant conventual visit often withdrew our Franciscan from the sight, but not from recollection, of the parishioners.

A chapter meeting of his order, about to be convened at Rome, required the imposing presence and sagacious counsel of Friar Cummings, during an important phase of his missionary career. The good parish priest and people of A—— must therefore reluctantly resign themselves to the loss of his invaluable ministrations and fascinating anecdotes, for the space of a long summer's season. But, with their heartfelt prayers for a pleasant and prosperous voyage to the Eternal City, our worthy religious began to make the necessary preparations for his departure. Father Cummings was not the man to keep his movements concealed from any of his friends—for foes he had none; and on the day appointed, after counting carefully over numerous articles of luggage consigned to the guard, he took the sole vacant seat on the outside of Peter Purcell's mail-coach, with a complacent and dignified demeanour. A numerous and noisy crowd of beggars were around. "Yer own Biddy Murphy, yer Riverence!" "Ah! thin, yer own Molly Kelly, Father dear; don't forget her and the childher." They vociferated a thousand benedictions on the "darlint of a charitable gintleman," in return for some loose copper distributed amongst them. One old crone in particular fervently exclaimed, "May every letther on the penny you gev me be a bright mould candle to light yer Riverence to glory!"

As the mail-coach moved away from the office at

A——, on to the Dublin highroad, nearly all the more substantial burgesses of their town crowded at street doors and upper windows to exchange a parting salute or a kindly word with the reverend voyager. Some, at least, supposed that the heads of Father Cummings's religious order in Rome might transfer the sphere of his usefulness, by making him superior of a respectable priory in the capital of the Catholic world; and that their old town would thenceforth cease to be blessed by his presence. This conclusion, it was thought, might be reasonably inferred from Father Gerald's mysterious innuendoes to Father Cummings himself on many previous occasions, and especially pending this anticipated event of his approaching visit to Rome. Whilst the friar humbly protested his inability and inexperience to assume any exalted dignity in the Church, the shrewd parishioners always fancied it cost his own convictions and feelings a strong effort to accord with these oft-repeated protestations.

Half a century ago, the strange idea of radiating iron railroads and running carriages by steam, from Dublin to the most distant coasts of Ireland, would have been considered an effort of imagination, too wild even for the disordered fancies of poet or romancist. The fire-ship, speeding on its course from the magnificent harbour of Cork over the broad Atlantic, while freighted with saloon and steerage passengers, telegrams, newspapers, letters, and merchandise, would have been classed amongst mythic creations of the Middle Age troubadours, or with some Oriental necromancy of the *Arabian Nights' Entertainments*. The patriot peer, Cloncurry himself, could hardly imagine such a state of things, when he projected a ship canal through the centre of Ireland, less with a view to define the ancient boundaries of Leath Cuinn and Leath Mogha, than to open a passage for Liverpool liners on their voyage to the western hemisphere. The Dargans and Malcolmsons were yet in embryo, and had hardly entertained, even as day-dreams, those enlightened projects and patriotic enterprises which must honourably perpetuate their names to future ages, in connection with the commercial and social prosperity of Ireland and the British empire. Canal boats, caravans, stage-coaches, and outside jaunting-cars, furnished the usual modes of internal conveyance by land and water; and the Bournes, Latouches, or Bianconis of the day were responsible for limbs and luggage of the subjects of our realm, when travelling through the Emerald Isle, for business purposes or on tourist excursions.

Beside him on the coach, Father Cummings soon discovered a brother clergyman's garb, hardly disguised under a dark kerseymere travelling overcoat, and a muffler like his own, with an umbrella spread to guard against the effects of a passing shower. Kindly greeting and conversation at once engaged the attention of the fellow-travellers, whose physical characteristics, age, and dress, bore a remarkable similitude. Condition of the weather, prospect of the crops, religious, political, and other topics, were duly discussed. Before their arrival at the metropolis, Father Cummings tendered the hospitalities of his residence in A—— to the Munster clergyman, if the latter could favour him with a visit on any future occasion. Printed cards were not the fashion of the day, at least amongst country priests; yet, an unimportant note, under an envelope, directed to Father Cummings, was transferred to the strange clergyman, and, of course, it furnished a correct address of the good-natured Franciscan. A formidable pile of luggage served as an effectual barricade, to screen the reverend Fathers from view of the coach-guard and passengers in the back seats. The *vis-à-vis* fellow-travellers of the clergymen appeared to have formed a coterie to themselves. The driver in front had his attention wholly occupied by an inquisitive English tourist, on his left, by the graceful winding of his flexible whip-cord, and by the easy flow of long reins, whilst directing the rapid movements of his four-in-hand team.

The usual scene of excitement ensued, when the mail-coach drew up at the office in Dublin. Mendicants were clamorous for halfpence; newsvendors proclaimed, with shrill cries, the titles of city newspapers; jarvey drivers with vehicles were jammed together, awaiting their expected fares. A selection once made by descending stage passengers, the guard and driver busied themselves in handing down trunks and hat-cases, superintending their distribution in the wells of jaunting-cars, whilst pocketing shillings and half-crowns bestowed in return for these services. Former occupants of outside seats on the mail-coach were soon dispersing to their several hotels or respective destinations. Father Cummings, with a warm shake of the hand, bade his brother priest adieu. Our traveller rattled off with his cumbersome appurtenances, to engage his passage across channel, on the Dublin and Liverpool packet. Soon afterwards she steamed out of the harbour, with her living freight of pigs and cattle, *spalpeens,* traders, and landed gentry.

When the bustle around Peter Purcell's coach had subsided, and all the passengers, with one exception, had parted in various directions, the fine portly, clerical, old gentleman, in travelling costume, was noticed moving slowly and painfully across the street, after having paid his fees to the driver and guard, who had placed his luggage on an outside jaunting-car. Suddenly he dropped on the pavement. An alarmed crowd collected around him. He was found struggling in a convulsive and unconscious state. Almost immediately afterwards the services of a doctor were in requisition. Scarcely had the patient been conveyed to an adjoining house, when the spark of life was found to be extinct. Immediate notice of the melancholy occurrence was conveyed to the city coroner. Preparations were accordingly made to empannel a jury, and hold the *post-mortem* examination usual in such cases. No friends appeared to claim his body, although an account of the circumstances attending the unknown gentleman's death, and a minute description of his *personnel*, appeared in evening and morning editions of the city daily papers. An intelligent jury having been selected, with a coroner at their head, they proceeded to examine the defunct body in the first instance. A very superficial inspection of the deceased gentleman's habiliments established as a fact, beyond all question, that he was a Catholic clergyman. A physician, who was first called to witness the death-agony of deceased, and one of the most eminent amongst the faculty—in a city renowned for the excellence of its medical practitioners—proved to the satisfaction of both coroner and jury, that apoplexy terminated the mortal career of the subject of their *post-mortem* investigation. Name and address of the reverend deceased were matters that presented somewhat greater difficulty, and his identification required a more prolonged investigation. Trunks and valises, which belonged to him, and which were as yet unopened, had been subjected to a careful scrutiny, without affording a clue to the information required. No linen or handkerchiefs could be discovered marked with initials; no name was found on the fly-leaf of his breviary; no card, no label, no bill or entry, in his pocketbook, serving to indicate the name and address of friend or correspondent. A note, however, was produced from an inside vest pocket, which served, to a certain extent, as a solution of this mystery. It was directed to the Rev. Father Cummings, A——,

and afforded strong grounds for supposing that the deceased clergyman was identical with the aforesaid renowned personage. The coach-guard and driver were awaiting examination at the time this letter was produced, and it was read before all who were present at the inquest. When afterwards called upon to furnish testimony in the case, a single glance at the corpse enabled both of them to recollect all the circumstances connected with their late departure from A——. The name of Father Cummings had been so often pronounced, by the good people of that town, previous to their starting for Dublin, and having been applied to the poor gentleman now stretched before them as a lifeless remnant of humanity, no further evidence was required, as no other seemed available, in enabling the coroner and jury to arrive at an official conclusion. Short-hand reporters were in attendance, as the public anxiously awaited the issue. On the day immediately succeeding this inquest, columns of the daily papers were filled with a report of testimony given by several parties examined in the case. This investigation concluded with the following verdict:—
"After a careful examination into all the particulars of this melancholy occurrence, we find that the deceased clergyman, Rev. Father Cummings, of A——, died suddenly of apoplexy, on the —— day of the present month, in Sackville Street, Dublin." A despatch was sent without delay to Father Gerald D——, as being a person most likely to communicate the result of this inquest to friends and relatives of the deceased; whose remains, having been duly shrouded and coffined, were intended to be consigned to those parties who might charge themselves with the duty of interment.

No sooner had this news arrived at A——, than a general gloom and lamentation spread amongst the townspeople of all classes and denominations; for

Father Cummings merited the rare distinction of having been a universal favourite. The sorrowing parish priest and some immediate friends of the friar at once started for Dublin, to make necessary arrangements for an interment of the body in their parish chapel. The hearse and mourning-coaches were met by numerous and respectable bodies of parishioners at various points along the route, and the funeral cortège occupied a full mile of road when approaching the immediate vicinity of A——. A large attendance of diocesan clergy, secular and regular, assisted at these funeral obsequies. Amidst tears and lamentations of an afflicted and impressible people, the remains were consigned to their resting-place. With a sympathetic feeling, Father Gerald faultered out the last prayers for the dead. Dull sounds of shovelled earth falling on the coffin gradually ceased as the grave closed over its victim, whilst the large assemblage of mourners dispersed to their respective homes. On the following Sunday, after mass, a meeting of parishioners was convened, a committee was formed, and resolutions were adopted to commemorate, in a suitable manner, the merits and virtues of the deceased, by the erection of a monument.

Meantime, the clerical gentleman, who had taken passage for Liverpool, passed direct to Dover, and soon journeyed on through the classic land of Italy, to his and Byron's "city of the soul," where he accepted their kindly-proffered hospitalities from his brethren at St. Isidore's convent. The necessary business connected with his mission having been fully transacted, time had been afforded for frequent visits to churches, convents, and charitable institutions. Even the well-known classic remains of pagan Rome proved objects of interest to our travelled Hibernian Father. It seemed strange, however, although he had left particular directions at home to have letters and newspapers posted to the quarters he actually occupied, in this "Niobe of nations;" yet his correspondents appeared to have been completely oblivious of his existence, as neither billet nor journal arrived from the island of his birth and affections. The longest tours of pleasure or business must have an end; and the object of Father Cummings's Roman visit having been accomplished to his satisfaction, a natural anxiety to learn what had been accomplished in Ireland during the interval, induced him to arrange his affairs and dispose his effects for departure. Having experienced a few of the usual inconveniences, as well as the pleasurable excitement, of continental travel, a rough channel passage and a distressing sea-sickness terminated his troubles, as he arrived at one of the Dublin hotels, where he procured rest and refreshment. On the following day, our continental traveller, with other passengers, might be seen mounted on the outside of Peter Purcell's coach, as it cleared the suburbs of the Irish metropolis, on its way towards the beautiful city of Cork.

As a matter of course, horses and passengers must be changed at the several stages. When the coach entered the principal street of A——, and drove onwards to the hotel, our clergyman on top recognized along his route familiar faces, which stared at him aghast, but with nothing of that friendly expression or recognition he evidently expected. Ejaculations of surprise and astonishment greeted his ears on all sides, as the gaping townspeople communicated to each other some mysterious intelligence. "Be jabers!" exclaimed one of the townsmen, "that gintleman on the coach is as like poor Father Cummins—God rest his sowl in glory!—as one egg is like another!" No sooner were the horses brought to a stand, however, and the Father had intimated to the guard his intention of proceeding no farther, when the bustling ostlers appeared leading fresh horses from their stables round to the street, to replace panting roadsters of the last stage.

At this moment, a portly figure in clerical costume stood erect from his seat, and shouted forth in a stentorian voice to the foremost of these advancing grooms,—" Tom, my boy—Tom, I say—lend a hand to the guard here, till ye take my baggage into yer decent master's bar-room." The familiar sound of Father Cummings's voice produced an electric shock on the astonished ostlers' nerves. Dropping the reins of their horses, they at once bolted right forward through the open hall door of the hotel, vociferating in an agony of terror,—" Och, masther, jewel! Och, misthress, dear! Molly, *alana machree!* May I never sin!—oh tundher and ages!—if the ghost ov Father Cummings—body and bones!—hasn't come up from Dublin on the coach, widh the outside passengers!"

The entire household was in commotion. " Arrah! none of yer nonsense, you ugly *gomalachs!*" cried the incredulous and excited innkeeper, hurrying forward in the passage; " I'm blest if the fools hav'nt taken lave of their seven sinses!"

" Tom!—Christy! for mercy's sake, what has happened?" gasped the helpless landlady, as the bounding ostlers, with averted stare, dashed against their mistress. They brushed past her prostrate figure, which nearly blocked up a narrow passage between the front and postern door.

" Goodness gracious!" chimed in the terrified parlour-maid, Molly, who rushed wildly to the front door; " what's that they say about Father Cummins's ghost?" And on the instant she observed the veritable apparition itself approaching with rapid strides from the middle of the street, bang went the massive door, as a barrier against this invading spirit; the bolt was hastily shot into its locker; and with consummate presence of mind, the fragment of a boiled potato was thrust into the keyhole.

Then came a reaction. Having taken these hasty measures in securing her retreat, the naturally rubicund cheeks of poor Molly became white as a sheet of paper; her strength and breath began to fail; her mental faculties became disordered; she reeled back on her mistress, now beginning to assume an upright position, and with a faint scream cried out, "Oh, the ghost! Father Cummins's ghost! the Lord purtect huz from the hands ov all our inimies!" A tremendous rub-a-dub-dub, rat-a-tat-tat, resounded without intermission from the hall door knocker. All the spring bells in the kitchen entry were ringing a furious peal, as both mistress and maid hurried away, filled with terror and confusion.

The sprite, finding his efforts to take this front line of intrenchments by storm ineffectual, popped round through the gateway to effect an entrance by the rear, just as a contingent of the retreating garrison was escaping on that quarter. Tom and Christy at once fell back to the sally-port that opened on the scullery porch. Molly's defensive strategy was successfully repeated in the face of an advancing enemy. Failing to enter through the door, his ghostship next appeared with the most prominent features grotesquely flattened against the glass of an adjoining window that commanded a view of the terrified figures in the passage. The setting of his portrait did not improve its outlines, nor heighten the colour of our ghost's distorted physiognomy. Every conscious member of the establishment beat a hasty retreat to the hotel upper stories. On venturing to peer out through one of the street casements, the innkeeper and his beleaguered household beheld their retreating and discomfited spectre retire from the gateway passage into the street. As he advanced, however, men, women, and children hastily withdrew on his approach; shopmen hurriedly secured their half-doors and shutters; front and rear entrances were strongly barricaded. Since the memorable sack of A―― by the Danes—"the bloody villains!"—its honest burghers never had their dreams more rudely disturbed than in this present instance, owing to the unexpected return of their ghostly fellow-citizen.

The rumour of Father Cummings's "sperrit" having appeared in town was soon conveyed to the rector, who happened to have called a vestry meeting of his congregation in the Protestant church. With no small degree of curiosity and disbelief, this whole conclave hurried towards the entrance gate, to learn the cause of all the strange commotion thus excited. On beholding the only group presenting itself in the street, our apparition rapidly advanced towards his separated brethren, with all his living proportions in full relief. When sufficiently near for purposes of identification, the rector and his flock were struck with a sudden panic. Through an instinct of self-preservation, each man felt desirous of placing himself in position to the rear of his more advanced companions. A slow, retrograde movement at first commenced. The ghost, calling the rector by name, requested him and his friends to stop until he should approach. But the minister fled within his own graveyard inclosure, followed by the disordered ranks of his hastily retreating parishioners.

Just at this moment appeared on the scene the parish priest, who had been called away to the country upon particular duty. He had heard, from some of his terror-stricken people, about the general consternation created in A―― by the friar's return *in the spirit*. When Father Gerald rode into town, his usual resolute air and determination served to inspire with confidence crowds that poured in from the country, and townspeople, who now ventured to leave their barricaded houses. They fully expected that their pastor, on producing his breviary, would read that portion of the ritual which must effectually relegate the perturbed spirit to its final resting-place, popularly believed to be somewhere near the shores of the Red Sea. Meanwhile, as our ghost appeared in view, and gradually approached along the deserted street, Father Gerald began to advance with greater caution, whilst his supports in the rear maintained a more respectful distance. With perspiring brow and rather difficult breathing, the parish priest suddenly reined his steed. In failing accents he faltered out: "My poor, dear friend!—Father Cummings!—will you speak?—in the name of all that's good!—and tell me what I can do for you, to give rest to your ——."

The personage addressed rushed forward with a preternatural illumination of eye and earnestness of action, crying out, "Ah! then, Father Gerald, it's myself that's delighted to see you again, after a long absence; and, as I'm blest, if you don't come along with me to my own happy home, when ——."

"Oh! the Lord have mercy on me!" exclaimed the parish priest; "sure enough, I find my mission on earth is drawing to a close!" Overcome with the intensity of his emotions, he dismounted from his horse on the street, and fell there apparently lifeless. A wild scream of horror immediately burst from his terrified parishioners. With the rearing quadruped, still bridled and saddled, they might be seen scattering in different directions.

The innocent subject of all this terror and confusion, in a state of perfect bewilderment, stood for some time over the parish priest's prostrate form. His chapel chanced to be near, and the entrance doors stood ajar, whilst a look cast in that direction prompted the thoughtful friar to raise his insensible friend in a pair of brawny arms, and bear him inside the porch. Here a little water, found in a vessel, was poured over the pastor's pallid forehead. His people, however, only saw disappearing figures enter the sacred building; and an impression was immediately conveyed to their sorrowing minds, that their reverend spiritual teacher had been summoned away from earth to receive the reward of his labours, and to enjoy for evermore beatific companionship with the deceased friar.

Meanwhile, the first unusual object that arrested Father Cummings's attention on entering the chapel was a handsome mural marble tablet, lately erected, and in a style of artistic excellence, betokening the hand of an accomplished sculptor. Finding all efforts to restore the parish priest to his senses ineffectual, the friar's curiosity induced him to approach nearer to the monument, on which he found the following inscription:—

UNDERNEATH LIE THE MORTAL REMAINS OF

THE REV. PATRICK CUMMINGS, O.S.F.,

WHO FOR MANY YEARS DISCHARGED THE DUTIES OF
HIS SACRED MINISTRY, WITH GREAT ZEAL AND
PIETY, IN THE TOWN AND PARISH OF A——,
AND WHO DIED SUDDENLY IN DUBLIN,
MAY THE —TH, 18—.

AS AN ENDURING TESTIMONIAL TO HIS TALENTS, VIRTUES,
AND MERITS, HIS FRIENDS AND ADMIRERS
HAVE ERECTED THIS MONUMENT,
BY PUBLIC SUBSCRIPTION.

REQUIESCAT IN PACE. AMEN.

The mystery attaching to the friar's strange reception, on his return to A——, was now fully solved. After a succession of fruitless attempts had been made to restore the parish priest to consciousness, Father Cummings was at last enabled to arouse him, and to explain that his Franciscan friend was yet in the land of the living. However, an account given of circumstances attending his own funeral by his friend, the resuscitated pastor, proved altogether inexplicable to the returned tourist. On being questioned about incidents connected with his late journey to Dublin, Father Cummings casually alluded to the name and physical characteristics of his clerical fellow-traveller on the coach. Then Father Gerald was enabled to recollect how, shortly after the celebration of our friar's obsequies, a notice appeared in some of the public papers, and to this effect, that a certain clergyman from the south of Ireland had taken his departure for the metropolis; whence, as no account had been transmitted from him at that particular date, his friends felt specially anxious to receive further information regarding him. The plot being thus fairly unravelled, fully accounted for a delusion under which the pastor and people of A—— laboured for so long a period. Father Cummings was heartily congratulated on the conclusion of an intricate investigation, which established as a fact his living presence in A——, when its inhabitants supposed his virtues already ripe for Heaven.

In a short time the parish priest was on the deserted street. But his appearance only alarmed the townspeople still more; for they felt fully convinced he was returning as an apparition. A vague dread of the result to be apprehended confined each individual to his house. The only friendly place of refuge afforded was the shelter of the Protestant church. The rector and his people not being witnesses of Father Gerald's late mishap, met him at the half-opened door, but with evident agitation depicted on their countenances. Mutual explanations were exchanged between the parish priest and the rector; a laugh of wild merriment succeeded; the whole Protestant body ventured into the street, with the priest at their head. The Catholics, gathering courage, ventured out by degrees, until the concourse comprised every inhabitant of that ancient town. Father Gerald, mounting a rostrum, addressed the multitude. He entered into a lucid statement explanatory of the grounds on which their false alarm had been based. The veritable Father Cummings made his appearance towards the close of this narrative; the people, with joyous acclamations, rushed to meet him, and heartily congratulated him on his safe, but heretofore dreaded, return amongst them.

Little time was lost in communicating with some Munster friends of the deceased priest, whose remains were interred in the chapel of A——. In a few days the corpse was exhumed, and translated to a family resting-place, in one of the southern graveyards. As a matter of course, the newly erected marble tablet was removed from its position, and the inscription was carefully effaced. A few years passed over, when both Friar Cummings and Father Gerald were gathered to the tomb. The monumental slab, however, served a future useful purpose. A town hall in A—— underwent certain building restorations. The monumental tablet filled a niche in the frontage afterwards erected, and it suitably contributed to general architectural effect. Had the epitaph remained, this sculptured memorial would furnish abundant testimony to the truth of our narrative already detailed. Yet local tradition preserves all circumstances connected with the friar's resuscitation. The ornamental slab, with its effaced inscription, is pointed out; and it will long continue to arrest the inquisitive traveller's attention, as he rambles for purposes of business or pleasure through the ancient town of A——.

It is a common fault with some persons, who have only limited sources for obtaining correct information on many points, and fallible judgment in combining circumstances which pass under observation, that they are very frequently urged to form hasty and erroneous conclusions. Such aptitude for self-deception depends greatly on allowing imagination to anticipate our reasoning faculties. Idle rumours are often taken for established facts. Sufficiently impartial inquiries rarely precede opinions at which men too easily arrive. A single false deduction in a chain of reasoning is enough to disturb true logical consequences. On almost every question, more than one special view should be taken. Nothing can be conceived more difficult in certain cases, than to reconcile appearances with facts. Besides, human testimony is liable to deceive, and to be deceived. It often happens that inconsiderateness likewise influences prepossessions or opinions, which issue through a distorted medium of preoccupation, interest, prejudice, or passion. But want of careful thought and of mental culture, even with the most conscientious desire of forming truthful opinions, tends especially towards incorrect judgments and decisions. One moment's sage reflection would often arrest a variety of absurdities and excesses into which several hot-brained people are apt to fall. Not always, indeed, are the results of such mistakes so fortunately solved, nor so happily ended, as in the *dénouément* of our present story.

CHAPTER II.

LACKEEN CASTLE, O'KENNEDY, AND THE PHOOKA.

" Tall are the towers of O'Ceinneidigh."
THOMAS DAVIS.

" The Phooka horse holds his frantic course
Over wood and mountain-fall."
R. D. WILLIAMS.

IN the townland of Lackeen, about one mile eastwards from the village of Lohra, and in the barony of Lower Ormond, County of Tipperary, there stands a fine old castle, in an almost perfect state of preservation. It is, indeed, well worthy of a visit; for the O'Kennedy's old castle of Lackeen has features of special attraction. Around its square keep and high battlements, the site of Piperstown village, Gortapeephra, and the Deer Park are pointed out, with an old, ruined church, and rich meadows or paddocks extended far and wide. A beautiful vale, through which a small stream gurgles along towards Lohra village, is an additional feature of interest. The scenery in this neighbourhood is highly picturesque, and the feudal fortress heightens its general effect. Long before the Anglo-Norman invasion, the O'Kennedys were lords of Ormond, and long subsequent they figure as chiefs and warriors in the Irish annals. The wars of the Stuarts and the Irish Brigade campaigns bear testimony to their fiery valour and earnest zeal in the cause for which their swords had been drawn. Their castle of Lackeen still exhibits rude grandeur, combined with the social discomforts of an Irish chief's residence during the

Middle Ages. There we yet trace the old vaulted understorey, cellar, or kitchen, and the geometrical, winding stone-stairs in one angle of the building; while narrow, ashlar-dressed doorways are seen leading into upper compartments of various sizes, from the fine old drawing or community room to the dimly-lighted chambers and guard-rooms. Narrow loophole windows, with some of larger size, penetrate those massive walls. Even the stone-built dove-cot, near the upper parapet, deserves inspection; while ruinous outworks, around this battlemented keep, give some idea regarding the capabilities of a fortalice, strong for purposes of offence and defence, in times long past. In the early part of last century this castle was inhabited; a few inexpensive restorations would even yet render it habitable. A modern roof, erected by the present owner, rises over the walls and parapets, which have sustained little damage from "time's effacing fingers." But the glories and the properties of the grand and high-spirited O'Kennedys have wasted away through confiscations, continental campaigning, and hospitable living; nor are there any representatives of the former estated gentlemen left. Still, well-to-do farmers and middle class occupiers, bearing the name, preserve respect for this much revered family, throughout the whole extent of Lower Ormond barony.

Beneath the castle walls, yet removed to a fair distance, an antique-looking, slated mansion, belonging to Mr. R——, the present proprietor of Lackeen lands, has its surroundings of an inclosed garden, out offices, and lawn. Aged hawthorns and other forest trees lend a sheltered and comfortable appearance to the place exteriorly; while within, domestic and kindly relations exist between master and man, the mistress and her handmaids.

"Yerra, musha, but it was a fine ould cashtle in its day, so it was, and many's the quare ould sthory's toult about it, so there is," said Owen Callanan, as he sat before a blazing turf fire in the kitchen of Mr. R——'s house, at Lackeen, with a large group of listeners, disposed in a semicircle around the grate. Reflected flames flickered over the ruddy faces of an attentive audience, and their eyes lighted still more brightly with expectation, as young curly-headed John R—— clung closer to Owen's side, and asked this aged fosterer to draw out one entertaining story from his well-treasured store of legends.

"Whethen bloody wars, Master John," said Owen, "I've so many to relate ti ye, that it's myself is puzzled to think which iv thim I'll sthart wid; but if yees ud wish to hear about O'Kinnidy's advinthers wid the Phooka, maybe it wouldn't tache that little rosy-cheeked, purty colleen, Maria Houlahan, over there on the creepeen, to bring in the sphring-wather from the meadow well at an earlier hour than she does, on next All-Hallow's Eve. For yees see, boys and girls," continued Owen, with a half-serious shake of the head, "yees might be doin' betther than sthrollin' over the big deer-park walk at the back of the cashtle, afther sundown, not knowing the stranger yees 'ud meet there by moonlight, or maybe in the pitch dark hours of night.

"Well, avourneens, long is the time ago, afore ould Noll Crumwell batthered the tall forthress wid his murtherin' artillery, me brave O'Kinnidy was the lord of the soil and the king of the cashtle, a great gintleman intirely, proud as a juke and bowld as a lion. The never a *shoneen* in the counthry about could budge a word in dishpraise or dishparishment of him or his tinents, nor dar' do a ha'p'orth that would bring sarra or throuble on mashter or sarvint. An' what was betther nor all, the O'Kinnidys wor a sthrong faction there, and ready for any fightin' or other divarshin on foot in shweet Tipperary. Their kith and kin wor ould residinthers in the barony of Lower Ormond, and all of the high up gintlemin of the family connection had their coorts and demesnes, as grand as the Lackeen O'Kinnidys. They sphent their time, like thrue Irish bloods, in huntin', racin', coursin', fishin', shootin', hurlin', and jewellin'; they had dinners, balls, and parties every week; maybe coortin' or carousin' once in a while; seein' lots of fine company all the year round, and givin' lashin's and lavin's of fine meat and dhrink to all comers and goers, gintle and simple.

"Lo and behould ye, thin, O'Kinnidy of Lackeen Cashtle wint over to attind the funeral of a lady in Aglishlohane churchyard, and afther to dine wid his cousin, O'Kinnidy of Ballyhough Cashtle. He rode back that fine evenin' on his thoroughbred hunther, 'Cock-o'-the-walk;' and afther a merry night of it he had, me bould O'Kinnidy of Lackeen mounts his high-flyer, and maybe he didn't flitther the sthones along the road that led near Eglish ould church, wid its ivy-covered gable. Soon and suddint, me darlints, he notished the light of a candle glimmerin' through the ind windy—for the church was betther preserved wid walls thin than now —an' he thought he heard and obsarved a pair of ould wimen athin the walls, very talkative and fussy, as wimen generally are, especially whin they get together bint upon mischief. Howsomever, the gintleman lighted from his horse, and tied the bridle to an ash-bough on the road shide. Thin he had the curiosity to schramble over the sthyle, tosthe the graveyard. He cautiously peeped in through the windy, and what do ye think he notished but the pair of vagabond sthrollers sittin' beside a coffin and the lid ov id off, wid the corpse of the rich lady, that was beried that day in Eglish, lyin' widin it, in her shroud! The villainous and onnatheral ould raps were jist in the act of sthrippin' from her corpse a fine pearl nick-lace, and real goold rings from

her ears, and jewels from her hair, and diamond rings
from her finger. Well, to be shure, if O'Kinnidy, who
feared neither man nor morthial, wasn't insinsed at the
wickedness of these hardened craythers, that had no
respict nor dacency in their doin's wid the poor deceased
gintlewoman. He cracked his ridin'-whip, an' thunderin'
out a great oath—the Lord presarve us! at the iday of
swearin' in such a lonely, solemn place—down he jumps
on the villains of witches over the crumblin' walls. I'll
engage they shouted wid fright, and cut and run for
their bare lives over the churchyard fince. O'Kinnidy
raised a loudher tally-ho than whin he rode afther his pack
of hounds, wid the fox in full chase. But it was amazin'
how their shrivelled sphindle-shanks carried thim off in
double-quick time; racin' they wor, like wild Ingins.
They shook their boney fists at him, darin' him, as it
were, to cotch thim, until at last they run him out in the
coorse.

"'Phooka, Phooka,' says the ould hags, 'up wid you
and take O'Kinnidy to the banks of the Red Say, and
let him find what little business he had in chasin' a pair
of honest wimen like huz from our proper business in
Eglish churchyard. Let him wandher there wid the Turks
and Haribs till he cools his head and heels, far from the
tall cashtle of Lackeen.'

"Then, alana-ma-chrees, up sphrings a big hairy monsther, from the bottom of a gripe, wid his red eyes and
nosthrils flamin' fire like the sphrigs on that roarin' turf
and bog-oak blaze forninst huz. 'I'm at ye, O'Kinnidy,'
siz he; 'an' maybe ye'll rue the night ye inthered the
ould anshent church of Eglish,' siz he; 'fine a fella as ye
think ye are in Lower Ormond.' 'Faith, an' perhaps
ye're mistaken,' siz O'Kinnidy, unbucklin' the belt of his
soord from his waist, and dhrawin' the blade from the
schabbart, as quick as lightnin'; 'ye'll find it a good

belly-band to tie ye wid, as tight as tuppence in a market-woman's thrash-bag, if ye're the divil himself, as ye seem to be.' No sooner said nor done, O'Kinnidy dhraws the soord and gives a slash right acrass the fore feet, and sint the Phooka's hoofs flyin' through the air. 'Now, maybe ye'll surrindher,' siz O'Kinnidy, siz he; 'for ye can't run any longer, I'll go bail.' Instantly, begorra, he thrun the soord-belt round the fore an' hind legs of the baste, sthrappin' him down shnug and tidy, an' thin curlin' him up on his back wid as much aise as if the Phooka was a hare or patthridge caught in a gin—for O'Kinnidy was powerful sthrong, I can tell ye. The Phooka kicked, and turned, and lashed, to no purpose. He cursed awful, for he was as mad as a hatther, to be tied and tethered in that fashin. Shpite of himself he was carried away by my bowld gintleman, who mounted Cock-o'-the-walk. He shlung the Phooka behind him over the saddle-crupper, an' he roarin' thremindous loud all the way, while O'Kinnidy galloped home to Lackeen, round by the *boreen* passing Sir Toby Butler's big house.

"Shure enough, Sir Toby was the hairo that lived in great sthate an' grandeur at Lisduff House in those times. I aften heerd my grandfather say it was the beautifulest place he iver seed; long ranges of elm and yew threes afore the hall doore, and leadin' off by a great avenue tosth Eglish; the ould manshin wid its high-pitched roof an' tall sthacks of chimblys lookin' over the whole surrounding counthry. More-be-token, Sir Toby niver wint out in grand sthyle athout four-an'-twinty sarvints in white liveries, wid a piper playin' afore him. Sir Toby was a great lawyer, bud he would dhrink port and claret like a fish; an' troth, I b'leeve, he wouldn't refuse his sthiff tumbler of punch of an evenin'. But he sthood up for the Threaty of Limerick like a man, and definded the rights of the Irish Catherlics at the bar in the houses of

Lords and Commons, whin we had a Parliament of our own in College Green. An' see what id all come to, like all earthly grandeur; he's now berried undher a fine old headsthone in St. James's churchyard in Dublin. An' throth, the last time I was up there wid the masther's cattle to Shmithfield market, the sarra one of myself bud must go to the berryin' ground, an' I seed his tomb and read the good karrecther on id wid the rale feelin' of a proud Tipperary man.

"Well, to reshume the sthory, it was afther twelve o'clock whin O'Kinnidy and the Phooka reached the court-yard gate of Lackeen, an' lights were in the Cashtle windys, for the sarvants were up expecting the masther home; but they were ashtonished shure enough to hear the baste bellowin' and shpittin' fire behind his back. 'Let me in, porther,' siz O'Kinnidy; 'I have the Phooka behind me on the saddle, and I mean to thrusth him down the dark murdherin' hole in the cashtle, and put a big sthone over it, like a cork on a bottle of sperrits. Troth and I'll keep him there as the king's prezner for life.'

"'If yez dare to do so, boys,' shouts the Phooka, 'yez 'ill rue it to the day of yer death—and that won't be long comin'; for I'll set the cashtle of Lackeen in a blaze wid my breath, from foundation to parapet. Thin every mother's son iv ye will go to blazes, shure enough; so let O'Kinnidy take care what he ordhers his sarvints to do.'

"'Open the gate, porther,' siz O'Kinnidy, mighty commanding like, for he was a fine sojerly young gintleman; 'whether do you obey yer masther's voice or this hairy ould villain, either widin or widout the walls of Lackeen?' 'Begorra, masther,' siz the faithful porther, 'no matther what the kinsequince be to me or mine, it must niver be said his sarvint feared to do the biddin' of an O'Kinnidy in Lackeen. But, masther aroon, for mercy's sake, put that horrible howlin' monsther somewhere athout the cashtle, or the never a wink of sleep you'll have to-night, nor pace nor aise for yourself or any of the family.'

"'Yer right, Tim O'Mara,' says O'Kinnidy; and then he unbuckled the Phooka. 'Go, you infernal baste, and schamper off toast the Shannon!' shouts O'Kinnidy, givin' him a sthroke of the sthrap; 'and if I cotch you comin' my way agin, purshoon take me, but I'll shweep the hind feet off you, you bloody rashcal, as well as the fore! Then I'd like to know how ye'll lay yer thraps for honest people, you mane, skulkin' vagabone!' Wid that he made the Phooka go on his knees, and beg pardon for his haynous offinces. But I warrent ye the ould thief—lookin' schow-ways at the angry gintleman—hadn't much conthrishin for his sins. Howsomever, O'Kinnidy was tindher-hearted as a lady, though bould as Brian Boru; he dishmished the schemin' rogue like a magisthrate at petty sessions. Yet, I tell ye, before releasin' him, O'Kinnidy med him go bail, although widhout takin' any securities, never to touch or meddle widh breed, seed, or gineration of the O'Kinnidys.

"But often in the heel of the evenin' there is a great big pookawn goat seen lurkin' about the cashtle and lands of Lackeen. Aithen I have my own suspicions the ould boy may be consealed under his cruckked horns, and hairy shkin, so I'd advise my darlin' Masther John and purty bright-eyed Maria Houlahan to mind their stheps, whin they vinthur out in the night, widhout Owen Callanan and Pincher, the tarrier, to keep off all inthrudhers. That's all I'll now say, by way of warnin'; the Lord save all Christhians from every misforthin'."

The rattle of hot potatoes on the kitchen table, and the clatter of sally noggins, filled with new milk, which furnished a full and wholesome meal, concluded Owen's narrative. Variously expressed was the wonderment of his attentive auditors, while sliding round to their several places at the supper table.

Having thus disposed of our legend, we may venture on some details or characteristics regarding the *Phooka.* He is supposed to appear in the shape of a dusky and large animal, resembling a horse or pony. Sometimes this sprite is seen like a monstrous bull, with eyes and nostrils gleaming fire. It has also been mentally conceived under the shape of a large eagle, or rather, like the great winged Roc, which carried Sinbad the Sailor on his airy course. The Phooka's appearance is especially to be looked for on or about All-Hallows Eve. Woe betide the mortal who ventures abroad after dusk, and in lonely places, at that particular time! The Phooka usually steals in a noiseless manner from behind; and if he once succeed by inserting the head between a mortal's legs, the unhappy individual is instantly whisked off his feet, to find himself astride on the hobgoblin's back. Then up to the moon he ascends, or he descends perhaps to the bottom of a lake, or he flies over the ocean; he jumps from the highest precipices to the lowest depths; he crosses mountains, streams, and glens. Frequently does he traverse realms of space to the most remote countries of the world. This is accomplished in the course of a single night, and to the rider's extreme discomfort. The Phooka is sometimes called the *gruagach,* or "hairy spirit." Its mischievous pranks are well illustrated in "The Fairy Rath of Lough Innin," a metrical composition of Alexander Henry; as also in the very beautiful poem, "Alice and Una," by Dennis Florence MacCarthy.

Several localities in Ireland appear to have received their nomenclature from some supposed connection with this much dreaded monster. In the county of Cork there are two castles called *Carrig Phooka,* or the Phooka's Rock. One of these adjoins Doneraile, and the other lies near Macroom. The celebrated waterfall of *Poula Phooka*, or the Phooka's Cavern, in the county of Wicklow, must have had some connection in tradition with a sprite, so well known in Irish fairy mythology. There is also a noted landmark or cairn, and a natural cave, at a place called Clopoke, in the Queen's County. This townland is said to have derived its denomination from being haunted by this uncouth spirit; the word *Cloch-a-Phuka* meaning "the Stone of the Phooka." No less than three townlands in the county of Clare have combinations with the term *Phuca*. Many old raths and lisses throughout Ireland are called *Rathpooka* and *Lissaphuka*, because they had been supposed suitable habitations for this mischievous sprite. Sometimes his name is found shortened to *Pook*, and hence the affinity in sound with Shakespeare's elfin, "Puck." Places connected with his name are usually of a wild, romantic, and solitary character.

CHAPTER III.

FAIRY MYTHOLOGY OF THE IRISH.

"When evening's dusky car,
Crown'd with her dewy star,
Steals o'er the fading sky in shadowy flight,
On leaves of aspen trees
We tremble to the breeze,
Veil'd from the grosser ken of mortal sight."

COLERIDGE.

EVENING is the time usually selected for Irish fairy migrations from raths and dells. It is also the favourite juncture for indulging in their peculiar pastimes or revels. In his "Songs of the Pixies," as we find, the poet attributes a like propensity to that Devonshire race of beings invisibly small, and harmless or friendly to man. Poetic and popular imagery is strongly united, in efforts required to depict fairy characteristics. These creatures of fancy ever delight the vagaries of thought, when called up by the enchanter of his own mental vision, and when transferring the ideal suffusion, in appropriate language, to the perception of cultivated intelligences. Having described the amusements of his Lilliputian elves, during this visionary hour, and with the day's decline following fancied sports of fairy trains, we luxuriate with him in the following beautiful apostrophe to night. It is, indeed, richly coloured with a glowing fervour of imagination:—

"Mother of wildly-working dreams! we view
The sombre hours that round thee stand
With downcast eyes (a duteous band!)
Their dark robes dripping with the heavy dew,
Sorceress of the ebon throne!
Thy power the Pixies own,

> When round thy raven brow
> Heaven's lucent roses glow,
> And clouds, in watery colours drest,
> Float in light drapery o'er thy sable vest;
> What time the pale moon sheds a softer day,
> Mellowing the woods beneath its pensive beam:
> For 'mid the quivering light 'tis ours to play,
> Aye dancing to the cadence of the stream."

Before entering upon fragmentary details of legendary lore, and their accessories of local scenery, it may be desirable to dwell, somewhat in advance, on more general outlines of Irish traditions, in reference to fairy and other preternatural creations of popular fantasy. This digression must necessarily be concise, and mainly suggestive of further development, through extraneous sources; but it is hoped, that the more curious or intellectual investigator will easily track his way to those by-paths of Irish localities and literature, which will doubtless richly reward his romantic, artistic, poetic, antiquarian, historic, and philosophical tastes or studies.

The ancient and early settlers of Ireland, called Tuatha de Danaans, are thought to have been the first professors of Druidism; but they are certainly known to have been adepts in the arts of sorcery and magic. It is said they were transformed into fairies at some remote period, and consigned to subterranean habitations, under green hill sides, raths, and cairns. Our most romantic dells and woods are reputed the favourite haunts of fairy resort. These are often denominated the "gentle-places." Fairies are also partial to "banks and braes," beside purling rivulets. In Brittany, also—a country which held many ancient usages and practices common in our own—trolds and spirits, with dwarfs and fairies, popular myths of eld, haunt woods, rocks, streams, and fountains. The raths of Ireland must have been very numerous in former time; and this can be ascertained, not only because of those yet remaining, but also from this fact, that the compound word, Rath, Raw, Rah, Ray, or Ra, is found connected with the nomenclature of more than one thousand different localities within our island. Here the spirit-people love to congregate, but difficult it must prove to collect perfectly authentic accounts, regarding their social economy, amusements, and pursuits.

Music heard beside these raths, on a fine evening, often induces mortals to linger with delight, although danger may be incurred, whilst listening to such syren melody. Benevolence is sometimes exercised towards mortals by the fairies, who are said to cure men and women of infirmities and diseases, or who are thought to remove deformities, disagreeable accidents, or misfortunes. They often communicate supernatural power to mortals, and invisibly assist them. Again, these creatures are found of a malevolent and mischievous disposition: frequently abducting mortals, to serve some selfish or degrading purpose, often paralyzing their energies and prospects of worldly happiness, or sometimes leaving a long inheritance of sickness and sorrow on afflicted individuals and families. A libation of cow's *beestheens*—some of the thick new milk given after calving—when poured on a rath, is believed to appease the anger of offended fairies. Many other similar practices are considered no less potent, when suitably employed.

The Irish word *sig*, or *sighe*, pronounced *shee*, is the usual generic title applied to that denomination of supernatural creatures, known in the sister kingdoms as fairies, elves, or pixies. The *fear-shee* is known as the "man-fairy;" while the *ban-shee* is recognized as the "woman-fairy." Sometimes we have the term *mna-shee*, "woman-fairies," used with peculiar diminutives known in the Irish language. The *Fear-sighes* are chiefly alluded to in ancient legendary lore; and the *Bean-sighes* are usually known as a distinctive class of imaginary beings, when wailing for anticipated deaths. In the fairy soldier-troops only men appear. Amongst the moonlight or fairy-palace revellers, fine-dressed lords and ladies are indiscriminately mingled in social enjoyments. Within their luxurious halls songs and strains of ravishing music and rhythm are heard, which transport with delicious enthusiasm the souls of mortals. Those sounds tingle on the ear with melodious cadences, that long haunt the memory and imagination.

During moonlight, fairies are often seen by mortals flitting in shadowy troops, between the eye and the mildly-beaming nightly orb. They are especially fond of revelling at midnight. Wild strains of unearthly music are heard, at this time, by an ingle nook, lonely rath, green hill side, or tangled wood. The summer or autumn nights were selected by our Irish fairies as most appropriate occasions, for congregating their dancing parties in secluded vales, on vernal banks, whilst the gurgling water trickles along its sheltered course. Sometimes they sport near old ivied castles, beside a lake or river, or oftentimes within the gloomy precincts of some graveyard, under the walls of its ruined church, or over lonely tombs of the dead. Harvest-time is remarkable for affording frequent glimpses of our Irish fairies. They are, however, very jealous of mortal intrusion, and commonly proceed to wreak vengeance on all unbidden interlopers on their revels. The wild harmonies of zephyr breezes are supposed to be the murmuring musical voices of fairies on their travels. Although elfin sports may continue during night, the first glow of morning is a signal for instant departure to their umbrageous raths, deep caverns, rocky crevices, or old *tumuli*, where their fabled dwellings are carefully concealed from the eye of mortal. On alighting at, or departing from, a particular spot, their rapid motion through air creates a noise somewhat resembling the loud humming of bees, when swarming from a hive. Sometimes, what is called *shee gaoithe*, Anglicè, *a whirlwind*, is supposed to have been raised by the passing fairy host.

Elves are often heard and seen hunting, with sound of horns, cry of dogs, tramp of horses, cracking of whips, and "tally-ho!" of huntsmen. These belong to the class known as Cluricaunes. Rushes and *bouliauns* often turn to horses, when the fairies get astride on them, as they usually do, when about to migrate in a body, or troop, from one place to another. Over hedges and ditches, walls and fences, brakes and briars, hills and valleys, lakes and rivers, they sweep with incredible velocity and airy lightness. Allingham thus alludes, in one of his ballads, to these fairy pastimes. His description principally refers to the northern province, and to the dread entertained by children, lest they might be abducted by a passing elfin band:—

> "Up the heathery mountain,
> Down the rushy glen,
> We daren't go a-hunting,
> For fear of little men.
> Wee folk, good folk,
> Trooping all together,
> Green Jacket, Red Cap,
> And White Owl's Feather."

Those strange sounds caused by crackling furze-blossoms, are attributed to fairy presence. They shelter beneath clumps of gorse thickets, love the scent of their flowers, and mark out beaten tracks through the wiry grass growing round their roots. They sip ambrosial dew from out the yellow cup-leaved blossoms. They also suck dew-drops from other leaves and flowers. In his ballad of "Tren, the Fairy," Joyce happily alludes to such a practice, in these lines:—

"From flower-bells of each hue,
   Crystal-white, or golden-yellow,
Purple, violet, red, or blue,
We drink the honey dew,
   Until we all get mellow—
   Until we all get mellow,
   And through our festal glee,
I'm the blithest little fellow
In the fairy companie."

In a somewhat similar strain, Francis Davis, "The Belfast Man," has poetically recorded, in his "Fairy Serenade," social customs of *Sheogues*, in the eastern parts of Ulster. Having regard to the light-footed, ethereal, dancing groups of dwarfish beings, when delicately touching the green grass, it is supposed they scarcely shake off these dew-drops, during their wildest evolutions. Filled with a passionate eagerness for music and revelry, they indulge whole nights, without intermission or weariness, in their favourite exercises and recreations, lightly-gliding in trails or circles through varied postures and figures. The fairies are generally represented as habited in green, or sometimes in white, silver-spangled raiment, with high-peaked or wide-brimmed scarlet caps on their heads. By moonlight they are often seen under the shade of oak-trees, dancing on or around large globular *fungi*, or umbrella-shaped mushrooms. Thus discourseth the northern poet:—

"Oh, broad are the lawns of your airy fairy king:
And we'll o'er them glide on the watery wing
   Of a love-sick maiden's sigh.
   And thy crown I'll plume
   With the golden bloom
Of the blue-robed violet's eye;
   And we'll fill our glass
   From a blade of grass,
And we'll drink to its emerald dye;
   While we dance those springs
   The young daisy sings,
When she's kissed by the twilight fly.

> Oh! the gay green bower,
> And the gray eve hour,
> When the dew lamps round us lie!"

To the philosophical investigator, it is curious to discover how local habits and pursuits leave their impress on even the superstitions of a people. The Whitehaven coal miners used to fancy they often found little mining tools and implements, belonging to a "swart fairy of the mine," in their dark subterraneous chambers. The Germans believed in two classes of gnomes,—the one species fierce and malevolent, the other gentle and harmless. These creatures appeared like little old men, about two feet in height, wandering through lodes and chambers of mines. Although apparently busily engaged cutting ore, heaping it in vessels, and turning windlasses, in reality they were doing nothing. Except provoked, however, no harm accrued to the miners, with whom they associated. Rarely do we find our native fairies devoted to any industrial pursuits, except those lighter and occasional in-door occupations, which serve to engage and amuse the merry Irish maiden or thrifty housewife. Pleasure and social enjoyment seem the all-engrossing delight of our airy elves, as they enter largely into the constituent elements of our light-hearted countrymen.

It is only at a distance the fairies appear graceful in figure, or handsome in countenance; but their costumes are always of rich material, or fine texture. Frequently they change their shapes; they suddenly appear, and as suddenly vanish. These elves, on a near inspection, are generally found to be old, withered, bent, and having very ugly features,—especially the men. Female fairies are endowed with characteristics of rare beauty, in several instances; and to such beings most marked attentions are always paid by the diminutive lords of their affections.

Fairies are generally thought, by the peasantry, to partake of a mixed human and spiritual nature. Their bodies are presumed to be immaterial, or, at least, of some almost impalpable substance. They are animated with feelings of benevolence or resentment, according to circumstances. Although invisible to men, particularly during day, they hear and see all that takes place amongst mortals, regarding matters in which they have any especial concern. Hence the peasantry are always anxious to secure their good opinion and kind offices, and to propitiate or avert their anger, by civil conversation and practices. Fairies are always mentioned with respect and reserve. It is also considered inhuman to strain potatoes, or spill hot water, on or over the threshold of a door, as thousands of spirits are supposed to congregate invisibly at such a spot, and to suffer from that infliction. Before drinking, a peasant would often spill a small portion of his draught on the ground, as a complimentary libation to the "good people."

The peasantry have formed some ill-defined belief that fairies are like the fallen angels, driven out from bliss, but condemned to wander on earth until the day of judgment. Campion, "the Kilkenny man," has versified the fall of these elves from their previous high estate. The fairies are said to doubt regarding their own future condition, although they have hopes of being one day restored to happiness. An intermixture of good and evil balances their actions and motives; and their passions are often vindictive, as their inclinations are frequently humane and generous. Desperate battles with opposing bands, hostile to each other, are waged; and they meet, like knights of old, armed *cap-à-pie*, for such encounters. The air bristles with their spears and flashing swords, and their helmets and red coats gleam in the bright sunshine, during the progress of these engagements,

Thus far have we dealt with the generalities of Irish fairy lore; but further details are best illustrated in legends connected with personages and localities. Real or imaginary, such alliances render our task more light, lively, and gossipping; perhaps, also, more intelligible and entertaining.

CHAPTER IV.

APPARITIONS AND FETCHES.

"'Tis thine to sing, how, framing hideous spells,
  In Skye's lone isle, the gifted wizard-seer,
  Lodg'd in the wintry cave with fate's fell spear,
Or in the depth of Uist's dark forest dwells.
  How they, whose sight such dreary dreams engross,
  With their own vision oft astonish'd droop,
  When o'er the wat'ry strath, or quaggy moss,
They see the gliding ghosts unbodied troop;
  Or, if in sport, or on the festive green,
  Their destin'd glance some fated youth descry,
  Who now, perhaps, in lusty vigour seen,
And rosy health, shall soon lamented die.
  For them the viewless forms of air obey;
  Their bidding heed, and at their beck repair.
  They know what spirit brews the stormful day,
  And heartless, oft like moody madness, stare
To see the phantom train their secret work prepare."
COLLINS.

So sung the poet, in his Ode on Scotland's popular superstitions; and thus far he aptly portrayed the "second sight," or peculiar divination of the Highlanders. Another master of English verse, the poet Gray, has rendered his ode of the Fatal Sisters, from a Norse composition, having reference to the battle of Clontarf. On the day of this celebrated contest—Good Friday, and not on Christmas day, as stated by this poet—a native of Caithness, in Scotland, saw a number of persons on horseback, and at a distance. They were riding full speed towards a hill, which they seemed to enter. Curiosity led him to follow them, when he saw twelve gigantic female figures, all employed in weaving. This ode in question is supposed to have been sung by them, at the same time. Having finished it, their web was torn in twelve pieces. Six of the Fatal Sisters galloped on black steeds to the north, and as many to the south. Each took her own portion of the web. These were known as Valkyriur, or female divinities, the servants of Odin, or Woden, the Gothic god of war. They are said to choose the slain on a field of battle, whilst mounted on their steeds, and with drawn swords in their hands, flying over the heads of combatants. After battle, departed heroes were conducted by them to Valkalla, the hall of Odin, or paradise of the brave. Here these sisters served them with horns of mead and ale.

The Fetch—a well-known Irish superstition—claims some affinity with the Highlanders' belief in "second sight." The Fetch is supposed to be a mere shadow, resembling in stature, features, and dress, a living person, and often mysteriously or suddenly seen by a very particular friend. If it appear in the morning, a happy longevity for the living original is confidently predicted; but if it be seen in the evening, immediate dissolution of the prototype is anticipated. Spirit-like, it flits before the sight, seeming to walk leisurely through the fields, and often disappearing through a gap or lane. The person it resembles is usually known to be labouring under some mortal illness at the time, and quite unable to leave his or her bed. When the Fetch appears agitated or eccentric in its motions, a violent or painful death is indicated for the doomed prototype. This phantom is also said to make its appearance, at the same time, and in the same place, to more than one person,—as we have heard related in a particular instance. What the Irish call Fetches, the English designate Doubles. It is supposed, likewise, that individuals may behold their own Fetches.

The renowned Irish novelist and poet, John Banim, has written both a novel and a ballad on this subject. Somewhat analogous to the Highland seer's gift of second sight—especially in reference to approaching doom—Aubrey tells us, that a well-known poet, the Earl of Roscommon, who was born in Ireland, 1633, had some preternatural knowledge of his father's death, whilst residing at Caen, in Normandy. Such forebodings were recognized by the early Northmen; and it is probable their origin amongst the people of these islands had been derived from a Scandinavian source. Oftentimes they were invested with circumstances of peculiar horror,—according to northern traditions, which were also transferred to the Hebride islanders. These latter adopted a strange admixture of superstition, from their former independent ancestors, and the invading pirate hordes, that colonized their exposed and defenceless homes.

In the northern province of Ireland, a belief in wild apparitions and shadowy Fetches is a prevailing characteristic of its people. "Sair is ma hawrt, ma colleen dhas," said old Aileen Mac Quillan to her young and lively grandchild, Maggie, as both sat together, one fine May morning, before a cottage door, which faced one of the loveliest glens of Antrim,—"sair is ma hawrt, sin' we'se maun baith pawrt, an aiblins afore monie hoors hae pawst the-day!"

The old woman suddenly changed in appearance. Her wasted cheeks, preserving still some appearance of youthful ruddiness, began to settle into a pallor altogether unusual. With the quick instinct of childhood's intelligence, and with a natural alarm for her grandmother's health, poor Maggie looked earnestly into the sadly-altered features, and tearfully exclaimed: "Mither o' mercy! sic a waefu' glour I wad na hae expectit ane ye ava, wi' yer hale leesome looks afore, noo turnit sae dour an' din. Guidness me! gin she aint gaun int' a swarf, or aboot to dee!"

"Puir bairn; I'se be as cauld as the snaw anc the hyre,

tap in winter, afore anither mornin' dawns;" and as the old woman's voice fell into a more sepulchral and weaker tone, she added,—" I'm sae cauld, that it seems as if somebody war e'en noo walkin' aboon ma grave!"

The aged grand-dame was borne within the cottage, leaning on her grand-daughter's shoulder, and laid on her bed. Soon afterwards the spark of life became extinct; while the child, greatly agitated, and aghast with dismay, wept bitterly, when thus left alone with the dead.

The young girl's father had left home the evening before for Ballymoney fair, where he had a cow and a calf to dispose of; and having effected a sale at an early hour that morning, towards noon he approached Cushendun. Sounds of wailing reached his ears, as he turned down the little pathway, and over a style, which led to his home. His daughter rushed to meet him with the news of his mother's sudden death. The father of the girl took her tenderly by the hand, and then said mournfully: "A weel, Maggie, I saw ma mither's Fetch yestere'en, on the sklint o' a hill side, on the road to Ballymoney, a glidin' amang the heather, an' I kenn'd she was na lang for this warld, though she lookit as braw as ony carlin. An' the mornin', as I gaed ower the staney rig, I saw yersel linkin' an' wimplin' athart the feal i' the grass, sae feat an' winsome, thet I thankit the Laird ye were leckly to lie lang on the lan', wi' the rest o' yer kin. Guidness bless us! unco strange glints we aften hae o' this an' the ither warld!"

Old Aileen Mac Quillan was buried in the ancient churchyard, known as the Grange of Leyd, in a sheltered dell, not far from Cushendall. Fifty years afterwards, her grand-daughter, Maggie, was seen to visit the spot, with her husband, and a rising generation of grown sons and daughters. All reverently knelt about the grave, smoothing its green sward, and placing fresh sods of grass to fill up the inequalities found on its surface.

CHAPTER V.

CHANGELINGS, FAIRY-MEN, AND FAIRY-WOMEN.

> "Oh! it cannot be my own sweet boy,
> For his eyes are dim and hollow,
> My little boy is gone to God,
> And his mother soon will follow.
>
> "The dirge for the dead will be sung for me,
> And the Mass be chanted sweetly;
> And I will sleep with my little boy,
> In the moonlight churchyard meetly."
>
> Dr. Anster.

A poetic license is usually supposed to claim departure from strict accuracy of idea; and in the present case, it is quite evident, the accomplished and well-remembered scholar, who composed an agreeable ballad on an Irish superstition, has mistaken popular traditions and opinions regarding his selected subject. The peasantry never supposed an abducted child to have been laid in mother earth, when taken away from his former home. On the contrary, they imagined it lived in fairy realms; and they thought, however reluctantly, that it was condemned to endure, if not enjoy, all the vicissitudes of a constrained exile from earth and heaven. When not restored again to its parents, it was assumed that existence must be prolonged to an indefinite period, while living in such a state.

No opinion was more prevalent amongst the peasantry than that of human abduction, practised by the elfin tribe. Young and lovely children were the special objects of desire; and often when these had been snatched away from the parental home, old, emaciated, decrepid, and ugly fairies were left in their stead. These latter are called *changelings.* To guard against such accidents, even in the Scottish Highlands, midwives were accustomed to give a small spoonful of whisky, mixed with earth, to newly-born children, as their first food. This was no doubt intended as a preservative from some preternatural spell. Highland babes are carefully watched and guarded until after their christening is over, lest they should be abducted, or changed for fairy deformities. The Irish peasant mother entertained similar fears for her newly-born child, especially when it presented a very attractive appearance. But children alone were not the only persons subject to such species of forced exile. Mortal women, recently confined, were also abducted to suckle children conveyed to fairy-land; and, in some cases, they were required to nurse fairy-born infants. On this subject, we have many popular tales and traditions current; whilst our ancient or modern literature abounds with allusions to such incidents. For instance, Edward Walsh has written a beautiful ballad—"The Fairy Nurse"—relating to a girl who had been led into the fairy fort of Lisroe, when she saw her little brother, who died a week before, lying in a rich cradle, whilst he was rocked to sleep by a fairy woman. These following are its opening stanzas:—

> "Sweet babe! a golden cradle holds thee,
> And soft the snow-white fleece infolds thee;
> In airy bower I'll watch thy sleeping,
> Where branchy trees to the breeze are sweeping.
> Shuheen sho! lulo lo!
>
> "When mothers languish broken-hearted,
> When young wives are from husbands parted,
> Ah! little think the keeners lonely,
> They weep some time-worn fairy only.
> Shuheen sho! lulo lo!"

Changelings are known to have an inclination for certain grotesque pranks. The fairy child often procures and yokes a set of bagpipes on his arm. He sits up in the cradle and performs a variety of fine airs, with great hilarity, and many strange grimaces. When he plays lively jigs, reels, and hornpipes, inmates of a cottage are often set insanely dancing, and greatly against their inclination. Until this sort of forced exercise concludes, they are ready to sink with fatigue. Notwithstanding all his hilarious whims and oddities, the changeling was always regarded as an unwelcome family intruder. Sometimes a fairy child was thrown across the hearth-fire to eject him from a household. He then vanished up the open chimney, with expressions of vengeance, curses, and all manner of ill names, directed against the family that had so long and so unwillingly harboured him.

Sometimes supposed *changelings* were removed from the peasant's cabin on a clean shovel, and were placed on the centre of a dunghill; parents, meantime, believing that their true children would be restored to them, even after a long absence. Certain prayers were muttered by the fairy-man or fairy-woman directing this strange operation. Some Irish verses were usually chanted during the process. Of these, the following lines may be deemed a pretty correct translation:—

> " Fairy-men and women all,
> List!—it is your baby's call:
> For on the dunghill's top he lies,
> Beneath the wide, inclement skies.
> Then come with coach and sumptuous train,
> And take him to your mote again.
> For if ye stay till cocks shall crow,
> You'll find him like a thing of snow,—
> A pallid lump, a child of scorn,
> A monstrous brat, of fairies born.
> But ere you bear the boy away,
>   Restore the child you took instead;
> When, like a thief, the other day,
>   You robbed my infant's cradle-bed.
> But give me back my only son,
> And I'll forgive the harm you done;

> And nightly, for your gambolling crew,
> I'll sweep the hearth and kitchen too;
> And leave you free your tricks to play,
> Whene'er you choose to pass this way.
> Then, like good people, do incline
> To take your child, and give back mine."

When such words had been recited, the assistants retired within an adjoining cottage, closing its door carefully, and awaiting the issue, whilst some additional prayers and incantations were repeated. Any noise, caused by the elements or by a passing vehicle, was then supposed to have been owing to the approach and departure of a fairy host. Afterwards, the door being opened, these impostors confidently declared the true child had been replaced. This poor, emaciated being was then brought into the cabin, and its deluded parents were told their child would not long survive. As such an event usually accorded with this prediction, it only confirmed a belief in the imposture, and added to the established reputation of that particular fairy-man or fairy-woman, amongst our humbler classes

We have been told of a circumstance occurring—one, too, in which the names of parties and place were mentioned—regarding a respectable farmer's family, on whom a changeling had been imposed. A beautiful and healthy infant, sleeping with its mother, was thought to have been rudely snatched from her arms one night. With the morning's dawn, a deformed and withered-looking old creature appeared instead. The child was doubtless attacked with some paralytic disease, which had suddenly changed its appearance. However, the parents, with all their friends and neighbours, were persuaded about the child having been carried off to fairy-land, whilst a fairy had been left to supply its place. The poor mother found this weakling, whom she still continued to suckle, wasting away her own strength, and she seemed fast falling into decline. The child became remarkably peevish, and would not look on "man or mortal." Its piercing screams sounded so unearthly, that it was agreed on all sides the services of a fairy-woman would be required to recover the lost one. This matter was arranged with the greatest secrecy, lest it should be known to the poor, deformed creature, whose flesh had become completely shrivelled, and whose limbs had shrunk to the most attenuated dimensions. With her usual exorcisms and charms, the fairy-woman employed put this supposed changeling on a shovel, and afterwards left him on a dung heap, before the farm-house offices. Meantime, he offered every resistance possible, and screamed with terrific cries. To the great delight of the mother and her friends, when going outside, expecting the return of their lost darling, it lay, on the same unsavoury dunghill, ruddy, plump, and smiling sweetly as of yore, the old man having altogether disappeared. So far as our recollection of this story serves us, the child lived for some time afterwards, yet died before it had fully attained the faculty of reason.

Children, however, are not the solely abducted denizens of raths. Fairies take a fancy to the instrumentation of accomplished pipers, or other famous musicians, who are abducted to their subterranean or subaqueous habitations. These sons of melody, until almost dead with fatigue, are kept engaged in furnishing music to finely-dressed, frisky little gentlemen and ladies. Refreshments, at the same time, are liberally dispensed by these sprites. The musician generally finds himself ejected from fairy realms before morning. Sometimes he is invited to remain with his entertainers; but he usually prefers returning to the land of the living. His fairy entertainers often take away the old pipes or instrument, bestowing one much more perfect, and sweeter-toned, in its stead. The reputation of having been abducted to elfin land, and thus rewarded, is sure to establish a musician's practice and resources.

Midwives are likewise taken away to the fairy raths on pillions, with fairy horsemen conducting them to invisible abodes. If these women partake of any food or drink, to which they are pressingly invited, as well by persuasion as by the luxurious repasts prepared, a spell of detention is placed over them. They cannot return again to their homes. Elves are less liberal in bestowing gold or silver as a reward. Such bounty, however, when offered, is found to be illusive. We are told, that money obtained from fairies usually turns into round slates, dry leaves, old bones, or something equally worthless.

The Irish fairy-man or fairy-woman was supposed to hold some mysterious sort of communication with denizens of *moats* or *raths*. In various cases, it was rumoured that these impostors had been changelings originally; and as they usually lived a solitary and retired life, no ordinary share of mystery shrouded their motions. They professed a familiar acquaintance with all secrets, past, present, and future; to cure all diseases affecting men and beasts; to discover and restore lost goods; to give a description and procure detection of the thief, if property had been stolen; fortune-telling, and a knowledge regarding all matters of personal concern; causing cream to produce butter in greater abundance; whilst they often took care to impress on ignorant minds an opinion that their friendship would be desirable, to prevent the certain evil effects of fairy resentment. Even in times very remote, such influence was regarded as fatal to the individual against whom it had been exercised. Thus, for instance, Muirchertach MacEarca is reported, in our traditions and annals, to have been drowned in a tub of wine, at a house called Cleteach, near Tara, on November eve, A.D. 527.

This action is said to have been effected through the agency of a fairy-woman.

Herbs and plants in raths or dells are collected, with various kinds of mummery, and used for charms and cures by "bone-setters," or "fairy-doctors." These herbs are considered specially impregnated by some mysterious fairy influence, efficacious for the healing art. Sometimes "knowledgable old women," as they are termed by our peasantry, venture on the exercise of charms, without exciting any great degree of confidence in a fortunate result, either in their own or in the minds of others. An herb, or a bit of burnt sod, taken from the bonfire of St. John's night, in midsummer, is often sewn into the clothes of women. This serves as a charm, it is supposed, against fairy plots and abductions. Ointment, obtained by midwives, to besmear fairy-children, if rubbed to the eye of mortal, will enable such person to see the prosaic skeleton of fairy illusions in underground halls and palaces. Old friends and neighbours are often discovered amongst the *sheoges*, in this manner. Fairies, during their revels, also become visible to the eye thus anointed. If a mortal make any sign of recognition or exclamation, one of the sprites may ask, "Do you see me?" Being answered in the affirmative, he asks, "With which eye?" When rightly informed, the fairy thrusts a finger, or sometimes puffs his breath into that eye, and thus blinds the incautious person. Thus is the charm dissolved.

Within the present century, one of these fairy-women, who was named Moll Anthony, lived near the Red Hills, at the "chair of Kildare," an antiquarian object of curiosity, within this county. Her reputation as a possessor of supernatural knowledge and divination drew crowds of distant visitants to her daily, and from the most remote parts of Ireland. In various instances, these were furnished with a bottle, containing some supposed curative liquid. They were then directed to return homewards, without falling asleep on their journey. The bottle given was filled with water, darkly coloured with a decoction of herbs gathered, with certain incantations, near a rath, which afforded the customary *materia medica* of the fairy doctors, for the cure of special diseases, regarding which consultation was required. The most accomplished and skilful member of the medical faculty seldom received a more remunerative fee for his services, on behalf of a patient, than this *wise woman* of the Red Hills pocketed from her credulous dupes. At one time, a young woman had been directed to return with the magic draught to her sick relative's home. She was especially cautioned to keep her eyes open along the way. Overcome with fatigue, however, and probably feverish with anxiety and excitement, this young person was obliged to rest by the road side. Wearied nature soon began to claim her usual requirement of "balmy sleep." No sooner had the girl dozed off into dreamy unconsciousness, than one of the ugliest beings imagination had ever created appeared to her disordered fancies. With wrinkled visage, the spectre seemed ready to clutch her in his extended arms. Giving a loud scream, she bounded to her feet, and through terror doubtless she would have left the curative potion behind, had she not already taken the precaution of securing it within her bosom. The rude monitor of her obligation was supposed to have been a friend among the *sheogues*. We knew the person thus supposed to have been warned, and who, in old age, related this adventure. After the death of Moll Anthony, her daughter followed the same profession, but never enjoyed a like celebrity. Such preternatural talent or profession, in our day, is seldom liberally rewarded. It was, however, extensively and well patronized among the people of past generations; and in the language of the poet, without regretting the innovation, we may truly exclaim—

"Old times are changed, old manners gone!"

Sometimes the fairy-man, also called a "charmer," or "cow-doctor," undertakes to remove fairy influences from sick cattle, by some prepared herbs, and nostrums performed at a spring well. He will not allow any one to approach during the progress of his operations. In the west of Ireland, cows are often driven into certain springs or loughs, reputed holy, in order to restore the usual supply of dairy milk and butter, supposed to have been supernaturally abstracted. Fresh butter is thrown into the water, as a necessary part of these incantations.

As an illustration of the fairy-man's professional pursuits, once only had we a full opportunity afforded for witnessing some mysterious quackery, practised by a noted *Sheogue* doctor, called *Paddy the Dash*, and, sometimes, *Paddy the cow-doctor*. This individual was thought to hold friendly communication with the "good people,"—for his cabin adjoined one of their raths. Paddy received his cognomen from a peculiar stammering, or defect of articulation, that obliged him to jerk out his words at irregular intervals, and with violent gesticulation. An old woman had fallen into decline, and the necromancer's process of treatment was considered desirable in this particular case. Having some knowledge of these circumstances, a group of young friends, with Paddy's grace especial, had been admitted to the patient's sick chamber. Separated by a partition wall from the principal apartment, this chamber served for all other domestic purposes of this poor family. We were but "wee bit bodies" at the time, and have only an indistinct recollection of Paddy drawing out of his *coatmore* pocket a large black bottle, with two or three packages of brown paper, containing dried herbs, and a bunch of *boughelawns*, or *boliauns*, on which the fairies are said to ride occasionally through the air. The blossoms and tops of these *boughelawn* weeds were put in a porringer, filled with water, that had been left simmering on the kitchen fire. Some unaccountable flourishes were made over the sick woman, then some strokes on her back and forehead, with three shakes,—" in the name of Father, Son, and Holy Ghost,"—when helped to an upright sitting posture by female friends assisting. Blessed water, we think, had been used during this sort of necromancy, and it was sprinkled on the sick person. Thus were sacred rites of the Church often travestied and brought into disrepute, by persons who were doubtless not wholly devoid of faith, but who mingled certain revered practices of religion with the most degrading extravagances of imposture and superstition. The patient's face, hands, and feet, were finally bathed with the warm mixture, contained in a porringer, before the more earnest-looking and bewildered attendants left her apartment. Well do we recollect, to Paddy's great displeasure, the junior portion of the spectators could scarcely restrain their hilarity at the oddity of his enunciation, and his strange method of conducting the entire proceedings.

CHAPTER VI.

BURIED TREASURES.

" But if in pursuit we go deeper,
 Allur'd by the gleam that shone,
Ah! false as the dream of the sleeper,
 Like Love, the bright ore is gone!"
MOORE.

No supposition is more general than the opinion that gold or silver may be found concealed under nearly all the raths, cairns, or old castles throughout this island. It is always a difficult task to exhume buried treasure; yet several families are thought to have grown rich in consequence of finding golden store concealed in the earth. Generally, some preternatural guardian or other will be met with, and on the alert.

Such treasure is usually discovered by a dream, three times repeated. The prize is deposited oftentimes within " a crock," or covered vault; but when any attempt may be made to lift it, some awful gorgon or menacing monster appears on the defensive and offensive. Sometimes a rushing wind, with destructive force, sweeps over the plain, or from the opening made. It instantly carries away the gold-seeker's hat or spade, or even, in various cases, the adventurer himself. He is frequently deposited with broken bones, or a paralyzed frame, at a respectful distance from the object of his quest.

A few legends are here inserted by way of illustration. On the banks of a beautiful northern river, the Lagan, and near Dromore, a green plot may be seen, on which two large moss-covered stones, over 600 feet apart, are shown. It is said, two immense "crocks" of gold lie buried under these conspicuous land-marks, and that various attempts have been made to dig around and beneath them. In all these instances, when any persistent effort had been made, a monk appeared in full habit, with a cross in his hand, to warn off sacrilegious intruders. It had been intended—so say the legend-mongers—to erect near this spot a church, equal in its dimensions and beauty to St. Peter's at Rome. The contents of one "crock" were destined to erect such a structure; and those of the other were intended for its complete decoration. This golden store, most likely, may have been supposed, as saved from the wreck of some ancient religious foundation, and therefore it was regarded as a sacred deposit for the erection of a church or monastery.

The ancient castle of Dagan, or Dagon, in Clare County, was built about the twelfth century period by the Mac Mahons, who were lords of the soil. A family portrait of a lady, connected with this family, and who was called *Wauria Ruadh*, or "Red-haired Mary," is still preserved at Ennistymon House, the residence of Colonel Mac Namara. In the neighbourhood of this castle, there lingers a tradition that its vaults contain a buried treasure, which can only be found by a person named O'Grady, and during Mass time. A black and white duck, at the same instant, will be seen floating on a stream in the vicinity. It is to be hoped, however, the aquatic bird so distinguished in colour may not tempt any one of the O'Gradys to make explorations most delusive in their results, as they have often proved most destructive to many of our interesting old ruins. Disappointment to the treasure-seeker is likewise sure to bring with it the ridicule of all his friends and neighbours.

To the ruins of Manning's Castle, near Carrickmacross, County of Monaghan, the following curious legend is attached. A former resident, during one of Ireland's civil wars, concealed a well-secured box of treasure in the side of a steep, precipitous bank. This overhung a small but unfathomable lake, which bounded the castle on one side. After residents of the fortalice made many fruitless attempts to recover the treasure, at length, thinking he had discovered the exact locality, one more adventurous than his fellows, and at considerable outlay, procured a machine, to which a large balancing stone was attached. This was worked by a windlass of some kind.

A great crowd gathered round the lake borders, boats were skimming the dark surface, and excitement became intense, when a large iron-bound box was seen ascending slowly to the very edge of the lough. This box was attached to a strong hook, affixed to the large stone before-mentioned. In another instant a triumphant shout of success would have made the welkin ring; but ere that moment arrived, the galloping of a horse, at a break-neck pace, was distinctly heard, as if approaching the vicinity. Soon a large black courser dashed into the excited crowd. His rider—a very diminutive man, wearing a scarlet cap and dark-blue uniform—gave a hasty glance at the windlass and the box. He then shouted in piercing accents to the people, "Is this the work you're all at, you vagabonds, and the whole country round in a blaze of fire?"

The startled crowd looked towards this new comer, and then in search of the fire he had outridden. That very instant, box, stone, and windlass tumbled into the fathomless lake. The legend runs,—its waters were heard gurgling for hours after the descent, as if murmuring at the advent of such a strange visitant. But the red-capped alarmist and his sable steed vanished from sight at the moment of this fall.

CHAPTER VII.

THE MERROW-MAIDEN AND MERROW-MAN.

"When, by moonlight, the waters were hush'd to repose,
 That beautiful spirit of ocean arose;
 Her hair, full of lustre, just floated and fell
 O'er her bosom, that heaved with a billowy swell.

* * * * * * *

"The maiden she gazed on the creature of earth,
 Whose voice in her breast to a feeling gave birth,
 Then smil'd; and abash'd, as a maiden might be,
 Looking down, gently sank to her home in the sea."

CROFTON CROKER.

FROM generic notions of our native folk lore, certain strange and peculiar creations of fancy have received an imaginative form and existence. The Merrow, or, as it is written in Irish, *Morúadh*, or *Morúach*, is a sort of fantastic sea-nymph, corresponding with the prevailing conception of a mermaid. It is supposed to partake of semi-human nature and figure. From head to waist it appears in such shape; and thence to the extremities it is covered with greenish-tinted scales, having a fish-like termination. Those creatures are said to partake of a modest, affectionate, gentle, and beneficent disposition. Their name seems a compound of *muir*, the sea, and *oigh*, a maid. These marine objects are also called by the Irish, *Muir-gheilt*, *Samhghubha*, *Muidhucha'n*, and *Suire*. They would seem to have basked around our shores from the most remote period; for, according to bardic chroniclers, when the Milesian ships bore onwards in quest of a friendly harbour to our coasts, the *Suire*, or sea-nymphs, played around them on their passage. These fictitious imaginings are probably traceable to an Eastern origin. The merrow was capable of attachment to human beings, and is reported to have intermarried and lived with them for years in succession. Some allegory is probably concealed under the fiction of certain families or races, living on the southern and western coasts of Ireland, being partly descended from these marine creatures. Natural instincts, however, are found to prevail over their love. The merrow usually feels desirous of returning to her former haunts and companions under the sea waves. She is represented as the daughter of a king, whose gorgeous palace lies deep beneath the ocean. Sometimes mermaidens live under our lakes. In Moore's *Irish Melodies*, we have the fine conceit of a merrow being metamorphosed into the national instrument, to which allusion occurs in these opening lines,—

" 'Tis believed that this harp, which I now wake for thee,
Was a syren of old, who sung under the sea;
And who often, at eve, through the bright waters rov'd
To meet, on the green shore, a youth whom she lov'd."

Mermaidens are said to allure youths of mortal mould to follow them beneath the waves, where they afterwards live in some enchanted state. Merrows wear a *cohuleen druith*, or little charmed cap, generally covered with feathers, and used for diving under water. If this be lost or stolen, they have no power to return beneath " waters of the vasty deep." Sometimes they are said to leave their outer skins behind, to assume others more magical and beauteous. The merrow has soft white webs between her fingers. She is often seen with a comb, parting her long green hair on either side of the head. Female merrows are represented as beautiful in features. Merrow music is frequently heard, coming up from the lowest depths of ocean, and sometimes floating over the surface

Merrows often dance to it on the shore, strand, or waves. With all their fascinations, practised to seduce the sons of men, the mermaidens are occasionally found to be vengeful. An old tract, contained in the Book of Lecain, states that a king of the Fomorians, when sailing over the Ictian sea, had been enchanted by the music of mermaids, until he came within reach of these syrens. Then they tore his limbs asunder, and scattered them on the waves.

From Dr. O'Donovan's *Annals of the Four Masters*, at the year of Christ 887, we find a curious entry regarding a mermaid cast ashore by the sea in the country of Alba, the modern Scotland. One hundred and ninety-five feet was her length, we are told, eighteen feet was the length of her hair, seven feet was the length of the fingers of her hand, seven feet also was the length of her nose, while she was whiter than the swan all over. Hence, it would seem, that the merrows were thought to have attained extraordinary large proportions; if, indeed, this be not the actual record of a fact, illustrating the natural history of our coasts.

The valour of certain Fenian heroes is celebrated on behalf of a mariner-lady, in Miss Brooke's beautifully translated poem of *Moira Borb*. This we find in her *Reliques of Irish Poetry*. The chiefs met her coming into a harbour from the waves, over which her bark swiftly glided. Her beauty was faultless; and on being questioned as to her parentage, by the son of Comhal, she replies,—

> "Truth, O great chief! my artless story frames:
> A mighty king my filial duty claims.
> But princely birth no safety could bestow;
> And, royal as I am, I fly from woe."

Miss Brooke tells us, in a note, that she has not rendered this stanza literally, because she found it difficult to interpret the Irish words: *As mé ingean rig fo trinn.*

They may be translated, *I am the daughter of the king under waves;* or the last words may be rendered, *king of waves,* or king of *Ton* (in the genitive), *Trin,* literally, *a wave;* but it may also mean some country, anciently bearing such name. It might even be a metaphorical phrase, implying either an island or some of the low countries.

Strange to say, the merrow is sometimes imagined to be a water-man; but in such case, he is deformed in shape and features. Merrow-men are also said to keep the spirits of drowned fishermen and sailors under cages, at the bottom of the sea. Doubtless, a belief in such fantasies and necromancy must have come down to us from the most remote times of Paganism.

CHAPTER VIII.

THE LIANHAUN SHEE.

" It was a beauteous fairy form
   That thus about the wanderer played;
And twined a garland bright and warm
   Around us twain, that ne'er can fade.

" She called me her beloved lord,—
   She called herself a wife's dear name;
And gave to me, with glad accord,
   Her wondrous, sweet, and tender frame."

DENIS FLORENCE MAC CARTHY.

THE Germans, who are imaginative and speculative in fairy lore as they are versed in more exact science, poesy, and literature, have ideas regarding an *elfin kind*, or fairy-child, somewhat resembling the Irish superstition of the Lianhaun Shee. De La Motte Fouque has versified in their noble and expressive language the affecting incident of an elfin being, who became attached to a youth of mortal mould. He was captivated by the spell thrown around him, and with a sympathetic feeling he loved the unearthly nymph. Their bridal union, however, was of brief duration, and did not last after the rays of morning's sun began to peep over the purpled peaks of the mountain. Their die was then cast; the elfin bride lingered too long with her *inamorato* in the verdant vale; the sun's beams surprised them during their first nightly interview; the beautiful fairy form was soon turned into marble; the doating and bereaved youth cast himself weeping beside the lifeless figure; while he determined to remain there, until death came to his relief. This pathetic ballad has been charmingly rendered into an English metrical translation by one, foremost among our living poets, Denis Florence Mac Carthy. In the September number of the *Dublin University Magazine* for 1849 it appears, with other scintillations of his genius and inspiration, drawn from foreign sources, yet coloured in the alembic of his own fertile thought and happy phrase.

The conception of this spirit, as known to the Continentals, and understood by our countrymen, revealed to the poet a further intellectual glimpse of an invisible sorceress and guide, waving a more potent wand than that of Prospero. She is represented as directing the noblest aspirations of youths' ambition. Under her newly-assumed poetic guise, she arises the tutelary spirit over persons who are called to the ministration of truth and beauty, whether by cultivating religion, patriotism, generous actions, science, literature, or art. These worthy aspirants she delights in; while she blesses and enlightens them during the period of their earthly career. Sadly, however, would she lament, if, after persistence in their noble course, her *protegés* might be tempted to abandon their vocation, through weak or unworthy motives. Then must she feel keenly the force of these concluding expressions:—

> "Ah me! to be subdued when all seemed won—
> That I should fly when I would fain have clung.
> Yet so it is,—our radiant course is run;—
> Here we must part, the deathless lay unsung,
> And, more than all, the deathless deed undone."

The *Lianhaun Shee* has thus become idealized as a superior and an intellectual spirit, while addressing other subordinate yet guardian *genii*. These may be considered as separately presiding, not alone over various mental efforts and excellencies, but even over life's ordinary duties and enjoyments. The elegant poem of our gifted friend, as bearing on this subject, has appeared in the October number, for 1851, of the literary periodical to which allusion has been already made, and which has been enriched by so many other graceful compositions, emanating from his rich and diversified fancies.

Our sprite is supposed to form a particular attachment for men, to whom it appears in the shape of a young and beautiful female. Whoever falls under the spells of this fairy spirit cannot marry; for, although invisible to a third party, she has a strong fascination for the person to whom she becomes attached, and she will not leave his presence for several years. As the man reciprocates this affection, she instructs and rewards him by communicating a knowledge of music, the art of healing, fairy mysteries, and various other accomplishments. Mr. Carleton has made this sprite the subject of a popular Irish story. It also forms the theme for one of Mr. J. E. Carpenter's interesting songs, published in London, 1849, and chiefly drawn from fairy lore conceits.

The *Lenauntshee* is implacable in resentment, and unalterable in friendship. Mr. O'Daly has rendered the Irish of this word into "a familiar spirit," in an interesting *Collection of Irish Songs,* published at Kilkenny in 1843. This volume is now rarely procurable. When a peasant may find himself overmatched in a party or faction fight, and yet maintain the struggle against considerable odds, it is supposed that the *Lenauntshee* affords invisible aid, and deals out blows for him with scientific skill. The rather misty state of a combatant's brain during the progress of a contest, with an indulgence in spirituous liquors, would readily account for the reception of many invisible strokes, and a casual superior prowess of individual champions over the opposing force of a great many adversaries.

The celebrated and affecting ballad of William Carleton,

and known as "Sir Turlough; or, the Churchyard Bride," seems illustrative of the Irish *Lianhan Shee*. The goblin's fascination for the mortal, and the reaction induced on his part, with the tragic results of such attachment, greatly resemble the vagaries of popular credence on this subject. This churchyard spirit sometimes assumes the guise of a young and handsome man, when appearing to a female. In either case it symbolizes death, which it forebodes.

CHAPTER IX.

O'CARROLL'S BANSHEE AND TERRYGLASS CASTLE.

"Hark! hark! on the wings of the night-wafted gale
Sweeps on, in its death-tones, the BANSHEE'S shrill wail!
Hark! hark! to the echoes which sadly prolong
Those dread notes of sorrow, her gloom-bringing song!
From the depths of the grave, from the darkness of hell,
The phantom comes forth with her death-breathing spell;
For the gleam of her dark eye, the hiss of her breath,
But herald the coming of sorrow and death!"

J. L. FORREST.

A BEAUTIFUL and an affecting tale, called "The Banshee," occurs in the *Legends of Connaught.* There a living creature and a maniac had been thoughtlessly fired upon and killed by a soldier, under an impression that she had been a supernatural being of the Banshee species. In this particular instance, however, it does not appear that the characteristic figure and voice of the Banshee had been discovered.

The Banshee, or "white-woman," is sometimes called the *Shee Frogh,* or "house-fairy." She is represented as a small, shrivelled, old woman,—sometimes, however, as young and beautiful,—with long flaxen hair. This she is often seen combing, while pouring forth the wildest and most startling strains of soul-piercing melody. A Banshee is supposed to herald the immediate demise of members belonging to certain old Irish families. She is always observed alone, and in a melancholy mood, when found near the doomed person's home. In various instances, the Banshee is believed to have been the ghost of some person who had formerly suffered violence from a family progenitor. She repeats her vengeful wail, from a particular spot, whilst announcing the approach of death to his descendants. Whether she is a friend or an enemy of the family to whom her warning has been conveyed, seems undefined and uncertain. Her cry often comes from a spring, river, or lake, with which her name is connected.

Amongst traditions of the Scottish Highlands there is mention often made of the *Bodach Glas*, or avenging Gray Spectre. It seems of kindred species with the Banshee, and it was supposed to appear on the eve of some great impending calamity to the descendant of that chief, who had been guilty of taking a fellow-creature's life. We all know what a fine dramatic use Sir Walter Scott makes of this phantom, in his novel of *Waverley*, when the noble chieftain of Glennaquoich, Fergus Mac-Ivor Vich Ian Vohr, beholds this evil spirit on the eve of his captivity, and again on the night previous to his execution.

The upper waters of Lough Derg, on the Shannon, are overlooked by the ruined castle of Terryglass, and its four circular bastions, on the four corners of the massive walls. These are of immense thickness; but, it is sufficiently evident, they do not rise to a third of their former height. On a fine breezy day in autumn, the rough waters of Lough Derg roll along with every sweep of the winds, and wavelets beat the shores, at some short distance from the foundations of this massive fortalice. It is called "Old Court," by the country people. The door-way opened towards the Shannon, and near it one of the corner bastions is entered. A broken and winding, but comparatively wide, circular stone stair conducts the visitor to the upper level of Terryglass Castle walls; and it is quite possible to walk above their remaining grass-covered tops, especially if no stiff breeze prevail, and if the adventurer be active and strong of nerve. He may then look down over the ground-plan of the building, which is nearly quadrangular. A thick dividing wall separates the interior into two nearly equal divisions. As the visitor reaches each angle of the fortress, on his way, he may see interiorly circular bastions beneath him, in a tolerably perfect state, with old elder or thorn shrubs growing in the lower soil, while narrow looped windows on the exterior are splayed inwards, dimly to light the various compartments. The whole rests on a limestone rock foundation; while rich meadows, pastures, corn-fields, and tangled thorn fences, stretch around, or slope gently downwards to the waters of Lough Derg. Beyond the wide extended lake, the bordering woods of Lord Clanricard's demesne, with the new and old castles and house-tops of Portumna, may be seen. Still farther off, the blue tops of the Clare mountains stretch to the south and west, in every variety and depth of shade, beneath the lighter clouded skies. Around Terryglass Castle the lower walls spread near the foundations, and incline inwardly to a certain height, so as greatly to strengthen their superstructure, in the approved modern military engineering style of construction. Hoary and worn are the remains, and choked around with briars and shrubs. Yet they present traces of grandeur and vastness; nor can we doubt, that in former times this lordly fortress raised its parapets high in air, and looked with frowning pride over the wide range of Lough Derg and its surrounding landscape.

In times now remote, a chieftain named O'Carroll, with his military retainers, tenanted the halls of Old Court. As usual within those walls, an evening entertainment had closed with the dances and songs then practised; and the aged harper having drawn the last tones from the wire of his clairseach, all retired to rest, but the warders of night, who took their station on the highest tower, to keep watch and ward. O'Carroll had ordered his wherry, with the forester, huntsman, and two stalworth clansmen, to be ready next morning, and at an early hour after breakfast, on the banks of Lough Dearg. He purposed having a row over to the lower shore of Thomond, on a visit to one of the O'Briens. The sun rose bright, and the day was perfectly calm, as they shot forth on the glistening surface of the wide lake. Soon the boat seemed a speck in the middle waters, and with well-drawn strokes, the voyagers landed on a distant foreland.

The chieftain's return was expected on the evening next succeeding. But while the warder prepared for his night-watch, and before the people in Old Court had sought repose, a loud, piercing, unearthly wail was heard, coming, as it were, from the nearest waters of Lough Dearg. It froze the very heart with terror; while the castle retainers ran to every loop-hole window on the upper storey, and even to the roof, to ascertain whence this lamentation proceeded. The moon had just appeared, and shed a mellow light over the surrounding landscape, bringing every object into sufficient prominence. Soon the beholders observed a beautiful female figure, clad in white, with long flowing locks streaming over her shoulders, and gliding slowly over the clear surface of the lake below, while the mournful dirge became momently more faint, until, at last, it died away in the distance. The figure also dissolved, like one of the passing night shadows. The people, who had heard and watched this strange visitant for some time, looked at one another in mute astonishment, or vented exclamations of wonder and foreboding. "It is, no doubt, O'Carroll's Banshee," cried one of the number; "and I fear some sad accident will soon cause the death of our chief!"

With intense anxiety, on the morning afterwards, all eyes were directed towards the far-off shores of Thomond

A boat had been even despatched thither, at an early hour, with intelligence regarding the strange portent. Yet was it too late to convey warning to the chief, in whose fate his clansmen were painfully interested. Towards the midnight before, an unfortunate misunderstanding arose between O'Carroll and a gentleman of the O'Brien sept,— an insult was supposed to have been conveyed, and nothing would satisfy the offended party but the arbitrament of a passage at arms. Every effort was made by mutual friends to prevent such a result, yet without effect. Both combatants insisted on ending the difference —on the lawn before O'Brien's castle—before morning had dawned. The skilful and gallant swordsmen for some time wielded their trusty weapons in attack and defence; but the wary O'Brien seized on an unguarded moment, and the very next instant ran his rapier through the heart of that brave adversary with whom he contended. The Castellan of Terryglass fell lifeless on the ground.

His clansmen, in wail and sorrow, brought their chieftain's remains towards the boat; and, with sadness of heart, stretched to their oars, until they rowed across the lake. No sooner were they descried on the water, than many persons lined the Terryglass shore, eagerly expecting their return. Grief and lamentation were loudly and angrily expressed on seeing the pale corpse of O'Carroll, and on hearing the unlooked-for cause of his untimely fate. The body was borne to Old Court. After the *keen* had been chanted, and the funeral ceremonies had been duly arranged, the remains were brought to the neighbouring churchyard of St. Columba Mac Crimthannan. Here they were consigned to earth, an immense concourse of weeping relatives and retainers surrounding his grave, at the time and place of interment.

CHAPTER X.

THE THREE WISHES; OR, ALL IS NOT GOLD THAT GLITTERS.

"Like fairy-gifts, fading away."
                    MOORE.

"Remind him of each wish pursued,
How rich it glowed with promised good;
Remind him of each wish enjoyed,
How soon his hopes possession cloyed."
                    SIR WALTER SCOTT.

IN the remote wilds of Erris, and overtopped by a high heath-clad mountain, the lonely cabin of Fergus O'Hara looked down towards the Owenmore, a rapid stream flowing into Tullaghan Bay, on the west coast of Mayo. His wife, Rose, and her old mother Norah, were the sole companions of his humble home. Indeed, it must be said, they lived in tolerable plight and contentment, on a few acres of poor land, let to them at a reasonable rent; while their goats, pigs, and poultry had an almost limitless range over the uninclosed hill sides. A potato garden and a field of oats were the chief care of Fergus every returning harvest.

One Sunday evening, in the beginning of winter, when the day's duties were nearly over, all three sat chatting before a turf fire that blazed on the hearth-stone. Many family affairs were discussed and arranged; plans for the coming winter were formed; and meantime, while the small pot of boiling potatoes was raising a foam, known as "the white horse," a little dripping or seasoned lard was left over live coals, and slowly simmering in a frying-pan. The table was likewise spread for their homely meal.

"Fwhy, thin, I wish to goodness we could have iverything our own fwhay, Rose," said Fergus, in reply to some observation of his wife; "and we needn't fwear bud all would go right with huz."

No sooner were these words pronounced, than a shrill voice from above cried out, "Well, you just hit on the exact moment, Fergus O'Hara, when you can have your wish; and Fir Danig, the fairy, will give another wish to Rose, and one to old Norah, her mother. So now think well over the matter, before you all make this choice."

On looking upwards, they saw a diminutive creature, dressed in scarlet, with a high-peaked cap on his head. He had sharp features, piercing eyes, a mouth grinning from ear to ear; while the latter appendages seemed sticking out on either side of his head, like those of a mouse. He sat cross-legged, like a tailor, on one of the couples, with silver-mounted pipes yoked on his tiny arms.

The trio of human beings below felt sore afraid at first; but on second thought, they were assured the benevolent little elf had resolved to crown them with fortune. They took council together for some time, to know what it would be proper to demand; but the more this matter was considered, as in many other cases, the more was the council perplexed to arrive at any decision. For a moment, Rose's thoughts were diverted to another idea, as she sat in a contemplative yet vacant mood, stroking the tongs through the ashes in front of the fire. "Well," she ejaculated, after a long pause, "as the good gintleman, sittin' on the couple above, hash put huz in the way of bein' ruch for the remaindher o' our lives, I'm sorry fwhin' I wash at the market yestherday that I didn't buy, from the price o' my brood o' chickens, the fine hog's puddin' in Kitty Flanagan's shap. Troth and I'd like to have it frying there in the pan for our supper this evenin'."

No sooner said than done. In a moment a fine plump hog's pudding appeared on the pan, and its fatty exudations were soon commingling with the melted dripping, while a savoury odour began to spread through the house. Fergus looked at this addition to the evening meal, and instantly losing temper, he turned in a passion towards his simple wife. Hoarse with rage, he then cried out, "Fwhy then, blood-an-agers! ye *sraoilleog!* isn't that a great wish o' yours, afther the chance you got! Ye heve no sinse fwhatever, to ax for fwhat 'ud be eat up tonight, and nothing at all left for to-morrow. Did ye ivir fwhind me sich an *omadhawn?*" And as he maddened at the thought, honest Fergus, too, forgot himself, and added in an excited strain, "I wish one end o' the hog's puddin' was sthuck to yer nose, you foolish craythur!"

Immediately the smoking viand flew from the pan, and formed an appendage to the member indicated; while poor Rose jumped in an agony of pain from the stool on which she sat, and shook her head with the vigour, but hardly with the grace, of a female elephant, winding her huge proboscis. She screamed and gesticulated hysterically, for the hog's pudding raised blisters around the top of her nose.

This grotesque appendage, and the agony in which her daughter was, soon roused the fears and ire of old Norah. Looking wildly and angrily at Fergus, she, in turn, exclaimed, "You unforthunate *tamhach*, to thrate your wife in that fashion! shure enough, ye ought to feel ashamed o' yoursel'; bud I only fwish the other ind o' the hog's puddin' was stuck out iv yer own nose: id 'ud be a just judgmint an ye!"

Here was the third wish exhausted in its actual accomplishment; for soon was the disengaged end affixed to Fergus's nasal organ; so that if Rose screamed loudly, her husband bellowed and roared with might and main.

Both danced about the apartment like persons bewitched; until the old crone, beside herself with horror, rushed forward to sever the connecting link. First she tried it with her attenuated fingers, which were burned to the very bone in her attempt. She next endeavoured to cool them by blowing with her breath or sucking them with her lips; but she too screamed and danced about the house bewildered and terrified.

Meantime, Fir Danig shook out his arms and began to ply the pipes vigorously; while his cackling, husky laughter was heard as he gave out, in quick succession, these well-known bagpipe tunes, "The Wind that Shakes the Barley," "God Speed the Plough," "Off she Goes," "The Humours of Glinn," with a host of other lively jigs and reels. Nothing but a chaos of strange noises was heard within the cabin; but the "Reel of Three" was never more fantastically executed than by the trio on the floor, who were nearly exhausted by the pain and the dancing, which continued without intermission for fully a quarter of an hour. On the expiration of that time, Fir Danig gathered up his pipes, crowed like a cock, and the next instant turned a scraw off the roof. The moon peeped in through the opening, while he, giving a somersault, was seen fleeting across its luminous surface.

No sooner had he disappeared, than old Norah recovered her presence of mind, rushed towards the dresser, and procuring a knife, with a quick stroke she severed the hog's pudding in the centre. After some little trouble and patience bestowed on the operation, she cut the remaining portions clean off the noses of both, yet not without leaving a mark behind, that appeared like a ringworm, when they afterwards ventured abroad. Notwithstanding all their promises to hush up the foregoing incidents, and keep them concealed from the knowledge of their neighbours, mutual recriminations were sometimes indulged, in reference to their disagreeable reminiscences. In fine, the story got vent through the country. At fair, market, or gathering, their kind friends would often cast a sly glance at those traces left on the most prominent facial developments of Fergus and Rose, reflect on the vanity of human wishes, and draw such a moral as comported with their feelings or ideas, generated by spleen, compassion, humour, or wisdom.

CHAPTER XI.

FAIRY HAUNTS AND FAIRY CELEBRITIES.

" I saw the Mourna's billows flow;
   I passed the walls of Shenady;
And stood in the hero-thronged Ardroe,
   Embosked amid greenwoods shady;
And visited that proud pile that stands
   Above the Boyne's broad waters,
Where Ængus dwells with his warrior-bands,
   And the fairest of Ulster's daughters.

" To the halls of Mac Lir, to Creevroe's height,
   To Tara, the glory of Erin,
To the fairy palace that glances bright
   On the peak of the blue Cnocfeerin,
I vainly hied. I went west and east—
   I travelled seaward and shoreward—
But thus was I greeted at field and at feast,—
   ' Thy way lies onward and forward!' "

JAMES CLARENCE MANGAN.

OUR native literature abounds in romantic tales, containing many beautiful fictions. Yet some of these *contes* are often disfigured by extravagant inventions, and wholly incredible incidents. Sometimes voyages to foreign countries are described, and wonderful or grotesque achievements wrought by heroes who set out in quest of adventures. Sometimes we find an account regarding what occurred to them, when, through accident or design, they entered into the realms of fairy-land. In many of these narratives, curious information is conveyed to us in reference to several mountains, hills, rivers, wells, caves, and cairns, situated in different parts of Ireland.

The ancient Irish were accustomed to call any hill or

artificial mound, under which burial vaults lay, by the denomination *Sidh*. Hence, also, arises the term *Sidhe*, meaning "one dead," or "one buried;" and, generally, because the entombed persons had been regarded as heroes or celebrities, vague notions concerning their prowess or adventures floated through the minds of the commonalty. It is believed by many, that the Sidh-na-Brogha, or " burial hill of the plain," was identical with the celebrated Pagan cemetery known as Brugh-na-Boinne, or " plain of the Boyne," now the *tumulus* of New Grange, on the north bank of that river. It is supposed to have been one of the most famous, among the many royal *Religs* or "burial mounds" in Ireland. Here were the Tuatha De Danann nobles and their wives interred, as Sir William Wilde shows more at length, in the eighth chapter of his most learned and charming guide-book, *The Beauties of the Boyne and Blackwater*. But the *Leabhar na h-Uidhre*, an old manuscript, compiled in the twelfth century at Clonmacnoise, contains a tract called *Senchas-na-Relec*, or *History of the Cemeteries*, which serves to illustrate the ancient topography of Erin with the funeral rites and customs of her earlier inhabitants.

If our Pagan ancestors had any definite ideas or belief concerning supernatural Divinities, these seem to have been regarded chiefly as spiritual or ethereal beings. Few gross conceptions of their characteristics or mystic acts, such as degraded the understanding of Greeks and Romans, were entertained about the Gentile Divinities of the ancient Irish. This is supposed, in a great measure, to have prepared their way for a ready appreciation and acceptance of the truths of Christianity. The local *genii* were usually known as "good people;" and, it was thought, they often desired an aggregation to their number, but only from among the beautiful, innocent, or amiable children of earth. Nor were they known to be vindictive towards men or women, if propitiated by them, or not provoked by the bad conduct of human beings.

Again, the Gentiles, or Tribes of the Glens, were considered to have been dark spirits, or monsters, generally dwelling in lonely valleys, wild-looking dells, and gloomy caverns. They were often overcome by valiant warriors, and, so far as known, they had little power seriously to injure mortals. Still were they regarded as revengeful, deceitful, and malevolent, when opportunities were presented; and a boding fear of their resentment or mischievous designs was apprehended by individuals, who were obliged to pass their haunts late in the evening, or after night-fall.

Certain weird places and personages are mentioned in Irish popular traditions, and have even found a record in our native literature. Their names have relation to celebrated storied chieftains or females, and to fairy haunts. In the *Book of Ballgmote*, there may be found a treatise, which gives an account regarding the origin of various renowned places throughout this island.

There is a very curious tract, contained in the *Book of Lecan*, which throws much traditional light on the origin of fairy hills, fairy chiefs, and fairyism in Ireland. Also, in the *Book of Lismore*, we find a list of all the Irish fairy chiefs. Both these MSS.—valuable for many historic tracts therein contained—are preserved in the Library of the Royal Irish Academy. Manahan Mac Lir is a fabled king of fairy-land, and the ruler of a happy kingdom. With his fair daughters, Aine and Æife, he sailed often round the headlands of Inishowen. Among some of our fine romantic legends, we are told that, whilst Brian Mac Fearbhall, a king of Ireland, was one day alone, and near his palace, he heard most ravishing strains of fairy music, which at last lulled him into a profound sleep. On awaking, he found the silver branch of a tree by his side. This he brought to the lords and ladies of his court. Amongst them appeared a strange lady, who invited the monarch to a fairy-land of happiness. The silver branch then passed from his hand into this lady's; and on the following morning, with a company of thirty persons, he sailed out on the ocean. After a voyage for a few days, he landed on an island inhabited only by women, of whom this stranger appeared to be the chieftainess. There he remained for several ages before returning to his own palace, near Lough Foyle.

Manahan M'Lir is regarded as the Irish Neptune, or sea-divinity; and he is said to lie buried in the Tonn Banks, off the coast of Donegal. Many shipwrecks here occur; and the spirit of Manahan is supposed to ride at intervals on the storm. The Tonns form one portion of a triad, known as the "Three Waves of Erin." The Wave of Rury, in Dundrum Bay; the Wave of Cliona, off Cape Clear, are the other divisions, the Tonns being known as the Northern Wave. Whenever Cuchulain lifted his shield and smote it, the three waves of Erin echoed this signal, and roared over ocean. When a storm is impending, the Northern Tonn is heard in loud commotion, and at a distance of several miles. From the fabled hero of whom we treat, the O'Malleys, who were celebrated sea-rovers, have been styled by their bards, "the Manahans of ocean." Manahan has been regarded as one of the Tuatha De Danann chiefs, who fell in battle, fighting against the Milesians. After death he was renowned as a sea-sprite, being surnamed MacLir, or Mac Léar, "Son of the ocean." From him, also, the Isle of Man, or Inis-Manannan, is said to have derived its name.

Another disembodied hero of local celebrity is Niall-na-ard, or Neil of the Heights, who is said to rule as Fairy King over the Hills of Knockameny, Knockglass, Lag, and Gorey, as also over the Gulf of Strabreagy, on the shores of Donegal. The Queen of this potentate is thought to hold divided jurisdiction with him, and to influence his decisions. Manannan is said to have submerged both of these, with their former castle and estate, under Strabreagy Lough.

In Irish legendary tales, we have also an account of a fairy chief from Sliabh Fuaid, who was accustomed to set all the company at Tara asleep, by the sweetness of his music, during the annual assemblies. He then set fire to the palace. This chief, named Aillen Mac Midhna, was afterwards killed by Fiun Mac Cumhal. This celebrated Fiun Mac Cumhail is likewise said to have found a preternatural and dwarfish harper, called Cnu Deroil, on the side of Sidh-Ban-Fiun, supposed to be identical with the present Sliabh-na-mban, in the county of Tipperary.

There is a king of the fairies in Munster, called *Donn Firineach*, or Donn the Truth-teller, or Truthful, who is said to live in the romantic hill of Cnock-firinn, county of Limerick. *Donn* in Irish has the English signification of *dun*, or *brown-coloured*. He is said, originally, to have been one of the sons of the celebrated Milesius, who came from Spain to colonize Ireland. This Donn is thought to have been shipwrecked, with all his mariners, on the coast of Munster. Amongst the old "Irish Popular Songs," so faithfully and expressively rendered into English metre by Edward Walsh, and published in 1847, we find the *Duan na Saoirse*, or "Song of Freedom," by the anonymous author, the *Mangaire Sugach*. In this, Donn is personified and introduced, as requiring the bard to proclaim that the hour had arrived for making a bold effort to restore the Stuart dynasty. The translation thus commences:—

> " All woful, long I wept, desponding,
> Dark-bosom'd, fainting, wearied, weak,
> The foeman's withering bondage wearing,
> Remote in gorge of mountain bleak.

"No friend to cheer my visions dreary,
Save generous Donn, the king of Faëry,
Who, mid the festal banquet airy,
Those strains prophetic thus did speak."

Donn, chief of the Sandhill fairies of Dooghmore, in Clare County, is addressed by Andrew Mac Curtin, a celebrated Irish scholar and bard, who flourished about the beginning of the last century.

Bodb was a fairy potentate, who, with his daughters, lived within Sidh-ar-Femhin—a hill or fairy mansion on the plain of Cashel. To this subterranean residence a famous old harper, named Cliach, is said to have obtained access, by playing his harp near the spot, until the ground opened, and admitted him to the fairy realms. Every seventh May morning, likewise, Ior, a fairy chief, steered his bark through Loch Cluthair. And the fairy fleet of the south was often seen by fishermen sailing round the Fastnet Rock and Carrigeen a Dhoolig. In Irish traditions we find Fiachna Mac Rœtach and Eochaidh Mac Sail mentioned as rival chiefs, amongst the Sidhe, or fairy-men. Ilbhreac was the elfin chief of Eas Roe, now Ballyshannon. There was a celebrated *sidhe* mansion at this place. In a rath on the road side, between Cork and Youghall, it is believed that a spectral chieftain, named Knop, holds his court. Sometimes music and merriment are heard from within this fort, and travellers often observe strange lights around it. Brigh Leith was anciently a famous fairy mount in Westmeath.

The White Shee, or Fairy Queen, has a recognized pre-eminence over others of her sex. It was probably owing to his familiarity with a tradition of this sort that the poet Spenser was induced to compose his magnificent allegorical and fanciful poem, *The Faerie Queen*. His favourite heroine, Una, is often named by the peasantry as regent of the preternatural *Sheog* tribes. The name probably occurs under other forms. We are told that Ounaheencha, a fairy queen of ocean, was accustomed to sail around the Kerry and Clare coasts in quest of handsome young men, who were captured, and conducted to her cave. Again, the fairy damsel Sidheng is said to have presented Finn Mac Cool with a battle stone, to which a chain of gold was attached. With this weapon he was rendered invincible on the field of contest.

Cleena, the elfin queen of South Munster, is said to reside within her invisible palace at Carrig Cleena, near Fermoy, county of Cork. Clidhna is said to have been of Tuath de Danann descent. There is a Cliodhna, written in Irish, *Tonn Cliodhna*, or *the Wave of Cleena*. The latter designation is applied to loud, roaring surges in Glandore harbour, in a southern part of this same county. There are sea-worn caverns, hollowed out of the rocks on this coast, from which the waves loudly resound, with a deep, monotonous roar. In the calm of night these moaning surges are most impressive, producing sensations of fear or melancholy. Such natural features and sounds have been graphically described by Dean Swift in his Latin poem, called *Carberiæ Rupes*, which he composed June, 1723, whilst on a visit in this neighbourhood. Alluding to the effects of a winter storm, he writes—

"Littora littoribus reboant: vicinia latè,
Gens assueta mari, et pedibus percurrere rupes,
Terretur tamen, et longe fugit, arva relinquens."

There is extant an Irish poem on the derivation of *Tonn Clidhna*, or Clidhna's wave, off the Cork coast. Allusion is thus made to the Fairy Queen of Munster by Edward Walsh, in his beautiful ballad, entitled ".O'Donovan's Daughter:"—

"God grant 'tis no fay from Cnoc-Firinn that woos me;
God grant 'tis not Cliodhna, the queen, that pursues me—
That my soul, lost and lone, has no witchery wrought her,
While I dream of dark groves and O'Donovan's daughter."

In one of Edward Walsh's translated Irish songs,
"The Banshee bright, of form Elysian,"
is represented as a most beautiful woman; but she may probably be regarded as the fairy queen; for in a vision she leads the imaginative Irish bard, John M'Donnell, through all the principal elfin haunts of Ireland.

Yet, perhaps, one of the most renowned heroines of our ancient history was the celebrated Queen of Connaught, Meadbh (pronounced Méav), who figures so prominently in the annals of our island. This princess was remarkable, not alone for her beauty, but likewise for her poetic abilities, and her masculine vigour of character. She contracted an unhappy marriage with Conor Mac Nessa, king of Ulster; but she soon separated from him, and formed an alliance with Ailill, a Connaught chieftain. He died shortly afterwards; and Méav next married another Ailill, son to Ross Ruadh, king of Leinster. Her warlike deeds were subjects for many old bardic ranns and romances. The *Cow-spoil of Cuilgne* is probably one of these best known; and this was regarded as a historic tale, which must have been committed to memory by the former poets of Erin, in order to entertain the kings and chiefs. This romance is yet recited by the peasantry in many parts of Ireland. "Meav's plain" was a poetical name among our bards for the western province. Many persons believe, that the celebrated Queen of Connaught furnished the original of Shakespeare's "Queen Mab," "the fairies' midwife," whose pranks are so graphically described in one of his most popular dramas.

In our youthful days—probably not much more than thirty years hence—the Irish peasantry numbered among them many excellent *raconteurs* and *raconteuses*, for the most part very old or middle-aged persons. At field-work, or by the fireside, or at fair, market, or merry-making, on a Sunday or holiday, it was customary to hear or recite some old story, with plot more intricate, yet quite as interesting, and well-drawn to a satisfactory conclusion, as any found in the romances of our best novelists. Often have we sat or stretched for hours under some shady tree or hedgerow, and heard with inexpressible delight the peasant's tale of wonder. Many a king or prince of the different Irish provinces figured as the hero of these tales; and usually, after a considerable share of fighting with giants or chiefs, some accomplished and beautiful princess became a bride of the conqueror, and returned with him to share the honours of his palace and kingdom. Such an incident always ended the story, but with the narrator's own concluding sentence,—"If they did not live happy in the future, that you and I may." Even when the chill of spring or autumnal evenings might be felt out of doors, we delighted frequently in mounting the ledge of a hay-rick, and, having cut a swarth with the hay-knife, to turn over our limbs as a coverlet, we engaged some field-labourer, wearied after the day's work, to pour forth, evening after evening, his inexhaustible stores of legend or tradition. Well we treasured in memory the thread of narrative for a time; but, it is needless to state, the names of heroes and heroines, with numberless incidents, have long since escaped from our recollection.

It is probably time to close our dissertation on old haunts of the Elfin tribe, and on those mythical individuals, who have achieved a registration in popular recollection, or on the rolls of historic romance, within the bounds of our Emerald Isle. It would require a little more time and researchful effort, to enumerate many additional incidents or illustrations; but imagination must yet take wing, and sport with further specific subjects of our theme.

CHAPTER XII.

LAKE HABITATIONS AND SPIRITS.

> "In their high-roofed halls,
> There, with the chiefs of other days, feel they
> The mingled joy pervade them? or beneath
> The mid-sea waters, did that crystal ark
> Down to the secret depths of ocean plunge
> Its fated crew? Dwell they in coral bowers
> With mermaid loves, teaching their paramours
> The songs that stir the sea, or make the winds
> Hush, and the waves be still? In fields of joy
> Have they their home, where central fires maintain
> Perpetual summer, where one emerald light
> Through the green element for ever flows?"
> SOUTHEY.

SUBAQUEOUS cities are supposed to lie under the surface of nearly all our Irish lakes. This belief has probably originated from frequently recurring optical deception, owing to the shadows of overhanging mountains and clouds being fantastically reflected from the unruffled surface of these loughs. Most of the Irish lakes are said to have sprung from Magic Wells, that bubbled up at certain times, until they had filled their valley basins. On this subject, there is a ballad by W. M. Downes, referring to the origin of Killarney. Spenser, also, in his *Faerie Queen*, seems to have in mind a nearly similar catastrophe, when he refers to—

"Sad Trowis, that once his people over-ran." *

In Moore's beautiful melody, "Let Erin remember the days of old," the tops of round towers are represented as shimmering beneath the waters of Lough Neagh. Again,

* Canto xi., book iv., stanza xli.

in that exquisite song, known as "O'Donohue's Mistress," we find allusion made to the lakes and local chieftain apparition of Lough Lene. Belonging to the Royal Irish Academy, there is a copy of a curious tract, usually entitled, *The Saltair* or *Psalter of the Pig*. This contains a legend regarding Caon Comrac, an ancient bishop of Clonmacnois, and it mentions an enchanted or a miraculous monastery and people, buried under the surface of Lough Ree, in the river Shannon. With almost every lake, throughout Ireland, some remarkable and highly poetic legend is connected. One of these romances we extract from documentary sources.

In times far remote, and while Crimthan Cas reigned, the princes and heroes of Connaught held a great provincial assembly on a certain occasion, and near a lake, situated in the beautiful plain of Magh Ai, and within the present county of Roscommon. Suddenly the magnates and people assembled beheld a stranger come up towards them from out of the lough. He wore a crimson mantle, a gold-bordered shield, and a golden-hilted sword. When Laeghaire Liban, son to Crimthan Cas, saw this unexpected visitor approach, the prince arose, welcomed him, and then asked about his name, and the object of his visit. The stranger answered, that his name was Fiachna Mac Reatach, that he was one of the *Sidhe*, or Fairy-men. He had come thither, he said, to claim assistance against another fairy chief, named Eochaidh Mac Sail. This latter had forcibly carried off Fiachna's wife, and the abductor now meditated an invasion of his territories. On that very day, a challenge had been sent to Fiachna, and he now asked the Conacian heroes to assist him, promising rewards of gold and silver to any brave combatants, who volunteered in his quarrel. After this announcement, the fairy chieftain courteously saluted the Prince of Connaught, and then departed towards the lake, into which he plunged, and instantly disappeared.

The courage and ardour of young Prince Leaghaire, and fifty other well-armed retainers, were roused at his sight, and moved by the appeal of their strange visitant. All followed excitedly towards the lake, and, as if with one mind, they dived beneath its waters. Soon they were ranged in martial array on a lawn, which stretched before a magnificent palace. There they found opposing armies in embattled ranks, and quite ready to engage in hostile encounter. Leaghaire and his men stood on the side of Fiachna Mac Reatach, and a furious contest ensued. It terminated in the death of the fairy chief, Eochaidh Mac Sail, who was killed by the prince's spear, while victory crowned the Conacians, and their allied fairy host.

The wife of Fiachna was soon restored to her rightful lord, and the mortal prince was next introduced to their beautiful daughter, Dergrene, "The Sun-tear." He fell in love with this charming princess; and his affection being reciprocated, he asked her parents' consent for their marriage. This was obtained, and the prince, with his retainers, thenceforth chose to dwell under the lake ever after, as denizens of a subaqueous region. Often by the lake side, and over its waters, these spirit people are seen; their music and revelry are also heard from beneath; nor are the mysteries of their enchanted kingdom known to mortals.

CHAPTER XIII.

MONUMENT BUSHES AND ROAD-SIDE CAIRNS.

"Here by thy pathway lone,
Where the thorn blossoms are bending
Over thy mouldered stone."
Mrs. Downing.

"For he told them tales of the Loup-garou in the forest,
And of the goblin that came in the night to water the horses,
And of the white Létiche, the ghost of a child who unchristened
Died, and was doomed to haunt unseen the chambers of children."
Longfellow.

WHO could have thought that, among the *contes* of an Acadian village notary, allusion would have been made, in the charming metrical tale of *Evangeline*, to superstitions, which prevail very generally in the minds of our Irish peasantry? Yet, such coincidences are deducible through a constant stream of tradition and from a common source of information. Those national *contes* have been borne by the unsophisticated emigrant of Normandy or Brittany from the shores of beautiful France to their primeval forest homes in the New World. Therefore may we trace, with a little exercise of judgment, certain affinities existing between the ancient Celts of Ireland and of Gaul, as revealed in the popular notions, not yet eradicated, even after a lapse of many centuries, and the progress of modern enlightenment.

Writers on Irish superstitions represent unbaptized children as sitting blindfolded within fairy moats, the peasantry supposing such souls "go into naught," as we are told. However, this belief by no means can be general, even amongst the most unenlightened of our peasantry.

All of those, with whom we have at any time conversed on this subject, believe that unbaptized infants suffer "the pain of loss," in accordance with the doctrine and teaching of Catholic Theologians. This teaching is also expressed in the sacred Scripture:—"Unless a man be born again of water and the Holy Ghost, he cannot enter into the kingdom of God" (John iii. 5). In other words, unbaptized persons are regarded as deprived of God's beatific vision, although not subject to the more extreme sufferings of those, who have lost the grace of baptismal innocence.

Unbaptized children and abortions are generally buried under "monument bushes;" and probably, owing to this circumstance, such names have been given them. It is remarkable, also, that when interments of this kind take place in consecrated churchyards throughout Ireland, the graves are always dug on the north side of a cemetery, apart from those deceased persons who had been baptized. "Monument bushes" are found, for the most part, in the centre of road crossings. Sometimes they are seen by a road side, but detached from adjoining fences. Often grouped together in gnarled and fantastic shapes, they present a picturesque and beautiful view to the passenger, especially when flowered over with hawthorn blossoms. Ghosts or monsters were occasionally conjured up, before the excited imaginations of credulous or timid persons, when passing those objects by night.

Ancient and solitary hawthorns, generally called "monument bushes," are held in great veneration by the commonality. It would be considered profanation to destroy them, or even to remove any of their branches. The fairies and phookas are supposed to frequent the sites of those bushes. The former dapper elves are often seen hanging from or flitting amongst their branches. But ghosts are more generally found about those haunts, and thus few persons desire to pass by them at a late hour, and without companions. Still, those fears are gradually losing force, because few of the old traditions are known to a rising generation.

Whenever a funeral cortège passed by these "monument bushes," it was customary for all the attendants to uncover their heads, while the *De Profundis* had been recited. Then the processionists continued their way with the corpse towards that graveyard chosen for interment.

A lady, dressed in a long, flowing, white robe, is often supposed to issue from beneath those "monument bushes," and to seat herself on the haunches of the horse, when a solitary horseman rides along the road. She usually clasps him around the waist, and her hands or arms are found to be deadly cold. She speaks not a word, and suddenly glides off, after riding a considerable distance with him. This apparition is supposed to indicate a near approach of the horseman's death; and thenceforward he begins to droop or fall into a lingering decline.

The following memorial customs, in reference to the dead, appear to have come down from a remote period. When a person had been murdered, or had died by some sudden death, on a particular spot or on a road side, our peasantry, when journeying there, as a mark of respect, carry a stone, which they throw on that site where the dead body was found. An accumulation of stones thus heaped together soon forms a pretty considerable pile. The hat is also taken off by those passing by, and a prayer is usually offered for the eternal repose of the departed soul. "Ni curfated me leach an der Cairne," *I would not even throw a stone on your grave,* is an expression used by the Irish peasantry to denote bitter enmity towards any person thus addressed. But it is very certain, that few of our generous people would carry their resentments so far, as to refuse the *Requiem* prayer after death, on behalf of those least amiable and popular while living.

CHAPTER XIV.

MR. PATRICK O'BYRNE IN THE DEVIL'S GLEN; OR, FOLLY HAS A FALL.

> "O wad some pow'r the giftie gie us
> *To see oursels as others see us!*
> It wad frae monie a blunder free us,
> And foolish notion."
> BURNS.

> "The purple peak, the tinted cliff,
> The glen where mountain-torrents rave,
> And foliage blinds their leaping wave."
> WILLIAM ALLINGHAM.

> "When I did hear
> The motley fool thus moral on the time,
> My lungs began to crow like chanticleer,
> That fools should be so deep contemplative."
> SHAKESPEARE.

THERE is scarcely a town or a country district in Ireland that cannot produce a few living specimens of marked originality. The inhabitants of each locality have a keen relish for genuine fun, presented to them in any fair form; but they seem to estimate it at a higher value, when they are more thoroughly conversant with the individual and his peculiar idiosyncrasies. Now, Mr. Patrick O'Byrne was a very distinctive type, representing an exceptional class of persons. He was a comfortable farmer; still was he a bachelor, and not over young. He was tall, well-built, and good-looking; he had received the benefit of "a little learning" in his earlier days; while he sedulously revised his knowledge of the classics, read the newspapers, almanacks, new and second-hand works, song books, and chap books, furnished through the enterprise of some itinerant pedlar, who wandered with his pack through the country hamlets, or who set up his booth at the provincial fairs and markets. He had some knowledge of Greek and Latin—not forgotten wholly since his days of classic study. He had often ventured into print, through the columns of a county newspaper. He had composed original charades, rebuses, and enigmas. He was especially admired, while he amused the peasantry, owing to his volubility of speech, peculiarity of thinking, affected pronunciation, and high-flown phraseology.

As every good and patriotic Irishman must also be a politician, on the right side, so Mr. Patrick O'Byrne, without neglecting the culture of his leased farm-holding, attended many a political meeting; he proposed many a resolution, and delivered many a telling speech, he being "a free and an independent elector" of his native county. He likewise dressed in a natty manner, yet with some eccentricities of costume, allowable to a personage who was denominated "Jintleman Paddy" by his neighbours, and behind his back; but invariably he was styled "Misther O'Byrne," before his face.

It so happened that the individual in question was remarkable for few serious blemishes of character, and he was liked by all classes. Yet had he one or two besetting faults. It was well known to his neighbours and intimates, that his quantum of self-esteem had rather exceeded the bounds of ordinary egotism, and in his conversations it was often amusingly displayed. If he had imbibed any considerable measure of whisky punch, to which—truth to tell—he was sometimes addicted, his thoughts seemed to become visionary and eccentric, in exact proportion as his head became more giddy or addled. Yet seldom did he exceed a tumbler or two at a sitting;

still, it must be acknowledged, even that was found rather potent, and quite sufficient to produce a little lively excitement in his brains.

The comfortable farm-stead of "Jintleman Paddy" was situated in one of the remote valleys, near the upper waters of the river Vartry, in Wicklow County. Having brought a young horse to the fair of its chief town, bearing a similar name, and having rejected the offers of many a shrewd horse-dealer, a satisfactory price was at length obtained from a sporting squire, who thought he observed "points" of great promise in the animal. This negotiation was not effected, however, without considerable hesitancy and chaffering. Indeed, it seemed rather a doubtful affair, whether any terms of bargain or sale could be finally arranged, until mid-day had passed. The knowing buyers were constantly moving through the throng of bipeds and quadrupeds, with stealthy glances, occasionally directed towards the frames and action of the latter, and towards that peculiar expression to be read on the faces of their owners. These were equally on the alert for chances that might determine the choice of the monied men. Mr. Patrick O'Byrne bestrode his own animal, with grace and dignity combined, and occasionally, in a dashing style, he put the well-trained young horse through various paces on the fair-green.

"Well, O'Byrne," said Squire Fortescue Cunninghame, who stood bolt upright, with his elbows angularly extended, and his hands resting on his hips, when the horse and rider approached, after one of those canters, "will you take my offer of forty pounds for your colt, now that you see how prices rule at the fair? and I have an engagement, that must take me from Wicklow within an hour."

"On the word of an honest mortal, Mr. Cunninghame, I had positively rather you had an abiding bargain of the brown colt, than any other honourable or right honourable gentleman of whom I have cognizance; and I am not absolutely disposed to ask a *bonus* on the price, above his real worth. He's inadequately cheap, indeed, at sixty pounds, for his pedigree is well known to every herald at arms and sporting character in this romantic county of Wicklow."

"I fear, then, after your refusal, O'Byrne, I must declare off," said Mr. Cunninghame.

"I'd regret exceedingly, sir, you would migrate from the fair without acquiring the *plenum dominium** of the animal. He would indubitably be acquired by some other buyer, as a consequence, and be brought an exile far away from his native pastures. I'd regret it extremely, Mr. Cunninghame, for your own peculiar interest. Here, too, I would remain by the loud resounding sea shore, moody as the hero Achilles, afar from the Grecian camp; and it might be predicated of me then, as old Homer sings of the sorrowful Chryses—you know the line, Mr. Cunninghame—

'Βῆ δ' ἀκέων παρα θῖνα πολυφλοίσβοιο θαλάσσης.'" †

Mr. Cunninghame laughed at this Homeric quotation, and so did "Jintleman Paddy."

"O'Byrne," cried the former, "I see you have not forgotten your classical authors! But will that help us the sooner, in this matter of sale or purchase?"

"'Pon honour and conscience, Mr. Cunninghame, I have reely refused, and irrevocably refused, sir, more than

* Full ownership.

† For the benefit of our readers having less acquaintance with Greek than Mr. O'Byrne, we must subjoin the following poetic version, by the blind old bard's celebrated translator:—

"Disconsolate, not daring to complain,
Silent he wander'd by the sounding main."
Pope's *Homer's Iliad*, Book i., vv. 49, 50.

that inconsiderable amount offered by you, over and over, from the army contractor and veterinary surgeon; this animal is a weight-carrier, I most solemnly assure you, without brack or vice; he is potential in taking the stiffest fences in grand style, sound in wind and limb. Say the even fifty, Mr. Cunninghame, and as you are an honourable gentleman, residing in our own dear, picturesque county of Wicklow, you must have the exalted preference of purchase, decidedly in advance of any other buyer at the fair. I won't say I want the money now, because I reely do; but the horse, noble as Bucephalus, will double the price in a year or two; the 'go' is in him, and the 'blood and bone' likewise; so don't let this uncommon chance escape your judicious penetration. You might peregrinate all Ireland's isle for his substantive equal, and certainly you could not discover his superior for anything like the price asked."

"Jintleman Paddy" waved his riding-whip and whip-hand, to give more oratorical and persuasive effect to his arguments. The bridle-reins were lightly moved through the fingers of his other hand, as the rider twisted in the saddle, casting an eye over the neck, sides, and limbs of his animal.

"Hold your hand, O'Byrne," said Mr. Cunninghame, who came down on the extended palm with the slap of a gold sovereign, "take five-and-forty, now or never!"

"Mr. Cunninghame, I reely wish to do you a fever. Come, sir, hold your hand for the gold which is yet yours; I want the *auri sacra fames,** until we reach a better issue. I must ride the animal to his comfortable stables, and try the fair of Castledermot, if I don't get superlatively more than that premium on his keeping. But I tell you what I'll honourably do—as you are a reel gentleman, and wouldn't take less—I'll agree to the subtrac-

* Wretched thirst of gold.

tion of a pound or a guinea for a 'luck-penny.' Now, sir, won't you reply in the affirmative, by pronouncing the monosyllable 'Yes ?'"

"I'll say no such thing, by Jove; for I have offered you more than the horse is worth already!"

"*Siste viator!** honoured sir, let us effect what is often transacted in similar cases. Let us adopt a vulgarism, and split the difference!"

"Well, O'Byrne, you are too hard and classical for my fair comprehension in your dealings; but, at a word, the money is yours, and the horse is now mine!"

"May he then thrive sempiternally with your honour, and the depreciation or loss in his price will be all on my side! No matter for that dolorous reflection, so far as I am concerned, it's now a settled bargain."

The cheque was duly drawn by Mr. Cunninghame, and the animal delivered to his groom. "Jintleman Paddy" packed away bridle and saddle, treated an acquaintance of his to a glass or two of whisky punch, and took another himself in company. It is somewhat remarkable, that at Irish fairs, markets, and gatherings, our people of the middle and humbler classes, although starting from home after an early breakfast, and fasting for a very considerable part of the day, hardly ever think of food, or a good luncheon or dinner, as a restorative, or as a necessary refreshment. On the contrary, a treat to some sort of spirituous or malt beverage is what most of them proffer to, or receive from, a friend. It is likewise rather a misfortune, as the Irishman is so social in his tastes and habits, that he can hardly ever indulge in a solitary drink, but he must treat his neighbours and acquaintance to some of the exhilarating draught, of which he feels disposed to partake. This usually provokes "a return," before the company separates; for his familiars cannot

* Stop, traveller.

bear to be outdone in generosity and so-called good-fellowship. Thus round after round may be indulged in, on certain occasions; and the results are anything but creditable to the good sense or sobriety of many persons. It is not wonderful, therefore, that many an Irishman should leave a fair-green with his brain somewhat misty and unsteady.

After the usual congratulations offered to Mr. O'Byrne on the price obtained for his horse, evening was approaching; and having been offered a jaunt on an outside car, belonging to his friend Mr. Hennessy, our hero took his departure from Wicklow, with the money obtained for his colt in a side-pocket. Pleasant conversation enlivened the journey, after they had cleared the fair-green and its yet discordant noises. A smart trot in a home direction, and on the road towards Newtownmountkennedy, brought them to the picturesquely situated village of Ashford, but at a late hour in the evening. Here, bidding a goodbye to his friend, Mr. O'Byrne turned alone into the celebrated Devil's Glen, and took the romantic walk, which led towards his own somewhat distant habitation, a few miles from Roundwood.

It happened to be a beautiful summer evening, and the moon had just risen, spreading a mellowed radiance on the roaring stream and deep broken valleys beneath, and on the gigantic trees, that spread below, around, and above, from the lowest ledge to the highest rocky pinnacles of that wild and romantic pass. Every object looked bright under the moonbeams; but this glow was contrasted by dark shadows settling over interior recesses, through the forest scenery. Ripplings of the Vartry water alone disturbed the solemn silence of the scene. It was a meet hour for contemplation or imagination to find play; and as our solitary traveller's brain was a little excited, and as his thoughts vaguely wandered in review over the day's incidents, or speculated on the past and future, they soon found vocal expression in the following discursive soliloquy.

"I'm superlatively blessed, Mr. O'Byrne, if you ever drained a nicer or wholesomer *vitrum* * of *scalteen* † than they chemically prepare at Michael Murphy's hotel; and it's myself ought to pronounce an encomium on the decent proprietor; for, indeed, he didn't forget to forward the cause of an old customer and a friend to-day, when he insinuated a word or two in the tympanum of Squire Fortescue Cunninghame's auricular organs. I obtained a capital transfer price for the horse, it's true; but I did not say one expression in his favour unbecoming a gentleman's exalted sensations of honour. Why should I do anything unworthy of a princely O'Byrne, the most superior blood in the county of Wicklow, as Irish history manifests? Ay, in troth, it could not be excelled in any other district or part of the island. Well, then, Mr. Patrick O'Byrne, *próspere procéde et regna;* ‡ you won't disgrace or be discarded by the respectable stock, indubitably, that's sure! Indeed, and I may repeat, *paulo majora canamus,*§ for you have the good drop in your veins, and kind for the *filius* ‖ of your father and mother. Were you not brought up tender and respectable, with education fit for a Bishop or Fellow of a college, and natural talents sufficient, at least, for a Member of Parliament? A clean, straight, and likely figure of an Adonis too! Well, that reminds me, is it not high time you'd think of selecting a wife from among the rich farmers' fair and fascinating daughters, that are breaking

* A glass.
† A mixture of hot milk, eggs, and sugar, with whisky, in a tumbler.
‡ "Prosperously advance and reign."
§ "Let us sing in a higher strain."
‖ "Son."

their hearts after your handsome self, your Sabine farm, your accomplishments, and your genteel appearance?" Here a toss upwards of the head, and a quick glance over the smart, swallow-tailed blue body-coat and gilt buttons, the green silk neck-tie, the brilliant plaid-pattern vest, and the Russia-duck pantaloons, down to the dusty, but well-shaped boots, interrupted the soliloquy for a moment. Occasionally he gave a light tap with the riding-whip, which he carried in his hand, to various parts of his habiliments; and this he always did with a sort of dignified nod. Again he resumed:—" Kathleen O'Toole is, no doubt, a well-favoured, decent, well-reared girl, with a superior fortune to boot; but still she wants the education and intellect to make a suitable companion for life. Yet, still, Mr. O'Byrne, if you expect intellect and learning, to compare favourably with your own, where are they to be found in this wild part of the country? Sure enough, there are ladies in Dublin that are smart and polished in their manner and expressions; and I was introduced to a succession of them while I stopped there on business matters; but the question is, could a life in the country suit them, although it might happen a respectable farmer like myself would take the fair creatures by storm? How would these lovely and delicate ladies admire, for their prandial refreshment, a good, juicy, Wicklow ham, the lacteal produce of a mountain farm, or the laughing portrait of a mealy potato, with its opened epidermis, smiling on a trencher? Ha! ha! Mr. O'Byrne; but that's a flowery metaphor, you must admit, and one worthy your classical taste and genius."

After a moment's pause, he again resumed:—" Ay, in troth, disguise it as we may—examine it in every shape and form—though I got the extreme of encouragement, and pleasant, lovely smiles, and elegant compliments from many of the finely-dressed and witty creatures, I doubt rather much, if they'd know how to manage the dairy produce, the swine and poultry, or other matters about my Sabine farm. So, I fear, Mr. O'Byrne, we must give up that half-formed notion. Indeed, I often think it a pity, you did not pursue the idea your progenitors had in view, when giving you the benefits of a classical education. But that is as Providence wills; only could I have had the auspicious fortune to have sailed over to London to manducate my dinners, and prosecute my studies at the bar, perhaps Councillor O'Connell himself, or Councillor Shiel, or even the Judges on the Bench, would not take such a lead of me in forensic business or legal attainments as they now do. Ay, in troth, I delivered as eloquent a speech at the Repeal Meeting, the other day, as the very best speaker among them; and I would have elaborated and ornamented it in the superlative degree; only the chairman and the parish priest contrived to have me move the last resolution on the list. The people commenced to disperse anterior to my being called on, and it was very advanced in the evening besides, when all must go home. So true is the adage, *sero venientibus ossa*.* Indeed, I find these meetings sempiternally mismanaged in this identical way. Some staunch friends of mine inform me, the great guns are jealous of my rising reputation as an orator, and keep me in the back scenes, until they have had their floods of declamation exhausted, and then they leave me almost nothing novel to advance. Ay, in troth, and I am much inclined to believe it. Indubitably, when I do obtain a chance, I delectate the populace, who are in the best of humour and spirits with themselves and the cause I advocate; and I necessitate them, men and women, to cheer, and wave their hats and handkerchiefs, as if the tide waves were rolling in on the sea shore. Why, I constructed and

* "Bones alone fall to the late comers."

answered more charades, rebuses, and enigmas, in the *Gentleman's and Farmer's Almanac,* than Larry Fogarty the schoolmaster did, with all his practice and time for book study. Ay, and composed as good songs as Tom Moore ever wrote or set to music; and that is saying a great deal for my own natural poetic ability."

At this moment, Mr. O'Byrne thought he heard some fluttering in the trees over him. He glanced an eye in that direction; but the next instant all was perfectly still. He supposed it must have been caused by one or other of the birds, that had not yet stilled down to enjoy repose in its nest for the night. He thus continued:—

"Ay, in troth, Mr. O'Byrne, you are a fine, well-to-do, respectable, intelligent farmer, sure enough; and didn't you perceive how Squire Fortescue Cunninghame paid you marked courtesy and compliments, while he was prognosticating with himself, at the same time, the probable purchase of your brown colt! Right hearty and blooming you looked in the fair to-day, in your splendid habiliments, suitable for an estated gentleman, or a lord; and you were 'high-fellow well met' with those that can fairly discover the manners, air, and education of a gentleman. Again, is there a more athletic figure of a man, or a more active, for his time of life, than yourself, in the whole county of Wicklow? At ball-playing, hurling, or wrestling, not one in the country-side could compare or contend with you." Here he gave several energetic flourishes with his arms, and cut off the tops of long grass or weeds on the road side with his riding-whip, and with as much energy as if he were wielding a sword and charging foremost among the advancing columns of the Irish Brigade, at the battle of Fontenoy. He tossed up his head, and resumed:—"In all physical and mental perfections, Mr. O'Byrne, I would like to know who dare challenge you, at home or abroad, in the vulgar monosyllabic term, *Boo!*"

The monosyllable *Boo!* was repeated with an energy corresponding to that in which it had been expressed by Mr. O'Byrne; and, to his great surprise, it seemed to come from out the forest recesses. But, again, Mr. O'Byrne, knowing that the Devil's Glen was remarkable at many points for repeating very distinctly and audibly sounds of the human voice, concluded that he had reached one of those spots, where reverberations might be localized. His classical recollections were even revived with a thought of the fabled wood-nymph, who might have been present. He again resumed his soliloquy:—

"Ha! ha! that sound certainly reminds me of a dialogue in the *Colloquia Familiaria* of Erasmus, and occurring between the Young Man and Echo. I'll hazard the experiment once more!" and Mr. O'Byrne shouted "*Boo! Boo!*" at the top of his voice.

"Boo! Boo!" reverberated from the adjoining rocks.

"Ha! ha! he! he!" next followed in an uncontrollable burst of laughter; while these monosyllables were well imitated, and exactly repeated. "Well, indubitably," continued Mr. O'Byrne, "that is most natural, and it reminds me of the lines in *Ovid:*—

'Forte puer, comitum seductus ab agmine fido
Dixerat, Ecquis adest? et, Adest, responderat Echo.'*

"Now, then, Echo, I'll just put you through your examination, and ascertain how far you are read in classical literature, and mediæval Latin. With respect to you, as the Young Man, I must open the colloquy—

---

* *Ovidii Metamorphoseon*, Liber iii., *vv.* 379, 380. Thus rendered in English verse:—

"By chance, the boy withdrawn, from comrades tried retreats,
'Who here is present?' said; 'Present,' a voice repeats."

"*Cupio paucis te consulere, si vacat.*" *

"*Vacat,*" † was the immediate response of the echo.

"Very good! very good! Now, answer me, *Et si venio tibi gratus juvenis.*" ‡

"*Venis,*" § replied Echo.

Then resumed Mr. O'Byrne, "*Sed potesne mihi et de futuris dicere verum, Echo ?*" ‖

"'Εχω," ¶ repeated the voice from the rocks.

"Bravo! bravo! Echo; then you speak both Greek and Latin, like Erasmus himself! Well, now, we'll pass over a few colloquies, until I ask one question that seriously concerns me for the future. Maybe Miss Kathleen O'Toole would look cross enough, if she understood your reply to my query, *Erit auspicatum si uxorem duxero !*" **

"*Sero,*" †† followed from the wood nymph.

"'Pon my word and honour, I had rather have heard the reply of Paddy Blake's echo, ' Pretty well, I thank you !' than the one you just now returned, in response to my question. Yet, it is ambiguous enough, I must confess; but it may have a prettier meaning and similitude, than I can now discover. Surely, it is never too late to mend, as the proverb has it; and it surprises me that Echo should pronounce the vocable *Sero.*"

Mr. O'Byrne mused a little, and then recommenced. "Now let us try a little dialogue on our own account."

* "I wish to consult you about a few matters, if you are at leisure."
† "*I am* at leisure."
‡ "And if, being a young man, I come to you under favourable circumstances."
§ "You come."
‖ "But can you tell me what is true regarding futurity, Echo ?"
¶ "I can."
** "If I marry, shall I prosper ?"
†† "Too late."

This he said in tolerable good humour with himself and the Echo. " Once more, *Quid dicis, Domine ?*" *

" Minæ," returned the Echo.

" Well, that means either *pounds* or *threats*. In the latter case it sounds very like *Boo!*"

" Boo !" again cried the unknown voice.

" I think that word hardly classical, and I'd like to know is it Greek, Latin, English, or Irish?"

" Irish," was very distinctly repeated.

" I believe you are perfectly right; and now that I recollect, as you are a nymph, I think, Miss Echo, I should have addressed you in the feminine form, and instead of calling you in the vocative, Domine,† it ought to have been Domina."‡

" Ah !" was the expression next heard ; and Mr. O'Byrne for a moment held down his head, a little vexed at the classical mistake, and puzzled to find words for a renewal of the dialogue.

At last he thought of concluding Erasmus's colloquies, for he desired to indulge in other reveries. " Before we say farewell, Miss Echo, I may venture to pay you the doubtful compliment of the Young Man, *Facundior esses, opinor, si longius abessem.*" §

" Essem,"|| again answered Echo.

" Wait awhile !" said Mr. O'Byrne, " for, *Non me delectant sermones dissyllabi.*" ¶

" Abi,"** repeated the Voice of the Rock, as Echo is poetically styled by the old Irish bards.

* " What say you, sir?"
† " Sir."
‡ " Mistress."
§ " I think you would be more eloquent, if I were at a greater distance."
|| " I would be."
¶ " Dissyllabic words do not please me."
** " Depart."

"I beg your pardon again," continued Mr. O'Byrne, "*Cœpi prior; video non posse vitari,* * *quin posterior desinas.*"

"*Sinas*,"† cried Echo.

"A word or two more, Miss Echo, *Jam igitur tibi videor satis instructus ad ea probe gerenda quæ sunt in vita.*"‡

"*Vita,*"§ was Echo's answer.

"Good-night, then! and it is nearly time for every honest man to be at home in his bed, *Proinde si me voles abire, dicito.*"‖

"*Ito,*"¶ resounded on the night air; and again Mr. O'Byrne was silent, yet highly delighted with his classic exercitations, and tickled after the conversation he had held with the imaginary Voice of the Rocks.

Suddenly, a rustling was heard once more among the branches and leaves of the trees overhead, and "Jintleman Paddy O'Byrne" looking upwards, perceived a diminutive creature astride on one of the oak boughs, that stretched across the roadway. He was dressed in a uniform of green and gold, with a black military cocked hat, and a pendant white feather falling over one of its brims. He wore a red vest, while white shorts and silk stockings, with nice little dancing sharp-toed pumps, fronted with gold clasps and buckles, nearly completed his costume. A pair of spurs was fastened on his heels. The extremities of his nose and chin seemed almost hooked together; while his mouth formed a crossing of two irregular rubied lines, through which long, yellowish, white teeth glittered; and his face was covered over with wrinkles or crows-feet,

---

* "I began first; but I see it is inevitable that you cease the last."
† "You allow it."
‡ "Wherefore, do I now seem to you sufficiently instructed rightly to apply those incidents which happen in life?"
§ "Be on your guard."
‖ "Then say the word, if you desire me to go.'
¶ "Go."

meeting at every conceivable angle. His eyes glittered like diamonds. This time he gave a loud laugh, but in the fairies' peculiar shrill key.

"Good-night, Mr. O'Byrne!" he at last cried; "I am right glad to have the pleasure of meeting you in this lonely glen, as you are an amusing character, and to form your acquaintance even now; for, as you know the old saying, 'Better late than never.' Don't you recollect your late conversation with Echo?"

The individual addressed trembled from head to foot, when he got a full glimpse of the goblin; and, notwithstanding that he was almost paralyzed with fear, when hearing these words, Mr. O'Byrne endeavoured to muster sufficient courage for another colloquy, which he knew to be inevitable. Making a low obeisance to the little man, not more than a few palms in stature, the mortal faltered out this return of the salute with a forced cough, to conceal his own nervousness and embarrassment.

"Ahem, sir! ahem! ahem! I'm exceedingly obliged for your kind, good wishes, my dear sir—or maybe I should call you your Royal Highness, or your Grace, or, at least, my Lord; for you seem, by your rich accoutrements, to hold some high military rank in the army. Maybe it's Captain, or Major, or General, I ought to style you; but you'll be kind enough to correct me, your Royal Highness, if I make any mistake. Might I beg, as a favour, a knowledge of the title, by which your Excellency is known?"

"I'm called the Cluricaune," said he very gruffly.

"And a highly respectable class of the 'good people' you belong to," chimed in Mr. O'Byrne, with the oil of flattery on his tongue; "indeed, it's well known you are full of talent, and fond of whim or frolic, wherever you may happen to be; and as for myself, I have a turn for fun and humour too, like most Irishmen."

"I'm right glad to hear it; and you were in great glee a while ago," returned the Cluricaune. "But I mean to show off, in a few entertainments, to-night, if you have no objection, Mr. O'Byrne."

"Not the least in life, your Royal Highness," said the mortal.

"Well, then, Mr. O'Byrne, would you like to hear a little of my mind about you, or about your perfections and accomplishments?" said the Cluricaune, with a laugh.

"With great pleasure, your Excellency," returned the personage addressed, yet with some hesitation.

"Do you wish to hear the naked truth?"

"Indeed and I do, your worship, especially from a highly intelligent gentleman like yourself."

"You are neither drunk nor sober precisely, at this present moment, Mr. O'Byrne. But maybe you will understand the force of my remarks to you on another subject."

"Indeed, your Excellency, I would not say but I am slightly elevated, sure enough; yet, on my word and honour, I did not take too much."

"Well, the very next thing to it. You took more than was good for your health of mind or body. Again, to be plain with you, I must declare you are full of self-conceit."

"I did not suppose I was, your Excellency."

"It is the case with every really conceited man," cried the Cluricaune.

"Well, your Excellency knows best; and I won't dispute the question with you."

"What pretensions, sir, could you, by possibility, have to a seat in Parliament, or to a position at the bar?"

"Oh! none whatever, your Excellency; only my natural talents and education might procure such distinctions for me, if I had more means, or a greater landed property; or maybe I might be helped there by an illustrious patron, like your Excellency, who is known to have vast treasures at your command."

"If I have them, be right sure I will not bestow any of my money on you, for you do not deserve any patronage from me. What are your ideas about politics?"

"Might I ask your Excellency whether you belong to the Liberal or Tory party?"

"Then, I presume, you would like to fall in with my opinions on public questions."

"Well, I would suppose your Worship ought to be a good judge about the wants and interests of the country, as you can see things more clearly and intelligently than we can. But I would like to act the part of a good patriot and Irishman on all occasions, and under all circumstances."

"I often heard the same thing said by many a humbug and time-server; but I must say, Mr. O'Byrne, you are neither one or the other; for you honestly act up to your political convictions and principles. Moreover, I think every man should have the public spirit to forward a good cause, according to the best of his abilities. Besides, you would make very excellent speeches, if you were not so fond of alluding to yourself—a theme on which every fool is most eloquent. But, what have you to boast of, in composing your wretched charades, rebuses, and enigmas? these can hardly be regarded as intellectual exercises: they only occupy the attention of small wits or idle persons. Every hedge-schoolmaster can do as much. And to compare yourself, as a poet, with Tom Moore! Well, to be sure, Mr. O'Byrne, is not that the height of impertinence?"

"Jintleman Paddy" hung down his head, and seemed rather confused, as he discovered all his soliloquies had been overheard by the Cluricaune. The latter recommenced his invectives,

"Now, Mr. O'Byrne, you also spoke slightingly about Miss Kathleen O'Toole, and thought she would not make a sufficiently good wife for you, because she does not indulge in any of your pedantry and nonsense. Yet, I can tell you, she comes from as good a stock and family as your own, in the county of Wicklow; she has a fortune that no comfortable farmer should despise; she is better-looking and younger than you by far; she is, at least, as careful and neat a housekeeper within doors as you are a proper manager without; she has sobriety and modesty, in both of which respects you are somewhat deficient; while she excels you greatly in every other fair quality. Shame! shame! Mr. O'Byrne, that you should overrate the showy, fashion-loving, dressy, talkative ladies of Dublin, and overlook the sterling character and good looks of an honest and simple, but decent and respectable, Wicklow farmer's daughter. Maybe, then, you will never meet with half as good a match all the dear days of your life!"

Mr. O'Byrne keenly felt those just reproaches; but he tried to appear as complaisant and repentant as possible. He also wished to keep up his spirits, and show no signs of fear, in company with the Cluricaune. This, however, cost him a great effort; for he was really anxious and uneasy to understand the sprite's object. The Cluricaune again began:—

"Mr. O'Byrne, for our special amusement, I would now like to indulge in a little fun, and to play off a few pranks in your presence."

"Well, your Highness, I am very fond of sport, and he is a churl that is not; so the moment you are ready to commence the fun, I'll enjoy it beyond measure. Ha! ha! ha!"

"Maybe, then, Mr. O'Byrne, you'll soon laugh at the wrong side of your mouth; for, in truth, I'm convinced already, you had sooner have my room than my company. Now, look out, stop a moment, and you'll see what I can do!"

With that the little man began to swing with both his arms from a cross bough, like Leotard from the trapeze, and then, with incredible speed and dexterity, he cast himself, by a series of somersaults, from one branch to another, before the gaze of the alarmed and astonished mortal. When somewhat tired of this exercise, the Cluricaune looked below, and thus continued:—

"What do you think of that performance, Mr. O'Byrne? Did you ever witness anything like it?"

"Jintleman Paddy" mentally acknowledged it was extraordinary enough, and most sincerely hoped he might never have a repetition of any similar performance under similar circumstances. But as he must reply to the question, he at last faltered:—

"I have not seen the equal of it, certainly, your High Mightiness, although I saw Mr. Merryman turn many an active head-over-heels on the stage in front of the show-box at the fair of Wicklow."

"Why do you compare me to that paint-daubed harlequin?" said the Cluricaune. "Do you think you are paying me a compliment, or that it is language one gentleman should use to another? Can you whistle, Mr. O'Byrne?"

"Well, only very indifferently, I apprehend, for your Excellency's musical ear; but sometimes I do. So, now, is there any particular tune your honour wishes me to whistle?"

"Do you know 'Tatther Jack Walsh,'" says the sprite: "it's a great favourite of mine."

"Well, I do," replied Mr. O'Byrne; "it's a very sprightly jig, when given in quick time."

"Then give it in quick time," cried the Cluricaune; "and without a moment's delay"—an admonition which Mr. O'Byrne instantly complied with; and, setting his lips in order, he proceeded to render it in his best possible style, and in the clearest and liveliest strains.

No sooner had he whistled the first bar, than the Cluricaune, curling over and over, with a quick and almost instantaneous rotary motion through air, alighted with his dancing pumps on the crown of Mr. O'Byrne's new Caroline hat. At once, the nimble atomy figure commenced pattering with heel and toe, to the sound of the music; he strained his knees, and threw outwards and upwards his tiny legs, like a pasteboard toy moved with strings; he cracked his fingers as an accompaniment, and, in the glee of his soul, he sometimes emitted an ejaculation of delight, in a "Whoop! hurra! bravo!" Every treble step and flourish sent the hat down more firmly over the eyebrows of Mr. O'Byrne; and the noise made on the crown of his prized Caroline was like that of hen-egg hailstones rattling on a slate roof.

"Oh! for the love of goodness and justice, your honour, don't spoil my bran-new Caroline hat, that I paid fifteen shillings for last week in Dublin, and it the only decent one I have to appear in on Sunday or holiday, at meeting, wedding, christening, fair, or market!"

"Hold your tongue, sir," replied the Cluricaune, "and keep up the tune, until I finish the jig. If you don't, it will be worse for you."

With a heavy heart and an agitated vocalism, Mr. O'Byrne resumed the tune, until the Cluricaune had finished the last beat with his feet. He then jumped off a perch or so on the path before the mortal, and first standing on his head, the sprite made one spring upwards, and his feet were locked together over another oak bough, with his head hanging down, and a sardonic grin on his face.

"Don't stir an inch from where you are, Mr. O'Byrne," he again cried, "until I make another proposal to you. Are you not proud of your wrestling, of which you were just now boasting? I would like, in this very spot, to see of what stuff you're made; and I now wish to try a fall with you."

"Well, your honour, I have not wrestled a fall this many a day; nor could I presume to try one with your Highness, who is so young and active. Indeed, sir, I grant you'd soon turn the soles of my boots to the moonlight, if I'd try."

"No matter for that, you must now do what you can; and mind, if I throw you at all, it will be over that ledge of rock, and maybe you'll tumble down into the very waters of the Vartry. So now do your best."

With that he jumped on the ground, once more alighting on his feet. He seized Mr. O'Byrne's whip, which he threw to one side, and then took him by collar and elbow. Both pulled and strained for the bare life. Now and then the mortal received a sore tip on the shin from the Cluricaune's spur, while his fairy antagonist wriggled his legs out of the way when a hook or trip was intended. After a considerable share of tugging and prancing about, the Cluricaune at last took Mr. O'Byrne at a disadvantage, touched him under the knee-joint, whipped the right foot upwards, and then with a light toss sent him right over the precipice. A heavy fall was the result, and the contest was at an end.

"Now, maybe, I have taken the conceit out of you," cried the Cluricaune, while Mr. O'Byrne rubbed down his side and shoulder, which had come in contact with some sharp rocks or roots on the surface. The vanquished man acknowledged he was fairly thrown, and he was again helped upon his feet. The sprite even extended his hand to pull his adversary once more on the upper bank. There at last Mr. O'Byrne, sore and jaded, stood, after his late trial of strength.

No sooner had "Jintleman Paddy" fairly recovered

from the first effects of his shock than the little fairy was resolved to put him under another ordeal. Taking up the whip, after a sudden step or two backwards, with a short run, he vaulted upon Mr. O'Byrne's back, and then alighted with each of his knees placed on either shoulder of the panting mortal. Suddenly he closed them round the neck of his poor victim, who felt for an instant as if he would be choked under the pressure; but the Cluricaune soon relaxed his hold, and then gliding downwards, got astride of Mr. O'Byrne's back. Then, flourishing the whip, he gave a smart tap, and cried out :—

"Come, now, Mr. O'Byrne, trot out in good style, for it's getting rather advanced in the night, and I want a ride on your back to the upper part of the Devil's Glen, when I'll leave you at the Waterfall. Step out, sir! step out!" he repeated, redoubling his strokes, with an occasional touch of the spur; and the mortal was obliged to quicken his paces over the course indicated, which lay also in the direction of his own home.

"Oh! would your worship sit more lightly on my back, and keep your knees looser on my ribs, and you'll find there will be no need of whip or spur to keep me moving as fast as I can. For, 'pon honour and conscience, I am tired and sore enough after the day's exercise and getting home from the fair, not to speak of the hard tussle I had with your honour just now. If your worship pleases, I'll move on quickly, without the necessity of your using whip or spur."

"Did you ever hear the old proverb, Mr. Patrick O'Byrne, that a spur in the head is worth two on the heel?" rejoined the Cluricaune.

"Jintleman Paddy's" conscience misgave him, on remembering those potations he had indulged at the fair of Wicklow, and he was at a loss for an answer. At last he ventured to remark :—

"Well, then, your honour, in that case, without your two spurs on the heel, my spur in the head ought to be enough to satisfy your Excellency that we'll get over the ground before us in very good time."

"Now, tell the truth, Mr. O'Byrne, didn't you get more than a spur in your head to-day before you left the fair-green?"

"There is no use in concealing anything from your honour, even if I were disposed; and I must say I did take a second tumbler of punch at Michael Murphy's hotel, on the head of our bargain."

"And anything else?"

"Well, just the dandy of *scalteen*, by way of *dhuc an dhurus*, before I got a seat with my good friend, Mr. Hennessy, who offered me the accommodation of his outside jaunting-car."

"Then, you ought to be 'pretty well, I thank you,' as they say in this part of the country. And don't you think you took a little too much already for your light head and addled brains, this blessed moonlight night?"

"I'm very sure I did, since your honour says it."

Mr. O'Byrne penitently gasped and panted, as he perspired and reeled under the weight of his unrelenting rider. At last, with much effort, both reached the top of the glen, where the waterfall's loud roar was distinctly heard. The Cluricaune hereupon relaxed his hold. Leaping off Mr. O'Byrne's back, he cried out:—"Here, then, I'll leave you, Mr. O'Byrne, and bid good-by to you; but take my advice for the future: mind how you stray about the Devil's Glen after dark, with nothing but the glasses of punch and your own small wits to guide you, or maybe you'll have a repetition of the pretty hard usage you received to-night, for your correction and improvement."

With that, drawing out his tiny foot, he gave Mr. O'Byrne a kick, which sent him clear across the waterfall. This blow completely stunned him; and he felt as if the huckle-bone of his hip were out of joint, after such rough treatment, in addition to his previous mishaps. In the morning early he was found by one of his neighbours, and snoring on the ground, at the bottom of a ravine, apparently quite unconscious of the exposed quarters in which his lodging had been taken. His new Caroline hat was battered on leaf and crown; his blue coat and pantaloons were soiled with the mud; his face was scraped, and his body stiff and sore. He told the story of what had occurred on the previous night, and attributed his series of misfortunes to the ill-timed practical jokes of the mischief-loving Cluricaune.

For the remainder of his days "Jintleman Paddy" was known to limp and halt; he lost his usual robust vigour and animal spirits; but he was careful, from his past experience, to guard against lonely walks, and late returns from fair or market; while he especially dreaded the effects of whisky punch; for he well recollected the Cluricaune's warning. The village doctor declared his patient to have been crippled with chronic rheumatism, from having lain so long under the damp dews of night; while the wise "herb woman" tried to persuade him that her *nostrums* would restore faded strength, and propitiate the malignity of his fairy tormentor. Yet Mr. O'Byrne could never make up his mind to follow out the prescriptions of either adviser for any considerable time, or to any satisfactory issue. A temperate course of life, and its moderated enjoyments, rendered him capable of spending the winter of his days in a state of "single blessedness" and comparative comfort. But it was noticed by his neighbours, that, when rational relaxation or business obliged him to visit Ashford, "Jintleman Paddy" had rather take two miles of a round, than venture, by day or night, through the lonely Devil's Glen.

I

CHAPTER XV.

HY-BREASAIL; OR, THE BLESSED ISLAND.

"On the ocean that hollows the rocks where ye dwell,
A shadowy land has appeared, as they tell;
Men thought it a region of sunshine and rest,
And they called it O'Brazil—the isle of the blest.

"From year unto year, on the ocean's blue rim,
The beautiful spectre showed lovely and dim;
The golden clouds curtained the deep where it lay,
And it looked like an Eden, away, far away!"
GERALD GRIFFIN.

ISLANDS, invisible to most mortals, lying out on the distant ocean, or in the narrower seas and channels near Ireland, are often said to have been seen by heroes who set out on some erratic expeditions. Magicians, or enchanted people, are met with, and their spells sometimes prevail against earthly intruders. In certain instances, the enchanted people are defeated by mortal skill and bravery. In such case, the adventurer is enabled to revisit Ireland. Thus the rich "Island of the Red Lake," where the birds warble melodiously, is mentioned; and it is even celebrated in some of our ancient or mediæval romances. This Red Lake is supposed by many to have been the present Mediterranean Sea. An island lay within it, on which a palace was built. Here fruit-trees also grew, and the immortals there living fed on their luscious produce.

The Firbolgs and Fomorian colonists of Ireland—for the most part seafaring men—are thought to have placed their Elysium far out in the ocean. It went by these various names:—Hy-Breasail, or the Island of Breasal; Oilean na m Beo, or Island of the Living; Hy na Beatha, or Islands of Life. These titles and opinions remind us of some striking analogy with the Μακάρων Νῆσοι, or Islands of the Happy, among the Greeks. Another title, applied to some of those fabled regions, was Tir na m Beo, or Land of the Living. Among our Pagan ancestors these latter were regarded as immortals. For in the fabled spirit-land of the Irish beatified, under the Atlantic waves, the good and brave had their special abodes and enjoyments. The Firbolgs were also thought to have had their residence under the waters of our lakes. A somewhat different account is given regarding other races and classes inhabiting Ireland. The Tuatha de Danaans, and the Druids, are said to have held their seminaries in caves and secluded subterranean abodes. Hence their Elysium was naturally supposed to have been situated under the earth. By many, however, it has been supposed, that the ocean paradise had been tenanted by the shades of brave mariners, whose vessels sunk in the wild solitudes of the Atlantic, when tempests arose, and those unfriended sailors perished in the seething waves.

One of those most distinguished islands is said to appear far away on the verge of the Atlantic's horizon, beyond the group of Arran islands, and removed to the shadowy distance fading from mortal sight. It is, however, sometimes visible; and it has been beautifully described by the graceful pen of the Irish novel writer, Gerald Griffin, in his poetical works. This description of Hy-Breasail is prefixed to the present chapter. The story runs, that a peasant, attracted by its tempting appearance, when it gleamed on his vision,—

"In the breeze of the Orient, loosened his sail."

But, on directing his course westward, this island seemed

to recede in proportion as he advanced. At last, a rising tempest submerged his bark, when,—

"Night fell on the deep, amidst tempest and spray,
And he died on the waters, away, far away!"

The "Great Land" was a denomination often applied to Hy-Breasail; and, as in many other instances, we may possibly trace the acceptance of a historic fact, through the mists of a popular tradition. Nor is this all; because, from an early period, the Irish and Scandinavian chroniclers have placed on record their accounts regarding an extensive western continent.

This *Irland it Mikla*, or Great Ireland, is frequently alluded to in the Northern Sagas. The route towards it, commencing from the north of Europe, is described in this manner. They relate that, to the south of habitable Greenland, there are uninhabited and wild tracts, with enormous icebergs floating around them. The country of the Skrælings lies beyond these tracts, Markland extends beyond them, and Vinland the Good stretches beyond the last-named country. Next to this, and some distance beyond it, lies Albania, — that is, Huitramannaland. Formerly, vessels are said to have gone from Ireland to this particular region.

In this vague sketch, modern antiquarians have laboured —and not unsuccessfully—to identify the country of the Skrælings with the Esquimaux coast, Markland has been regarded as Labrador, Vinland is supposed to have been the same as New England. But the territory designated Huitramannaland, was thought to have been the country stretching farther southward, and reaching beyond the Chesapeake Bay.

It is now generally believed by all, who have made the subject of American maritime exploration a special study, that Columbus was not the first European who landed on the shores of the western hemisphere. From our earliest Irish annals and biographies, there are accounts of an adventurous ecclesiastic having gone forth from our island, to spread the truths of Christianity in a land, only conjectured to have had an existence, but still with correct information, grounded on a well-understood primitive tradition. They credit the first voyage westwards to St. Brendan, patron and bishop of Clonfert and Ardfert, on the south-west coast. It is recorded that he flourished from the year A.D. 550 till the beginning of the following century, and that he made no less than two voyages in search of the promised land. The precise point of departure is related to have been the foot of Brandan Mountain, now Tralee Bay. His sea-store consisted of live swine, while his companions were monks. His first voyage abounded in adventures, which have the poetic glow of a fervid Celtic imagination to give them both range and colour. The dates in these legends are well fixed, whatever else may be dubious, concerning the details of this very extraordinary voyage. A general tradition of the Western Continent's existence was widely received before the birth of Christopher Columbus; nor can we reject, as entirely incredible, repeated allusions to this tradition, contained in early chronicles of northern nations in the old world. To the ancient Irish, as to the mediæval Spaniards and Portuguese, the distant land was the Eldorado of romance; but our insular mariners set forth on an adventurous voyage, with more unselfish and holier purposes. Little, indeed, could they have thought, at the time, that from Ireland would afterwards issue that drain of modern emigration, which has contributed so materially to increase the wealth, progress, power, and resources of the vast Transatlantic Republic.

An old Scandinavian chronicle, known as the Landnamabock, and which had been compiled in the thirteenth century, relates, that Ulf the Squinter, son of Hogni, the White, occupied the whole of *Reykianess*, a south-west promontory of Iceland, which was situated between Thorskafiord and Hafrafell. He had a wife named Biorg, who was daughter to Eyvind the East-countryman. They had a son named Atili the Red, who married Thorkotu, daughter to Hergil. They had a son named Ari, and he was driven by a tempest to Huitramannaland, or the "White man's land," which some called Irland it Mikla, or Great Ireland. This region was placed in the western ocean, near to Vinland the Good, and west from Ireland. Ari is said to have been baptized in this newly-discovered country, whence he was not permitted to take his departure.

The narrative proceeds, that Ari had a wife named Thorgerd, daughter to Alf of Dolum. Their sons were Thorgils, Gudlief, and Illugi. The family of Reykianess was thus known. Eirck, the Red, was connected with the family of this Ari Marson, whose voyage from Ireland occurred in 983. It may not be amiss to repeat what has been placed on record, as all these historical allusions afford corroboration respecting the authenticity of different narratives. Jorund was the son of Ulf the Squinter. He married Thobiorg Knarrarbring. They had a daughter, Thjodhild, whom Eirck the Red married. They had a son, Leif the Lucky, of Greenland. It is worthy of remark, that the writer of this account was Ari the Learned, who was born 1067, and who flourished towards the end of the eleventh century; therefore he lived within a century after Ari Marson's departure from Ireland. He was immediately descended from Ari Marson. Of course, he would naturally be anxious and careful to obtain the most accurate accounts regarding his ancestors, before committing them to writing.

Again, it is related, that a certain person, named Rafn,

a Limerick merchant, lived for a long time in Limerick city, in Ireland. Rafn was a kinsman to Ari Marson, and he flourished at the beginning or about the middle of the eleventh century. So Thorkel, the son of Geller, and who was grandson to Ari Marson, says, that certain Icelanders stated, who heard Thorfinn, Jarl of the Orkneys—also kinsman to Ari Marson, and born 1008, died 1064—relate, that Ari had been seen and known in Huitramannaland. Although not suffered to depart thence, he was there held in great honour, having been selected as their chief, by the inhabitants of that distant region.

There various *Irishmen* and *Icelanders* visited and recognized Ari, the son of Mar and Kotlu, of Reykianess, and regarding whom nothing had been heard for a long time. Several modern American writers, who treat concerning the arrival of Northmen in New England, consider Huitramannaland as deserving to be identified with it, if not further coextensive with the midland and southern states of the great Western Republic.

At a later period, an adventurer, named Biorn, followed on the track of Ari Marson. Afterwards Gudlief, son of Gudlang, towards the middle of the eleventh century, proceeded to the distant land, and conversed with Biorn, in Huitramannaland, or *Irland it Mikla*, beyond the Atlantic. If so disposed, it would not be difficult to accumulate proofs of America's discovery or colonization by seafaring men, who feared not to brave the perils of a trackless ocean, when losing sight of our rock-bound promontories.

We have but briefly summed up the evidence, which established more than a dreamy consciousness regarding the distant Atlantic's realms, in the minds of thinking men throughout the European continent, in mediæval times.

There is quite sufficient reason to infer, that many believed in the existence of a Great Ireland, extending far towards the west, even before Columbus's discovery. Assuredly, if they were mistaken, we are in a fair way to see the doubtful vision of their days become a reality; for there are few Irish families, at the present day, who have not formed alliances with that "land of the west," and whose dearest hopes are not bound with its progressive prosperity, and those influences it is likely to exercise on the current of modern civilization. Hy-Breasail now dissolves, as a popular vision; yet, through its mists, a more distant region reproduces the spell of an Irishman's enchantment.

In Plato's *Timæus* there is mention made of an Atlantic island, said to have been greater than all Libya and Asia together, and it afforded an easy passage to other neighbouring islands. It was even supposed, that facilities of access to a continent, bordering on the Atlantic ocean, were attainable from these islands. Storms, earthquakes, and a deluge taking place, caused this island, called Atlantis, to disappear, with all its dwellers, under the surface of ocean. It was inhabited by a race of Athenians, and they were suddenly merged under earth in one day and night. The Rev. George Croly has produced some pleasing verses on this subject. This sudden visitation the poet attributes to the crimes of its inhabitants, and to their scoffing at Heaven. He ends the account with these lines,—

> " Now on its hills of ivory
>   Lie giant weed and ocean slime,
> Burying from man and angel's eye
>   The land of crime."

Here we find traces of ancient tradition, referring to the destruction of Sodom and Gomorrha, with all the country around, the inhabitants and all things springing from the earth, as recorded in the book of Genesis. Ashes arose from the earth, as the smoke of a furnace. In many similar instances, Gentile traditions tend to confirm the arguments of those commentators, who rightly interpret the Mosaic accounts of early history, as contained in the sacred Scriptures.

Somewhat similar accounts are told about various other localities. At Rosnaree, near Tara, there was a tradition, that two hundred persons were swallowed up by the earth, for blaspheming the true God. This is said to have occurred before the introduction of Christianity to Ireland. And subsequent to this period, in Armorica, an old city, known as Chris, or Keris, sometimes called Is, and situated on the sea shore, was ruled over by a Prince Grandlon, surnamed Meur. This royal personage had been a friend to Gwénnolé, founder and first abbot over the earliest monastery erected in that part of France. This saint predicted the submersion of Gradlon the Great's chief city. His prophecy was thus fulfilled. The city of Is had been protected from inroads of the sea by means of an immense pond, or basin, which received superfluous waters, during the prevalence of high tides. A sluice-gate opened and admitted the king to the basin, whenever he deemed it necessary; but he always kept the key of this secret opening. The princess Dahut, his daughter, secretly entertained her lover at a banquet one night, and both purposing to escape from the palace, she stole the key while her father slept. On opening the flood-gate, the high waters burst through and submerged the city with its inhabitants. The offending princess was drowned, and afterwards she was metamorphosed into a syren. Often was she seen on the sea shore, combing her golden hair; while her plaintive songs were heard in cadenzas, melancholy as the murmur of ocean's waves on the strand. In that charming work of Le Vicomte Hersart de la Villemarqué, the *Barzaz Breiz*, or Popular Songs of Brittany, the foregoing legend is metrically given, with commentaries of the distinguished editor. Local tradition maintains, that Gradlon escaped the rising waters, mounted on his white steed; and thus was he represented, between the two towers of Quimper cathedral, before the period of the French Revolution, while an annual popular *fête* commemorated the old poetic story. The editor compares this Breton legend, and other French traditions, with the Lough Neagh submerged city, as immortalized in the *Irish Melodies* of Moore.

A very curious vellum MS., on medical subjects, written in Latin and Irish, is yet preserved in the Royal Irish Academy. When purchased, many years ago, in the west of Ireland, it was traditionally believed, that one Morough O'Ley, a resident of Connemara, some time in the seventeenth century, after having been transported by supernatural means to the enchanted island of O'Brasil, there received a full course of instruction regarding all diseases and their cure, together with this MS., to direct him in medical practice. The O'Leys, or O'Lees, who were for a long time physicians to the O'Flaherties, did not fail to increase their hereditary and professional celebrity, by the acquisition of this treatise.

There was an island of Caire Cennfinn, concealed in the sea between Ireland and Scotland, according to an ancient tradition recorded in the book of Lecan. This may have had some connection with another Scotch tradition, *Flathinnis*, otherwise known as the Noble Island. It is said by Macpherson, to stretch out in the western ocean, but it is surrounded by clouds, and beaten by tempests. Within this island every prospect constitutes a paradise for the virtuous sons of Druids, who enjoy peculiar pleasures. Yet are they excluded from the Christian's heaven. Certain practised incantations cause this fabled land to appear. Departed persons, during their peculiar happy state, were believed to have been warmly attached to their former country and living friends. Among the ancient Celts, females were said to have passed to the Fortunate Islands. In the words of an old bard, their beauty increased with this change, and they were regarded as ruddy lights in the Island of Joy. This enchanted country, called Hy-Breasail, or O'Brazil, signified "the Royal Island," according to General Vallancey's interpretation. It was regarded as having been the Paradise of Pagan Irish. The poet of all circles, and the idol of his own, Thomas Moore, has not forgotten the commemoration of Arranmore, near the Eden of immortals, in those inimitable "Melodies," which have so much redounded to his own and to his country's fame. In this fabled region brave spirits are described as dwelling in a land of peace, in delightful bowers and mansions.

The Poet Claudian* speaks of a land, situated at the very extreme part of Gaul, and beaten by the ocean waves. Here, it was said, a ruler named Ulixes ruled over a people that were silent, after he had offered a libation of blood. Here, also, were heard the plaintive wailings of shades that passed by with a slight rustling noise. And the people living on those coasts saw pale phantoms of departed persons flitting through air. Loud lamentations escaped from their troop, while all the adjoining shores re-echoed to their terrific howls. It is clear, however, that those unhappy ghosts must have differed in degree from fabled denizens inhabiting the Island of Joy.

In Southey's poem of "Madoc," allusion is made, likewise, to certain green islands on the western ocean. Thither "the sons of Garvan," and "Merlin with his band of bards," sailed. Thence they were not known to have

* In Rufinum, lib. i., v. 123-133.

returned. It was believed they reached a "land of the departed;" and as the poet resumes his description,—

> "There, belike,
> They in the clime of immortality,
> Themselves immortal, drink the gales of bliss,
> That o'er Flathinnis breathe eternal Spring;
> That blend whatever odours make the gale
> Of evening sweet, whatever melody
> Charms the wood-traveller." *

In a very rare publication, called *The Ulster Miscellany*, and printed in 1753, there is an ingenious political satire, entitled, "A Voyage to O'Brazeel, a Submarine Island, lying west off the Coast of Ireland." It is, doubtless, modelled on the design of Dean Swift's voyages to Lilliput and Brobdignag. The mode of descent to O'Brazeel is represented as very peculiar. The island itself is described as flecked with mellowed, well-distributed light, covered with beautiful landscapes, producing corn, fruits, trees, grass, and flowers; abounding in streams, fountains, flocks and herds, fertile fields and pastures, with a happy state of society, religion, and government.

Gerald Griffin alludes to a nearly similar subject, in one of his beautiful lyrics, regarding the supposed frequent appearance of a phantom city, situated amidst the wide Atlantic waves. According to another account, its walls are yellow, and in it dwell certain fairy denizens. These lines contain the tradition,—

> "A story I heard on the cliffs of the west,
> That oft through the breakers dividing,
> A city is seen on the ocean's wild breast,
> In turreted majesty riding.
> But brief is the glimpse of that phantom so bright,
> Soon close the white waters to screen it;
> And the bodement, they say, of the wonderful sight,
> Is death to the eyes that have seen it."

* First Part, Section xi.

It is very probable, a belief in the existence of this fabled island comes down from a very remote period. It may have given rise to the traditionary transatlantic voyage of St. Brendan of Clonfert, called also the Navigator. This holy and adventurous man is said to have spent seven Easters away from Ireland, having landed on a distant island,—

"The freshest, sunniest, smiling land that e'er
Held o'er the waves its arms of sheltering green."

The adventures of this holy Navigator and his companions have been most exquisitely described in Denis Florence M'Carthy's *Voyage of St. Brendan,*—a poem, which, for felicity of expression, and ideality of subject, has nothing superior to it in our own, or perhaps in any other language.

CHAPTER XVI.

THE FÉAR GORTHA; OR, HUNGRY GRASS: A TALE OF THE IRISH FAMINE.

"But no! thine heart is broke, thine arm is weak,
Who thus could see God's image not to sigh,
Famine hath plough'd his journeys on thy cheek,
Despair hath made her dwelling in thine eye."
J. J. CALLANAN.

"Alas!
Nor wife, nor children, more shall he behold!
Nor friends, nor sacred home. On every nerve
The deadly winter seizes, shuts up sense,
And, o'er his inmost vitals creeping cold,
Lays him along the snows, a stiffen'd corse,
Stretch'd out and bleaching in the northern blast!"
THOMSON.

THE Féar Gortha, or Hungry Grass, is a peculiar Irish superstition; and we may easily suppose there is nothing analogous to it in other countries. It is said by the peasantry, that when an *al fresco* meal is partaken of on a certain spot, if its fragments be not thrown to the fairies, a crop of hungry grass will there grow, and whoever passes over it must fall into such a weak state, that death will ensue, if he be not immediately relieved. A gaunt spectre, only skin and bone, and miserably clad, is thought, likewise, to wander through Ireland at certain seasons, in the shape of a travelling mendicant. He is called *Fear Gurtha*, or the Man of Hunger. The Irish word *Fear* signifies both *man* and *grass*, but by a difference in pronunciation. Who ever gives relief to the Man of Hunger will enjoy unfailing prosperity, even during the worst periods of famine and death. These visitations, as public calamities, are sure to follow immediately after his appearance. Uncharitable individuals will be found among the most miserable sufferers on the approach of such national inflictions. There is a beautiful moral conveyed in this fiction; and, at all events, it does not tend to repress the Irishman's kindly feelings, or generous disposition.

Maxwell, in his interesting sketches, called *Wild Sports of the West*, alludes to the *faragurtha*, or "hungry disease," which is assigned to various causes. Some are of opinion it is attributable to fairy influence; whilst others affirm, it is contracted while passing a spot where a corpse had lain. Many assert, it is owing to the traveller putting his foot on a poisonous plant. The natural cause, however, is overlooked, for a supernatural explanation. It is quite evident, that want of food, fatigue, destitution, with many other predisposing causes, will account for the sudden death, or ravenous sense of appetite experienced, especially by the peasant class, while on their long and laborious rambles over rough and wild mountains.

Near the most remote extremity of Cork County, there is a high mountain, known as Hungry Hill, which rises in bare and solitary isolation over the estuary of Bear Haven and Bantry Bay. This mountain has an elevation exceeding 2,000 feet above the ocean, which swells along its base. A singular and picturesque waterfall descends over ledges of projecting rocks, and from a height of nearly 800 feet. Its source is supplied by a lake at the very summit, and the mountain torrent, issuing therefrom, falls in a broken course; so that, it forms a truly magnificent and loudly-roaring cascade, as it hurries down along the steeps. After its descent, the waters wind onwards in a rushing stream by Ardrigoole, and then enter the Bay of Bantry. Various remains of great antiquity are traceable in the country immediately surrounding Hungry Hill.

It is said, this place takes its name from the circumstance of Féar Gortha growing on it. There are certain localities in Ireland where this *hungry grass* abounds. These places are supposed to be enchanted. The *Féar Gortha* causes people, when crossing over it, to take sudden weaknesses, especially after a long journey. The fit of hunger coming on them is sometimes so excessive, that they find themselves unable to pass particular spots, held in horror by the peasantry. If relief be not afforded, therefore, by some companion or casual passenger, death immediately ensues under such circumstances. When recovering from this weakness, the famished sufferers often fall into a poor state of health. A bit of oaten cake is thought to be the best antidote against this hungry grass affection. As a further illustration concerning this popular belief, we find the following account of compassionate sympathy for human woe, existing among the spirits of our raths and glens. Grose relates, that the Irish fairies frequently left bannocks or oaten cakes in the way of travellers. If the latter did not consume this food, some accident of an unlucky nature was likely to befall them.

Around the wilds of Hungry Hill, in this remote district to which allusion has been made, the famine years of 1847 and 1848 came with a wide-spread severity; while the poor fishermen and cottagers along the coast were sorely distressed, when sea and land refused a return for their humble industry. The tales that are still told about whole families, men, women, and children, pining away in hopeless misery, with the pangs of hunger wasting day by day frames once athletic and vigorous, are fearful even yet to remember. Fevers followed in the train of famine; whole villages felt the dire scourge, the inhabitants sunk into yawning graves, unshrouded and uncoffined, while utter ruin and dispersion scattered hundreds of wretched survivors into the workhouses, or on board the emigrant ship, or on the shores of far distant countries.

Poor Teige O'Driscoll, with his wife and seven children, tenanted a small reed-covered shieling near Castletown, and for many years he had wrought out a tolerably decent livelihood for himself and his charge. But, in the autumn of 1846, his potato-fields were marked with the blight, which then began to appear, and soon the expected winter's produce was found, on digging out, to be blackened and rotten. Still, he put out boldly to sea, with two of his grown boys. The elder son, Daniel, had barely attained the years of manhood. Spreading out his nets and lines, Teige was enabled to weather many storms and adversities of the physical and moral atmosphere, both on sea and land. The small means, so hardly obtainable, were honestly won, and economically laid out for the hundred of oatmeal, or the Indian corn, then beginning to be introduced as an article of provision for the poor. But nothing was relished so much as the potato, with the fine fish, captured out at sea, by our peasantry. These sources of supply began to fail; however, a hope was entertained that better times would shortly dawn. The spring sowing was resumed, often with indifferent and diseased seed-potatoes. Summer passed, and autumn returned, with its disappointing mass of vegetable unwholesomeness.

The usual hopeful spirit of our poor people was utterly broken. Individual benevolence could render little assistance, unaided by Governmental action; and sad, indeed, are the records of those days, when cries unheeded went up from the wilderness. Despair of effecting anything commensurate with the crisis seemed to have paralyzed, for a time, every well-devised attempt, in bringing relief to impoverished homes,

K

Miserable and inefficient were the measures at last adopted to meet that impending calamity, under which a whole nation bowed. The workhouses were found quite insufficient to accommodate a tithe of the wretched applicants for shelter; and after various suggestions had been offered from all quarters, it was resolved to commence public works in various districts, and give out-door relief, but without adopting any settled system for judicious or economic administration. Depôts for the distribution of provisions were established, and Relief Committees formed, often in very inconvenient localities, for those who were to be the recipients of public and private dole. The day was often wasted before work could be obtained; a miserable pittance was the reward of those gaunt spectres of humanity, hardly able to wield spade or hammer on the road side; provisions were at famine prices; while whole families were stricken with the typhus fever, or unable to crawl from their wretched hovels, with the pangs of hunger wasting their very vitals.

The political and social conditions of life are deplorably arranged, in a country teeming with fertility, and admirably circumstanced for manufacturing and commercial industry, where a whole people is rendered dependent on one single article of food, and when its possible scarcity or failure may leave them subject to fearful trials, such as have been witnessed during the famine years in Ireland. Yet, periodically have we had experience of these recurring evils. Such a state of things could not occur, however, had we a proprietory of land cultivators here, or such a class of peasant tillers, as exists in many countries on the Continent of Europe, and in more distant parts of the world. A profound thinker has wisely said, that a country where the holder of the plough is in most cases the complete proprietor of the land he cultivates, can never become an impoverished one, and must afford the best social conditions of life for all ranks of its people. At this time of which we treat, the Irish landholder, as well as the tenant-at-will, suffered from our defective economic arrangements. Hereditary estates passed away from families at less than half of their value, under better circumstances. A purely agricultural country, however, cannot be a rich or a prosperous one. But those who professed to feel an interest in Ireland's welfare, had no better regard for her industry than to wish her existing as the fruitful mother of herds and flocks, or as the mere draw-farm for the subsistence of a people more favoured in the peculiar circumstances of their position. Even our rulers and journalists, at the time, and subsequently, considered Ireland's depopulation a subject for gratulation, rather than for regret.

Teige O'Driscoll and his family weathered this severe storm as best they could; but soon their means of subsistence, from being precarious, became entirely hopeless. Everything in their poor cabin had disappeared; the rent was not paid, nor could the landlord expect it under the circumstances. Honest pride prevented this humble household from giving up possession, and retiring for shelter to the workhouse. But soon no other alternative remained. Efforts were made to procure such a temporary, or, perhaps, abiding roof, for the starving O'Driscolls. The workhouse was filled with inmates, however, at the time of their application; and their last distressing effort was to seek once more the covering of their humble roof, with want and woe stalking around, and utter ruin staring them in the face.

The poor relieved those still poorer during this depressing time; but all were now placed on a dead level of want and wretchedness. Some works, without any more definite object than affording temporary aid to the starving, were undertaken near Kenmare river. In the winter of 1847, the wife of Teige O'Driscoll had been attacked by the typhus fever, and then rapidly followed the prostration of other members belonging to this afflicted family. Spiritual and medical assistance was afforded; but weakly indeed were the patients, when Teige and his eldest son started out to try and procure employment, at a spot far distant from their home. They were successful so far; but with their threadbare, scanty clothing, and their emaciated frames, father and son bent over the heap of stones they were engaged in breaking for a public road. That peculiar slender voice, induced by complete physical prostration, that lack-lustre eye, and that downy white hair covering over the wan face, when complete destitution has long been the companion of hunger, were perceptible in the case of both exhausted toilers. Yet these poor strugglers wrought with a holy purpose, if with relaxed energy; for they shivered and starved through the chill winter's day, and obtained their trifling wages towards its close. Then, with heavy hearts, they paced homewards over the rough path, which led them by a toilsome course up the steep and bare sides of Hungry Hill.

The wind blew keen and biting, as the shades of night closed in; sleet followed in a drifting and benumbing shower. Father and son, with wasted strength, had neared the summit, when a fit of weakness seized on the former, and he was obliged to rest on the exposed mountain side. The son looked in his face, which was growing pale and livid by turns; and then, throwing his feeble arms around his parent, young Daniel sank exhausted beside him. The storm howled over them, and no human eye beheld their closing death-struggle.

Those fever-suffering inmates of the cabin were happily unconscious of the fate which had befallen the only bread-earners of the family circle. One by one, and after a few days' illness, death followed death in quick succession; while the corpses were hurriedly coffined by the charity of friends, and removed to an adjoining burial-ground. The father and son were missing for a day and night; but when a third day had gloomily dawned, the stiffened corpses of both were found, wreathed round with a snow-drift as their only shroud. Their wasted frames, and thin, sharp features, were rigid as marble, and actually fastened by the frost to the bleak mountain's side. Their eyes were glazed and wildly staring; but their hands were clasped and joined over their breasts, as if the forlorn sufferers had abandoned all this world's consolations in a last prayer of resignation to the will of that Almighty Being who often chastens humanity by temporal afflictions, although we cannot doubt in the Providence that directs all the concerns of life and its mysteries.

Soon were these poor remnants of mortality united with their kindred of generations in the dust. The green sward of their graves has not yet sunk to the obliterating level, which would remove it from the recollection of surviving friends. On the sea shore a roofless stone cabin is still crumbling to decay, and a trace of broken fences surrounds it. A memorial of individual suffering it remains, but not a solitary one, in the district around; for many a humble roof-tree has fallen within the comfortless walls, and many a once happy home has become desolate, while its inmates have been sent to premature graves, or scattered to all quarters of this habitable globe. No wonder that bitter memories of the past should survive in the recollections of the Irish peasant.

Many of their former neighbours said poor Teige O'Driscoll and his son Daniel had trod on the hungry grass, and that both were relieved by the near approach of death, from witnessing the further miseries of those most dear to them in life. Yet, it unfortunately needed no preternatural cause to account for their premature departure from this world; since, like many others of their country-people, they fell victims to the wide-spread calamities of this sad period in our island's history.

The natural, political, and social causes, which may at any future period reproduce a similar state of things, are yet suffered to continue; nor are the means and machinery of administrative power available to dissipate those clouds, whenever they gather over and darken the national horizon. We have heard and read statements, offered by superficial or prejudiced persons, that the prosperity of our farmers and peasantry has advanced in a general ratio, since the years of famine. We know, from practical experience and observation—we could even prove from available statistics, unsifted for peculiar purposes, and only applied or combined in the process of legitimate deductions—that the national wealth and material resources of Ireland have deteriorated, and are yet declining. Nor can these improve, until complete security for the return of his outlay in labour and money reward the industry of a tenant-renter; since comparatively few of our great landed proprietors are considerable improvers of land, or extensive employers of the working classes; while in general they are consumers rather than producers of wealth, for their own, and for the benefit of their humble dependants.

CHAPTER XVII.

VARIOUS POPULAR FANCIES.

> Yet bright memory still reaches,
> All athwart thy glistening beams,
> Where, beneath the shading beeches,
> Lay the sunny child of dreams;
>
> "Weaving fancies bright as morning,
> With its purple and its gold;
> Strong to trample down earth's scorning,
> With the faith of men of old."—LADY WILDE.

THE symbolism which connects natural objects with devotional or high-toned moral sentiments, must be productive of elevated emotions in the mind. This inference seems deducible from many prevailing opinions in Ireland. Some of these are worth placing on record, and they may serve for purposes of comparison with the traditions of other nations.

The Irish, in common with other Celtic tribes, cherish a peculiar veneration for those tiny birds, the robin and the wren. The killing of a wren is said to entail on the perpetrator some injury to person or property by fire. The legend of this little bird having brought fire from heaven is pretty generally known. In Ireland it is still a custom to hunt the wren on St. Stephen's day, and to carry its body from door to door, while at each halting-place the bearers shout and sing a rhyme commencing thus,—

> "The wren, the wren, the king of all birds,
> St. Stephen's day was caught in the furze;
> Although he is little, his honour is great,
> So rise up, landlady, and give us a treat!"

This rough usage would seem to jar with the received idea of ill-luck being attached to the wren's destruction; but the apparent discrepancy can be reconciled, it is said, in this manner: such a custom once had a mystic meaning, in relation to the great festive season, during the first twelve nights of the sun's return from the winter solstice. A sacrificial killing of the sacred bird, on such an occasion, was justified by former usages. A custom, similar to the Irish one, prevails in the Celtic districts of France; and there the wren is commonly called, "poulette au bon Dieu."

In a common rann, or verse, this little bird has thus been linked with the robin,—

> "Robin Redbreast and Jenny Wren,
> Are God Almighty's cock and hen."

Respecting the favour with which the robin is regarded, there exists, in Ireland at least, a very generally accepted tradition, that during the awful period of our Saviour's crucifixion, one of these venerated little birds was seen endeavouring with its beak to pluck out those cruel nails by which His Divine hands had been fastened to the cross. But, in attempting this fruitless task of love, the robin had its tiny breast stained with the sacred blood,— the stain of which, it is said, is to exist for ever, as a venerated sign upon the feathery covering of the race. It is stated that, in Pagan times, the robin was under the immediate protection of Thor, by virtue of that blood-dyed colour which is dear to the thundering god. We may then ask, Could the Christian tradition have arisen to extirpate the Pagan one? It seems belonging to the same class of legends, which assigns those marks upon the haddock to be perpetuations of the traces left by the finger and thumb of our Divine Lord when He took one in His hand, it is popularly supposed, to bless this particular kind of fish for the famishing multitude who followed him into the desert.

The well-known passion-flower is also said to have been first noticed at the time of our blessed Redeemer's crucifixion. Thenceforward it bore those emblems of torture, to which the innocent victim of man's impiety had been subjected; but chiefly in the popular estimation this fancy has taken root. Such an impress of so great an event, in the Christian's recollection, and on a beautiful natural ornament of our gardens, must blend in the memory and feeling, however faintly, a type with the reality of that affecting sacrifice once witnessed on Mount Calvary.

Akin to these legends is a tradition that the ass was unmarked by a cross, until the period when our Divine Lord entered Jerusalem, meek, and sitting upon one of these animals, to "cast out all who were selling and buying in the temple." Frequently have we heard the peasantry say, as the very acmé of reproach to a person remarkable for thievish propensities: "You'd steal the cross from off an ass's back!" A few years ago, a lady of our acquaintance chanced to see, for the only time in her life, an ass without a cross on its back, or even the slightest trace of its ever having had one there. The fact might have escaped observation, but that the animal had been unharnessed at the time. She did not fail humorously to ask the owner: "Who stole the cross from off the ass's back?" To this question the ready and good-natured reply was: "Bedad, ma'am, that is more than I could tell you; although I would not charge the taker before any court!"

In parts of Ireland—especially throughout the dioceses of Kildare and Leighlin—it was customary with the young people to assemble on the eve of St. Bridget's festival, observed the 1st day of February, and to carry with them what had been denominated a *Bride-oge*, which means in English, The Virgin-Brigid. This was formed of a churn-dash, covered with stuff or materials, to fashion it, as near as possible, like a female figure. These materials were usually covered with white calico. A dress of some village *belle* covered the whole, with an elegant bonnet and fashionable cap surmounting the figure's head. The *Bride-ogé's* face, however, was round, and perfectly featureless. Frills, tuckers, necklace, and a handsome sash usually decorated this grotesque figure. A piper or fiddler marched before, playing lively and popular airs; and especially when the crowd of accompanying idlers stopped at each door, in country places and villages, the *Bride-oge* always obtained an entrance for its bearer. Young children were often greatly frightened at the unexpected arrival of this uncouth visitant. A lad and lass were told off, footing it merrily to a jig or reel, and, after its conclusion, the director of such proceedings, —his hat decorated with boughs or ribbons,—went round with a purse to collect offerings for the *Bride-oge*. These were seldom or ever refused, and they were usually in keeping with the means or liberality of the householder. Proceeds thus collected were expended, on St. Bridget's day, in getting up a rustic ball, where tea, cakes, and punch, were in requisition as refreshments. A dance and plays were also organized as part of the evening's amusements. This festive celebration was probably derived from carrying St. Bridget's shrine in procession, at some remote period. The later travesty, and disorders accompanying it, induced many of the Catholic clergy to discourage such odd practices, and we believe they are at present almost entirely obsolete.

CHAPTER XVIII.

TRACES OF DRUIDISM IN IRELAND.

> " In flaming robe, of spotless white,
> The Arch-Druid issued forth to light;
> Brow-bound with leaf of holy oak,
> That never felt the woodman's stroke.
> Behind his head a crescent shone,
> Like to the new-discovered moon;
> While, flaming from his snowy vest,
> The plate of judgment clasp'd his breast.
> Around him press'd the illumin'd throng,
> Above him rose the light of song;
> And from the rocks and woods around,
> Return'd the fleet-wing'd sons of sound."
>
> WILLIAM DRENNAN.

AT this period little can be known with accuracy regarding the state and condition of Druidism in Ireland. We possess accounts, no doubt, applying to the continental Druids, and from classical sources. Cæsar, Diodorus Siculus, Strabo, Pomponius Mela, and Ammianus Marcellinus, treat concerning them, in their respective writings. We are told that the Druids were instructors of the people, and depositories of learning, which they carefully retained among their order, so that the vulgar should not have an opportunity of discovering their mysteries, and that the understanding of their pupils might be improved by the exercise of memory. They committed none of their tenets to writing, though they were acquainted with the use of letters, according to Cæsar. In their academies all precepts were delivered in verse. Even yet, in Brittany, its people recite an old chant or recapitulation of the

Druidic doctrines on destiny, cosmogony, geography, chronology, astronomy, magic, medicine, metempsychosis, &c. It is in the form of a dialogue between a Druid and a child, contained in twelve questions and twelve answers. It appears to have come down from a very remote period. Such students as aspired to honours in literature, under the Druids, were for about twenty years employed in committing didactic compositions to memory. These Druids, also, decided in matters of law and equity; while their decisions were regarded as absolute, and these decrees were enforced by a species of Druidical proscription, which was dreaded both by princes and people.

The Druids are supposed to have formed numerous schools for the instruction of youth, whose minds they impressed with a reverence for their peculiar mysteries. It is said their priests were clad in white garments, and that they gathered the mistletoe from an oak tree with a gold pruning-knife. Druidesses took part in their celebrations and rites.

Entertaining an opinion that it was derogatory to the sublimity and immensity of the Divine essence to confine their adoration within the limits of roofed edifices, they are said to have worshipped within open circles of erect stones, resembling rude obelisks. Many of these are yet standing in the British Isles and in Ireland. It is also believed that they set apart consecrated groves for celebrating their sacred rites and solemnities. As the oak was an especial object of their esteem, their places of worship were surrounded with oak trees, whence they were called *Druids*, according to several writers, who deduce their title from the Greek word δρυσ, an *oak tree*. But, it is altogether more likely, their name must be derived from a Celtic source. Cæsar informs us that the Gaulish Druids convoked a general assembly of their order, which assembled in a consecrated grove, in the country of the Carnutes, and within the most central part of Gaul. The period assigned for this meeting was at a particular time of the year.

In Ireland, also, it is said, the Arch-Druid lived within the Meathian territory; and, on the first of August, the other Druids assembled annually on the hill of Uisnech, which had been considered as one of the most central places in this island.

Owing to the Druids' noble efforts on the Continent, in animating the people with courage and patriotism, to resist tyrannic invasions of the all-conquering Romans, that influential order incurred the inveterate hostility and vengeance of these plunderers. Whereupon they were first expelled, by the Roman invaders, from Germany and Gaul. Thence they are said to have gone to South and North Britain. Anglesea, the Isle of Man, and Ireland, were subsequent places of refuge. In the latter country the fugitives were hospitably received by the native Druids. It is also thought their skill in the continental arts and sciences, with a profession and practice of these branches of knowledge in Ireland, must have contributed somewhat to effect a civilizing influence, during this Gentile period of our history.

The Druids ordered the religion and ceremonies of the people, whose directors they were. It is said they regulated the decisions of princes in matters of public policy, while they enjoyed various immunities and privileges. Here, as well as in Gaul and Britain, Druids are supposed to have had the management of sacrifices, and were intrusted with the decision of controversies, both public and private. So great was their power and influence, that such as abided not by their judicial verdicts were interdicted from being present at their religious rites. This was regarded as a powerful and grievous punishment in those days. The Druids were distinguished for profound learning, and consequently they were intellectually superior to the superstitious and ignorant priests of the heathens. The veneration in which they were held induced many ambitious spirits to embrace their profession.

Britain was thought, in Cæsar's time, to have been the original seat of the Druids, and that their institutes were better cultivated there than in Gaul, where they also flourished. Various writers concur in stating that here, in Ireland, they believed in one God, in the immortality of the soul, and that men were, after death, to be rewarded according to their actions during mortal life. The austerity of their lives, as likewise the prudence and policy with which they regulated their own order, gained them the veneration and respect of their people. They had provincial conferences annually, and they also assembled as a constituent part of those triennial conventions held at Tara. A mound of the Druids was pointed out in connection with the topography of this place. It is thought they had a very considerable knowledge of natural philosophy, and particularly regarding the magnitude, motions, and distances of the heavenly bodies.

Old Irish and British books contained considerable matter relating to the Druids' magic practices. Before St. Patrick's arrival in Ireland, the Magi are traditionally believed to have possessed many books, and several of these were burned by the Irish apostle. If this be a fact, it is more than probable, such an example had been followed by many of our early missionaries. The Druids —called Magi by Latin writers—are known to have possessed great political influence. Dion Chrysostom declares, that kings were not permitted to act without consulting the Druids, nor hold any deliberative meeting in which they did not participate. The king had at all times a Druid about his person, to pray and sacrifice for him; as also to advise him in difficulties, and to determine on occasions of emergency. Every noble, also, was attended by his Druid. This appears to accord well with the state of Druidism in Ireland, so far as can be gleaned from existing records; yet, according to some accounts, the Druids and their disciples only formed a class of the Irish population, inconsiderable in number, and restricted in point of time, however respected or feared, on account of their incantations and magic practices.

The Tuatha de Danann, who possessed Ireland when it had been invaded by the Milesians, were altogether devoted to Druidism and the black art. They were conquered, however, by the newly-arrived colonists; and it has been imagined, that the chiefs, among the older inhabitants, disdaining subjection to a less spiritual power than their own, assumed the garb of a Gentile immortality. Then they are fabled to have selected the most beautiful hills, lakes, or islands, within or around the coasts of Ireland. To these they retired, and became invisible to mortals, although they observed all that happened among the children of earth. These chiefs lived in fine halls and palaces, with their courtiers and retainers. From mortals they often spirited away husbands and wives, young and beautiful, with children not yet fully grown. These lived in a region of enchantment, until released by some happy chance or form of invocation. In one of St. Patrick's lives, it is related that the daughters of King Leaghrie thought he and his clerics, clad in white, were gods or phantoms of the Sidhe, or Druidic mansions, as at this early period the connection between fairies and Druids had been more clearly understood than at the present time.

Some of our ancient writers deny, however, that the Tuatha de Dananns retired into the hills or lakes of Ireland, or that they were demons or human bodies possessed by demoniac spirits, as many modern writers have not hesitated to assert. Those people were real human beings, and continued to live only in the natural manner, but having a knowledge regarding the occult science and literature of those countries through which they passed, before landing on this island. Here, it is thought, they introduced and perpetuated, for a long time, the practices of magic and necromancy.

It is related that the Tuatha de Danann colony brought precious relics to Ireland. Among the rest, that *Lia-Fail*, or "Stone of Destiny," on which the Irish kings were subsequently inaugurated, is noted. Concerning this piece of antiquity, curious tales are current. Indeed, its celebrity has caused the more distant British islanders to preserve some knowledge of its mysterious history; but we cannot enter upon all the romantic incidents recorded, in relation to its origin, use, or preservation.

In that most authentic account of his mission in Ireland, known as his Confessions, St. Patrick declares that the Pagan Irish had no knowledge of the true God, and that they only worshipped unclean idols. This account is quite consistent with his acts; for, during his missionary career, he is related to have replaced such idols, and the haunts of superstition, by the erection of temples to the Christian's God. There is yet extant a hymn of great antiquity, and attributed to St. Patrick. It purports to have been composed for his own and the protection of his monks, against the death's enemies lying in ambush for himself and his clerics, when he approached Leaghrie's court, at Tara, to preach the Gospel. It is likewise called a corselet of faith, to defend body and soul against demons, persons, and vices. In it he prays to be protected from dangerous, merciless powers; against false prophets, idols, heretics; against the spells of women, and of smiths, and of Druids; as also against poison, burning, drowning, slaying, and magic.

In various old tracts we meet with accounts of Druids having been attached to the court or person of our former Gentile monarchs and princes. Thus, Dubhchomar is said to have been chief Druid to one of those kings of Ireland who was called Fiacha. His Druid, likewise, was a very courageous warrior. Again, Cathbadh, the Druid, was father to Conor Mac Nessa, king of Ulster, who also had a Druid for his instructor. Bacrach was one of his chief Druids; and he is said to have described the Passion of Jesus Christ to the king, in so moving a manner, that the latter burst into a fit of ungovernable rage. This caused his death. The Arch-Druid to Niall of the Nine Hostages was Laighichin Mac Barrecheadha, who, with other Druids, excited that king to a war against Eochy, king of Munster. It is related that king Dathi had a Druid, named Finnchaemh, about his person; and Doghra, we are told, was chief of the Druids in his time. Our ancient historians state that king Læghaire's Druids predicted regarding St. Patrick's arrival and mission in this island.

Several noted Druids are named in our old records. Among the most remarkable of these may be enumerated Amergin, who was a Milesian Druid and bard. Mac Dachurr, a Druid, is mentioned in a tract on the first settlement of the tribes of Laoighis, or Leix, contained in the Book of Lecain. A Druid, named Treuilngith-Teorach, is recorded in the book of Ballymote; but in the Book of Leinster he is called Treuilnig Treorach. We also read about Cleitheach, who was a Druid.

Another Druid, named Trosdan, is said to have found an antidote which cured wounds inflicted by the arrows of certain British invaders. We are told that Cabadius was grandfather to the celebrated champion Cuchullain, and a Druid. Tadhg, the Druid, was father to Morna, who was the mother of Finn Mac Cumhail, so renowned in the romantic period of Irish history. Dadar was a Druid, and he was killed by Eogain, son to Olill Olum, king of Munster. This Eogain had been married to Moinie, daughter to the Druid Dill. We are likewise informed that Fearchios, the Druid, treacherously slew Lugad Mac Conn, the abdicated king of Ireland, by running him through the body with a spear.

Ida and Ona, Druids, were the chiefs of Corcachlann, near Roscommon; and of these, Ono made a gift of his fortress, Imleach Ono, to St. Patrick, who converted it into the religious house of Elphin. Afterwards this place was constituted an Episcopal see. The peasantry have some lingering traditions regarding this extinct order of men. It is popularly believed, there is a Druid living enchanted within a mountain, between Bunncrana and Fahen, in Donegall County. He is called Lambhdearg, or *the Bloody-handed.* Among the Bethan MSS. we find a poetic account, attributed to Oisin, about Finn Mac Cool, in the garb of a Druid, meeting with Laighne Mor. He was a Fomorian warrior, who came from Scotland to raise tribute in Erinn. A treaty of peace and amity, however, confirmed a friendship between these redoubtable champions.

The Druids were always classed among the most respectable representatives of our past social state. There is an Irish poem extant, and it enumerates the five chief heroes of Ireland, together with the five most hospitable of its men, the five chief Druids, the five best poets, the five best surgeons or physicians, the five best artists, the five best musicians, the five best harpers, the five lovemakers, the five chief mariners, and the five sages of Ireland.

An idea seems to have been entertained, that our Irish Druids must have borne some relation with the Eastern Magi, and that their doctrines and ceremonies were severally almost identical. Our unpublished literature gives some degree of countenance to such a supposition. A very curious MS. in the Irish language, and intituled, *Soibhsgeal Seamuis*, or "Gospel of James," contains a curious account of the seventeen wonders seen over the world, on the night of our blessed Lord's nativity. In the seventh chapter, the journey of the three Druids from the East, their arrival at Jerusalem, and their interview with Herod, are related. Then follows their meeting with Joseph, to whom they recount the object and circumstances of their journey. The succeeding chapter (eighth) states, that Joseph showed these Druids to where the Infant lay. Him they then adored, and offered precious gifts.

To the early Druids many of our later Irish writers have attributed a knowledge of charms, magic, necromancy, enchantments, and the black art. In the Irish language, their very name is rendered into English by the word *magician*. We may find a variety of accounts, regarding Druids and Druidism, in the Book of Lismore, belonging to the Duke of Devonshire. And in the Royal Irish Academy, which contains a copy of this same MS., we may discover a paper treating on the offices, laws, privileges, and social habits of the Druids. This tract was written by the late Edward O'Reilly, of Harold's Cross, in 1824. Much of the matter contained in it, however, is of a purely speculative kind.

An ancient copy of the learned and accomplished Cormac Mac Cullinan's *Glossary* is preserved in the Royal Irish Academy. It contains an account of the Druidical ceremonies, known by the designation of *Teinm Laeghdha* and *Imbas for Osnae*. These rites are said to have been interdicted by St. Patrick. This Glossary, also, professes to give an account respecting the Pagan Divinities and customs of our ancestors. Here are mentioned the goddess Buanan, corresponding with Minerva; Bineid, with Bellona; Neid, with Mars; Brigid, the Muse; and Dianceacht, with Æsculapius. A description of the *Fe*, or sepulchral wand for measuring graves in Pagan cemeteries, and always left there, may be met with in this MS. Whether the sepulchral wand was identical with the *Slatnan Druidheacht*, or "Rod of Druidism," cannot be determined. Allusion is made in this Glossary to many curious ancient tracts known to the author, but now supposed to be lost. In the absence of correct information on this subject, our bards and *shanachies* have indulged greatly in unreliable speculation regarding the religion and rites of the Druids. We find in his poem on Glendalloch, written in 1802, that William Drennan has fancifully described the appearance of a chief Druid engaged in some of the mystic ceremonies of his order, as seen in the poetic quotation prefixed to this chapter. It has been extracted from a small volume of his, intituled, *Fugitive Pieces in Verse and Prose*, and published at Belfast, in 1815.

A prose and verse tract, purporting to have been taken from the Yellow Book of Slane, relates the Decline of Cuchulain, and the jealousy of his wife Eimir. It is preserved in the Royal Irish Academy, and written in a very old dialect of Irish. It describes curious cases of Druidism and witchcraft, while it relates the interference of evil spirits and fairies in the concerns of men. A contention of the Druids forms the subject of a separate narrative.

Amongst the traditions referring to Druidic or Pagan incantations, practices, magic, and *diablerie*, these following are on record. On the first of May, we are told that our Druids drove cattle through Bael fires, in order to preserve such animals from disorders during the remainder of that year. This Pagan custom, to a comparatively late period, had been practised in Munster and Connaught, where the farmers and peasants burned wisps of straw near their cattle, and through a like motive, to ward off all manner of disease.

Amongst the Highland traditions, we are informed that crystal gems, sometimes set in silver, are called *Clach Bhuai*, (*recte*, "Buadhach"), or "The powerful stone." Another sort of amulet was called *Glein Naidr*, or "The adder stone," as we are told by Pennant in his *Scottish Tour*. Some necromancy is connected with the possession of these relics, for it is believed they insure good luck for their owners. In certain cases the Highlander was known to travel over 100 miles, bringing water with him, in which the *Clach Bhuai* was to be dipped. Such practices were required to produce the intended effect. These were supposed to have been the magical gems, or stones, used by the Druids, and which, when inspected by a chaste boy, would enable him to see an apparition in them, so as to foretell future events. We have not been able to discover if a similar custom ever prevailed in Ireland.

Since the Druidic times, Irish spring wells are said to have been invested with some sacred character. To desecrate a holy spring is considered profanity. Sometimes this desecration will cause it to become dry, or to remove far from its first position. Severe chastisement is believed to be visited oftentimes on the wanton delinquent. Incantations were also practised. As an instance of *diablerie*, forming part of our Pagan superstitions, the following account remains on record. Two women are spoken of in some ancient tracts, and who are said to have come over from Scotland for the express purpose of subjecting Cormac Mac Art, monarch of Ireland, to the influences of demonism.

The Druidical doctrines appear, from what we can now glean regarding them, to have been very accommodating in ministration to popular delusions of the most benighted classes. Though the majority of the people embraced the true faith, still there were some pertinacious sticklers for Paganism, and who believed that the new doctrine did not satisfy the material wants of the people, or gratify their natural cravings. The people, who could not possibly abolish at once all reminiscences of the religion they had only recently abandoned, gave them a tacit toleration. The magicians still exercised their arts in a covert way, and affected to employ preternatural agencies. These pretenders to spirituality dwindled down to the charm-mongers and fairy-herb doctors of our own day. It may be added, their last tangible personification subsided into those wicked *bocoachs*, or mendicants, who had, or pretended to have, been attended by familiar spirits, who enabled them to cure diseases, and to tell all about the world of mystery and fable. These were the precursors of those spiritual mediums, practising on the credulity of fashionables and fools at the present day. The clergy opposed many impostors and vagabonds with their powers of persuasion at all times; but, nevertheless, these strollers kept hold on the people's affections, and cheated many credulous dupes out of their hard-earned money in a variety of instances. Fortune-telling and cup-tossing now form the half-sportive, but yet improper, deceptions of several young and ignorant persons.

Almost effaced from popular remembrance, at the present day, are the former accounts of those magicians, once so celebrated in Ireland. Yet Druid's altars, Druid's idols, and Druid's houses, are mentioned in the bardic remains of ancient Erinn. Besides these, various localities have a traditional connection with the Druids. Some of these we must particularise, with their associated stories.

An ancient historic tale, called *Cath Cumair*, which

gives us some account regarding the battle of Cumar, fought shortly before the death of Eochy Feileach, which happened A.M. 5069. This tract relates how his three sons rebelled against the king, and at their mother's instigation. She had been divorced from her husband. This battle, in which Eochy's sons were defeated and killed, in retreating from the field, is said to have been fought near Athlone. The Druids are here introduced as endeavouring to promote peace; but their vocation, united with the justness of their remonstrances, did not screen them from the wrath of those rebellious princes. Two of them were put to death on the spot, and at a place afterwards called *Dumha nan Druadh*, or, the Druid's Mount. It arose to the north side of Cruachain, the royal residence of the Conacian monarchs.

There was a place known as Feart-an-Druadh, or the Druid's Grave, on Sliabh-na-mBan, in the County of Tipperary. Here had been fought a great battle between two parties of the Tuatha de Danann, or fairies. The celebrated Finn Mac Cumhail and his heroes took part in this engagement. This renowned warrior is said to have possessed Druidic powers, and a wonderful gift of prophecy.

There is a poem in the Royal Irish Academy which gives an account of Cormac Mac Art's famous hostile expedition into Munster, to demand tribute from its king, about A.D. 220. Then he encamped at Drom Damhghaire, now Knocklong, in the County of Limerick. His Druids were consulted, and by their incantations they dried up all the rivers and springs of water in Munster. This caused the greatest consternation to the king, and to the inhabitants in that part of the country. However, they procured ultimate relief from Mogh Ruith, the Druid, who lived at Valencia, on the Kerry coast. The magic arts of this latter, thus exercised, prevailed over the efforts of his discomfited brethren; for he is stated to have shot an arrow into the air, and where it fell, a rushing torrent issued. This relieved the men and flocks of Munster. The spring was afterwards called Tobar or Tipra Ceann Mor, or "Well of the Great Head," in the County of Limerick. A river that ran from it was called Sruth Cheanna Mor, or "Stream of the Great Head."

In the Book of Lismore is to be found the speech of Mogh Roith, the Druid, in the encampment of Dromdamhgaire. He was the son of Sinduinn, and a renowned warrior. His name is also written Mogruth. In the same MS. we find the speeches of Cormac Mac Airt's Druids.

The hill of Druim Suamaigh, on the Meath side of Athlone, is said to have derived its name from a learned Druid. Many other places might be mentioned as connected with Druidism, were we inclined to enter more minutely upon this subject.

A transformation, or transmigration, of certain remarkable persons into one of the lower animals, or from one object into another, is frequently found in the relations of our early Irish bards. Demoniac influences are supposed to have caused this metempsychosis, and it would appear to have formed a part of our Pagan ancestors' irreligious creed. Instances abound in our oldest MSS. yet extant. In the Book of Ballymote, we have a poem containing an account of Tuan, the nephew of Partholan, and sole survivor of the plague which carried off all the Irish people. He is fabled to have assumed various shapes and transformations into the appearance of several animals. He lived on for several centuries before he returned to human shape. He then related to Saints Columbkille and Finian, of Maghbile, the history of the different colonizations of the island until their time. This is not the sole instance that could be cited. The exquisite song of Fionnuala, by Moore, represents her as transformed into a swan, and condemned to sail over the lakes and rivers of Ireland, until the dawn of a Christian period.

There appears to have been a Morrigain, likewise, in Irish, as in Breton, traditionary stories. Her name occurs in the *Tain Bo Cualnge*, where she takes the shape of a bird, perched on a pillar stone, in one instance. Again, she appears to the champion Cu, in the form of a beautiful female, and declares her love for him, although her advances are rejected. Next, in the shape of a serpent, she winds round his feet, while engaged in combat; but he extricates himself, and wounds her. Afterwards she was healed unconsciously by the author of her misfortune.

The well-known story of the swan of Mac Coise, the poet, sufficiently illustrates this Druidic notion of metempsychosis. We give the account as transmitted by our ancient bards. On a certain day, Mac Coise was at the Boyne, where he saw a flock of swans: whereupon he cast a stone at them, and it struck one of the swans while on the wing. He ran immediately to catch it, when he found it was a woman. He demanded intelligence from her as to what happened to her, and how she came to exist under that shape. She then informed him. "I was in sickness," said she, "and it appeared to my friends that I died; but wandering spirits and demons solely spirited me away with them." After hearing this account from her, the poet restored the woman to her friends, and the enchantment was thus dissolved.

But Druidic incantations are supposed to have lost their efficacy whenever the Irish saints chose to exert their supernatural powers in opposition to them. An old MS. life of St. Caillin informs us how this holy man turned some hostile Druids into stones. These were afterwards to be seen, near his own church, at Fenagh, in Breifney. We find nearly similar accounts, about the magicians having been foiled in all contests with the heroes of Christianity. The pages of Irish Hagiology furnish a great variety of such incidents.

According to some accounts, Irish Druids were accustomed to utter certain mysterious and rhapsodical speeches, in an extemporaneous manner; and several of these reputed improvisos have been preserved by our scribes.

In another Irish MS., transcribed by James Maguire, in 1746, and from older sources, there is a metrical composition, called a *Riotharg*, or rhetorical speech, delivered by Amergin, poet and Druid, when first placing foot on Irish ground, at Inver Colpa, near the mouth of the river Boyne. The term *Riotharg*, often occurring in old Irish MSS., is almost invariably applied to some obscure or mysterious speech, delivered extempore by a Druid.

According to Mr. O'Curry, it would appear that the perfect poet, or Ollamh, in ancient times, was expected to know and practise the Teinim Laegha. This is supposed to have been a peculiar kind of Druidical verse or incantation, which was thought to confer on the Druid, or poet a power of understanding everything he ought to treat.

Irish traditions, also, mention a wonderful ring, by which the upright judge, Moran, tested guilt and innocence. This ordeal is supposed to have originated in a Druidic charm. It is likewise mentioned in the Brehon laws, as being one of the former ordeals of Ireland. Their publication will doubtless throw a considerable share of light on our more ancient customs, superstitions, habits, and traditional lore. But we have great reasons for believing that the late Professor O'Curry's forthcoming lectures on the social life, manners, and civilization of the people of ancient Erinn, will add much to the imperfect knowledge acquired at present regarding this special subject.

CHAPTER XIX.

THE WIZARD EARL OF KILDARE.

"The wizard was brought to the great Castle Hall—
Weird was his aspect and gloomy his eye."—M. HOGAN.

"And still it is the peasant's hope upon the Cuirreach's mere,
They live, who'll see ten thousand men with good Lord Edward here,—
So let them dream till brighter days, when, not by Edward's shade,
But by some leader true as he, their lines shall be arrayed!"
THOMAS DAVIS.

THE Castle of Kilkea, in the southern part of Kildare County, never presented a lordlier aspect than at the present moment, tenanted as it is by a worthy scion of the historic Geraldine race. It has witnessed many strange scenes, and numberless legends are current in the adjacent neighbourhood, since its first erection. At present, its magnificent exterior carries us in recollection to ages far distant, for its features, under a tasteful restoration, have undergone few unnecessary changes. The castle is a perfect model of a grand chieftain's feudal residence interiorly, while fitted up with all the luxuries of modern refinement. Fine gardens, woods, and waters surround this noble mansion of the Marquis of Kildare.

Within Kilkea Castle a small room is to be found, and it receives for name "the enchanted chamber." Into this we have been once in our lifetime conducted. Here, it is said, a former Earl of Kildare, to whom the castle belonged, studied the "black art." This earl was nursed by a fairy, according to the popular tradition, and thus he became addicted to pursuits which caused him to be feared and suspected. He was a noble-looking and handsome young man, however, and he married a beautiful and an accomplished lady. This wife, being aware of her husband's favourite studies and preternatural powers, felt an uncontrollable curiosity to witness some of his enchantments. She besought him to gratify this curiosity, by exerting his peculiar powers, and by changing himself into some other shape.

The earl for a long time resisted her solicitations; but no refusal could overcome the lady's persevering petitions. At last, he warned her not to persist in her request, because if he should comply with it, and change his shape, she must be greatly terrified. Then he would be obliged to leave her for ever. His wife declared she had nerve and affection sufficient, not to feel afraid in his presence, under whatever form this transmigration might take place. His remonstrances proving vain, the earl finally yielded, and prepared to exhibit his skill in necromancy.

He then changed his human form into the shape of an enormous eel, or serpent, which wound itself round the castle, and in and out through its windows. Next, its head issued through the window of the enchanted chamber; but protruding therefrom, his features appeared so monstrously deformed and hideous, that his wife completely lost her presence of mind, raised a loud scream, and instantly fainted. Away flew the earl, and never more was he seen by the countess or his retainers, within the Castle of Kilkea.

Afterwards was he condemned to ride round and round the Curragh of Kildare, on a white horse, shod with silver shoes. When these plates of silver are worn out, it is traditionally said, he shall return once more to the Castle of Kilkea. Before the close of the last century, it was currently believed the silver shoes were then worn as thin as a sixpence.

One day a blacksmith was coming from Newbridge with a load of coals for the supply of his forge, in the town of Kildare. He overtook a travelling tinker, with a budget on his back, near the famous pit known as Donnelly's Hollow, where the celebrated Irish pugilist encountered and defeated Cooper, the English champion of the prize ring.

"Good night, and a good journey to you, tinker!" cried the smith, accosting his fellow-traveller.

The latter looked gruffly enough at the smith, and replied: "There are more men tinkers than carry the budget. Take your change out of that, if you like!"

"Arrah, friend, don't be angry," said the good-humoured smith; "for, do you know that the great Henry Grattan was called by the newspaper, that intended to praise him, *the greatest tinker in Ireland;* and, begorra! you have no rayson to feel ashamed of the ladein' man of your thrade, although the prenther set the types wrong, when he should make

> 'The gallant man,
> That led the van
> Of Irish volunteers,'

the greatest thinker in Ireland. So come along; murther alive! put your budget on the coals, and I'll give you a lift, on the slat of the car, beyant the lonely rath, where the poor fellows were massacreed by the fox-hunthers, in the year of '98!"

This merry sally and sad allusion put the tinker in good humour with the smith. He accepted the proffered lift for his budget thankfully, as he travelled in that direction; but he preferred trudging it on foot himself, being thus lightened of his ordinary load. On the way, they entered into familiar and friendly conversation regarding the events of the memorable year and spot to which their reminiscences had been drawn; nor did they forget Lord Edward Fitzgerald, whom they had often seen, and had intended to serve, in case he survived. The smith told how many pikes he had forged, and the tinker how many cans and canisters he had made and mended for the powder, shot, and provender of the insurgents, with other affairs, in which both had taken a leading part. But, as they approached the rath, suddenly a tremendous whisk of wind, rushing near their faces, was supposed to indicate the near passage of elves, and proximate danger to persons then exposed, even when escaping the effects of a fairy stroke, which might permanently paralyze them. Soon were seen whole troops of horsemen sweeping by, with glittering helmets and nodding plumes, with splendid banners, and clattering swords dangling by their sides, and all covered with bright armour. At their head rode the fairy Earl of Kildare, as they afterwards learned; for instantly he ordered the horsemen to wheel into lines and halt, while he pushed forward, and obliged the pedestrians to examine the hoofs of his horse, to discover if they wanted shoeing. Both the tinker and the smith inspected the shoe-plates, but found all the nails were fast. Had but one of them been loose, says the legend, the earl would have regained his freedom, and live once more in Kilkea Castle. As it happened otherwise, he was condemned to ride onwards with his troop, and to leave the frightened tradesmen to their own reflections regarding this surprising vision.

In the Duke of Leinster's princely mansion at Carton, near Maynooth, the visitor will yet see a well-executed painting of the fairy Geraldine, dressed in the costume of his age. We have gazed on it with great interest. But we looked in vain for some account of this half-historic, half-mythic personage, in the Marquis of Kildare's memoirs of his popular family, once regarded "as more Irish than the Irish themselves." The traditions of the palesmen, however, seem to have come down to our times; and it is only becoming they should be placed on record, for the perusal of our Irish public.

CHAPTER XX.

THE REALMS OF FAIRYDOM.

"Nor scream can any raise, nor prayer can any say,
But wild, wild, the terror of the speechless three,
For they feel fair Anna Grace drawn silently away,
By whom they dare not look to see."
SAMUEL FERGUSON.

IN Ulster, the hawthorn seems associated with fairy revels, and some mysterious undefined feeling causes the peasantry to regard it as a favourite place of resort or shelter, for those dreaded spirits of the raths and lisses. This prevailing opinion has been poetically illustrated in that most musical and imaginative Northern ballad, "The Fairy Thorn." Written, as it has been, by one of Ulster's and of Ireland's poets, so highly distinguished for a strikingly descriptive and dramatic power in the conception and versification of his subjects, we may rest assured it reveals, with more than pictorial effect, the expression of local thoughts and legends. A fairy host is introduced, and issuing from every point of the compass around an enchanted hawthorn. Four beautiful young maidens are engaged in dancing beneath it, when

"They hear the silky footsteps of the silent fairy crowd,
Like a river in the air, gliding round."

While clasping each other in terror, one of their number is forcibly abducted. Her companions fall into a trance, in which they remain until the following morning. The three maidens, who were left behind on earth by the fairy host, soon afterwards

"pined away and died, within the year and day,
And ne'er was Anna Grace seen again."

Such persons, it is supposed, may be recovered again, and restored to their friends; but not without recourse to knowledgeable practitioners and to charms. Rarely, however, are all the conditions complied with, so as to insure a favourable result. Then does it follow, that the fairy doctor or sorcerer can frame arguments sufficient to continue the delusion regarding his own skill, even when the trial has been unsuccessful.

A circle made round a place, with certain incantations, it is thought, will ward off the fairies' intrusion, or nullify their power. This practice is often adopted by persons who wish to dig for money about a rath. It is also used by those who take their stand within it, at a certain pass, to draw any spell-bound friend from a state of spirit durance. Fairy women often profess to point out the person thus detained, by some token or peculiarity of dress indicated to the living relative, before the spectre troop sweeps past this spot. If a fairy intend the abduction of any mortal, and if the latter have some intimation or fear of his incarceration in spirit-land, it is thought that a well-directed stroke of a sword, knife, or any other sharp steel weapon, to a vulnerable part will prove an effectual preservative. But this stroke must not be repeated by the mortal, even in self-defence; for the second stroke is calculated to cure the first, and strengthen the detaining fairy; so that, under certain conditions, the captive is supposed to pass away from his band of sprites.

Superstition spreads the cloud of fear over that mind, leaning to its absurdities. When it is thought persons have been spirited away to the realms of fairydom, the mystery attaching to such agency involves the ignorant in further aberrations of intellect. This doctrine appears to have embodied with it a strong admixture of that belief in the Irish Pagan Elysium, since persons, who, to all natural appearances, had died and had been buried, really existed, as often was supposed, in fairy subterranean abodes, and under unpleasant bondage. It was imagined that some of these unfortunate persons were wont to be restored to their friends. Living relatives generally left food, and even clothing, beside those raths, when it was thought abducted mortals were kept in confinement. This was intended to save the captives from any necessity for partaking of the rich banquets prepared for them by the fairies. Should they do so at any time, an opinion was entertained, that those persons could not escape from elfin thraldom, or return to their relatives on earth.

In the South of Ireland, especially, every parish has its grassy green, and fairy thorn, where it is supposed these elves hold merry-meetings, and dance their rounds. Fairy rings are circular patches of stunted and burned-looking grass, frequently found amid fine verdant fields. Those are pointed out by people in the country as places where fairies had a ball and supper over night. Sometimes their amusements become visible to belated travellers, and an extraordinary light shines around them. Something of a like character is believed in by the people of other nationalities. It is curious to trace such coincidences. Princesses and queens are often found presiding over these moonlight revels, or joining, with greater agility and grace than other fairies, in their evolutions. These, and their lady attendants, are especially noticed to have exceedingly beautiful and tiny feet, remarkable for their whiteness. Old cairns are also held to be sacred to the "good people." It would be considered unlucky to remove these remnants of antiquity for that very reason.

At the present day, it would appear that, in the northern parts of France, poems have come down by tradition, or writing, from the most remote times. These relate to Druidic superstitions, festivals, and ceremonies, the origin and object of which are now obscure, if not incomprehensible. Enchantments, enchanters, and enchantresses form the burden of many such compositions. In Brittany, especially, curious popular opinions yet prevail in reference to the local *genii*.

There is a female fairy sprite, or sorceress, called the *Corrigaun*,—thought to have been formerly a Druidess,— who is said to hate the sight of any priest or holy water. She was regarded as a prophetess, and sometimes she falls in love with mortals. She also carries off healthy children, replacing them by changelings. The Corrigaun is of small stature, but exquisitely proportioned. It is said their bodies are diaphanous, and their beauty appears to great advantage during the night; whereas in the day their visages are wrinkled. The Breton peasantry think these had been great princesses in former times, but that they refused to embrace Christianity, when preached by the first apostles in Armoric Britain. Hence they are supposed to have incurred the malediction of heaven, and to have become fallen intelligences. The Welsh people have nearly a similar tradition; and among them the Corrigauns are thought to have been Druidesses, condemned to expiate their sins under such a guise. From one of the fine legends related in Taylor's *Ballads and Songs of Brittany*, translated from the "Barsaz-Breiz" of Vicomte Hersart de la Villemarqué, the following picture of this sprite is presented. The incident recorded bears some affinity to the personal habits of our Irish *Banshee*:—

> "The Corrigaun sat by the fountain fair,
> A-combing her long and yellow hair."

The Corrigauns practised the healing art by means of charms, which are communicated by them to their favoured disciples. On the return of spring-time each year, the Corrigauns held a nightly festival, usually beside a fountain, and near one of the Breton dolmens. Here they were seen seated on the grass, with a snow-white cloth, covered with every delicacy, set before them. A crystal cup sparkled on its centre, and spread a marvellous light about them; from this they drank a knowledge-inspiring liquor when their feast had ended. But if the slightest human sound were heard, this whole apparition vanished from mortal sight. Yet those who disturbed them were almost sure to suffer some calamity, if they escaped immediate death. The Morgans, or Spirits of the Waters, with the hideous dwarfs, among the Bretons, are regarded as magicians. In these several traditions about them, we find many traits exactly resembling the opinions of our Irish peasants, and their forefathers, in reference to the spirits of evil.

The "good people" often perch, like cocks and hens, on the couples of Irish cabins, to enjoy some diversion at marriage-feasts, christenings, or other merry-meetings. Flint arrow-heads, of which so many have been collected in different parts of Ireland, and preserved in our antiquarian museums, are supposed by the commonalty to have been shot at cattle, which are objects of aversion to the fairies. This is one of their peculiar sports. The flints are popularly called "elf-arrows," despite the different nomenclature and theory of our most distinguished antiquarians. What the peasants call an "elf-arrow" was frequently set in silver, and worn about the neck. It was used as an amulet, to preserve the person from an elf-shot. Small and oddly-shaped smoking instruments, sometimes found, and which have been termed "Danes' pipes," are said to have been dropped by the "good people," in a variety of instances. Shoes are also lost on their travels. It is thought to be very lucky to find a fairy's shoe, of tiny shape, or grotesque fashion, and to keep it concealed from the eye of mortal. If seen by a third person, the luck vanishes. Many other antique objects are supposed by rustics to have been forgotten by the "wee people." These articles are, unfortunately, often destroyed, to avert the dreaded consequences of retaining property that might afterwards be discovered, or claimed, by their supposed previous owners.

It would seem, that the most cultivated minds entertained very singular conceptions respecting fairy influences over the affairs of men. This may be instanced in very ancient or mediæval literary fragments. In an ancient Irish poem, attributed to Donough, the great abbot of Boyle, Death is introduced as engaged in a dialogue with a dying sinner. The fatal visitor is made to speak regarding the fairies in this manner:—

> "I am found on the sea as well as on land,
> I am found in the woods amongst the fairies,
> And these are not the souls of men
> Who come to an unprovided death,
> But aërial demons that madly rebelled,
> And committed treason against the King of kings;
> For which crimes thousands of them were hurled from heaven,
> And shall burn in hell for all eternity."

Yet, it must be acknowledged, that we can have no absolute certainty of many compositions, still preserved in our libraries, dating back to the time of their presumed authors. In most cases, however, we cannot but consider them as undoubtedly genuine and authentic productions.

We have already seen, that the idea of Irish fairies having been fallen spiritual intelligences, or angels, was prevalent among the people. Yet, again, with a strange confusion of thought, they are believed to have lived, at one time, as habitants of earth. The notion in the existence of fairies, or wandering demons, is very ancient; and, perhaps, it may be considered as coeval with the dispersion at Babylon. It was not confined to Ireland and the

British Isles, for we find it existing in Persia, Egypt, Hindustan, and almost all oriental countries where the doctrines of the Magi held sway. It was known to the ancient Greeks and Romans under different phases. We might probably trace it through many other nations, were it necessary to multiply proofs of its very general prevalence.

Demonology and fairyism have intimate relations; but we may conceive forms of both, varying from the grotesque and ludicrous, to the more hideous and revolting superstitions. Fairyism, however, more survives in the popular remembrance after a long lapse of ages. It, in fact, existed in every country where the ancient Celts formed settlements, or sojourned in course of their transit to the west. In France, England, Scotland, Wales, and Ireland, its dogmas and enchantments survive in song and story. It is curious to examine the analogy subsisting between the origin attributed by ancient Greek mythologists and the Irish to fairies. The Titans, who made war upon the gods, are regarded as representatives of our rebel angels, in Greek and Roman mythology. Hesiod informs us that those wicked disturbers of celestial felicity were transformed after death into wandering demons; while it is likewise asserted that they interested themselves in human affairs. Another Greek writer supports such an assertion by stating that the souls of the wicked giants were dispersed over earth as wandering demons. How far the fabled giants of the Middle Ages, and the stories or strains of the troubadours, had relation with the heroes of Celtic mythology, would require whole pages of essay or digression rightly to elucidate.

CHAPTER XXI.

THE WATER-SHEERRIE; OR, BOG-SPRITE.

" Will-o'-Wisp misleads night-faring clowns,
O'er hills, and sinking bogs, and pathless downs."—GAY.

"As when a wandering fire,
Compact of unctuous vapour, which the night
Condenses, and the cold environs round,
Kindled through agitation to a flame,
Which oft, they say, some evil spirit attends,
Hovering and blazing with delusive light,
Misleads the amaz'd night-wanderer from his way,—
To bogs and mires, and oft through pond or pool,
There swallow'd up and lost, from succour far."—MILTON.

" Now quivering like the ray
On which it seems to play;
Now fading down the main of splendour, spirit-like, away."
T. C. IRWIN.

THE Bog-sprite appears in the shape of a distant light, or fiery meteor, which often presents objects distorted and misplaced to the traveller's gaze, until he is led into the midst of a swamp or pool of water, where he sinks and is lost. The Hanoverian "Tuckbold," and the English "Will-o'-the-Wisp," partake of the same description. In England this object is called "elf-fire;" and when it assumes the appearance of flitting about in the night, as an exhalation, it was formerly called a "fire-drake," from some fancied resemblance to a dragon.

At a distance, such gaseous light appears like that of a taper gleaming from some cottage window. It is generally thought to be the product of inflammable gas, which exudes from certain decayed animal or vegetable matter, contained in stagnant pools, or in damp, marshy, or peaty

THE WATER-SHEERRIE; OR, BOG-SPRITE. 167

spots. Sometimes it has a white, cloudy appearance, but most generally it is very luminous and brilliant. Bubbles of gas have been observed to rise from stagnant water in the day-time; and, at night, bluish phosphoric flames were noticed moving over the surface. It is said such flames have been known to shift their position, owing to the very motion of the air caused by an experimenter on approaching, and when he remained perfectly still they returned. Attempting to light a piece of paper by them, his breath kept these flames at too great a distance; but on turning away his head, and holding up a cloth screen, he was able to ignite the paper. He succeeded in extinguishing this meteoric fire by driving it before him to a part of the ground where no gas could be produced. Afterwards applying a flame to that marshy surface, whence the gas bubbles issued, a kind of explosion was heard, and a red light succeeded. Then it diminished in lustre to a blue flame, about three feet in height from the ground. This burned with an unsteady motion until morning dawned. Then all the flames became paler, seeming to approach nearer and nearer to earth, when at length they totally faded from sight. The experimenter, Major Blesson, of Berlin, was of opinion that when once the thin stream of inflammable air had been set on fire, it would continue to burn by day as well as by night. In the former case, however, it is not probable the pale lights of this "vain fire" would be visible. Where damp soils have been well drained and cultivated, it has been noticed, this *ignis-fatuus* no longer appears hovering over their surface.

In some places on the Continent of Europe, these wandering wild-fires, when seen, are thought by the peasants to be forerunners of their demise: hence they are called "death-fires." In these islands, no such opinion is known to prevail, unless the traveller be induced, by some mesmeric influence, to pursue their unaccountable vagaries.

The poet Milton, as we have already seen, gives us the received opinion of philosophers in his day, with that of the commonalty, regarding the composition and nature of this "wandering fire." In one of his minor poems, too, allusion is doubtless made to it, when the swain spins out his tale by the fireside, and acknowledges how he had been led by "friar's lantern." This term seems to suggest some local or general legend prevailing at the time, and the clue to which cannot be discovered at present.

In Collins's "Ode on the Popular Superstitions of the Highlands of Scotland," he graphically alludes to this glinting phantom of the moors:—

> "Ah, homely swains! your homeward steps ne'er lose,
>   Let not dank Will mislead you to the heath:
> Dancing in mirky night, o'er fen and lake,
>   He glows, to draw you downward to your death,
> In his bewitch'd, low, marshy, willow brake!
>   What though, far off, from some dark dell espied,
> His glimmering mazes cheer th' excursive sight,
>   Yet turn, ye wanderers, turn your steps aside,
> Nor trust the guidance of that faithless light;
>   For watchful, lurking, 'mid th' unrustling reed,
> At those mirk hours the wily monster lies,
>   And listens oft to hear the passing steed,
> And frequent round him rolls his sullen eyes,
>   If chance his savage wrath may some weak wretch surprise."

According to the Highlander's conceptions of "dank Will," he flits over fens, and among sedgy weeds, covering soft, marshy, and dangerous bog-holes. He is considered as a water fiend, anxious for the destruction of some belated traveller. The poor wanderer is led on, step by step, with dissolving views of firm footing and of rising ground before him. At last the grim and grisly monster, clad in all its terrors, appears to his unfortunate victim.

It is supposed this Jack-o'-the-Lanthorn, as he is often called, lures the mortal into some muddy hollow, where the water will rise around him on every side, thus precluding all hope of escape, until

> "His fear-shook limbs have lost their youthly force,
> And down the waves he floats, a pale and breathless corse!"

The perturbed motions of this departed mortal are described by Collins with that power of pointed and poetic delineation so peculiarly possessed by him. Doubtless the Irish, from whom the Scotch derived so many of their superstitions, had some such idea of the spirit's unrest; for, in nearly all such cases when mortals came to a tragic end, ghosts were thought to haunt scenes and friends known during their pilgrimage on earth. Thus, continues the poet last quoted, in reference to his lost traveller,—

> "For him in vain his anxious wife shall wait,
>   Or wander forth to meet him on his way;
> For him in vain, at to-fall of the day,
>   His babes shall linger at the unclosing gate.
> Ah, ne'er shall he return! Alone, if night
>   Her travell'd limbs in broken slumbers sleep,
> With drooping willows drest, his mournful sprite
>   Shall visit sad, perchance, her silent sleep:
> Then he, perhaps, with moist and watery hand,
>   Shall fondly seem to press her shuddering cheek,
> And with his blue, swoll'n face, before her stand,
>   And, shivering cold, those piteous accents speak:
> 'Pursue, dear wife, thy daily toils pursue,
>   At dawn or dusk, industrious as before,
> Nor e'er of me one helpless thought renew,
>   While I lie weltering on the osier'd shore,
> Drown'd by the Kelpie's wrath, nor e'er shall aid thee more.'"

In Ireland, the Bog-spirit, we have reason to believe, has been classed with the *sowlth*,—a bodiless or misshapen ghost,—which is thought to wander about lonely places in a state of unrest. But it is called the Water-Sheerrie in most of the Irish-speaking districts. Whether the *Dine-maitha*, or good people—as the fairies, by courtesy, are called—claim him for one of their *attachés*, can hardly be decided on positive grounds; but there are probable traditions of the people to countenance such a conjecture. If this latter view of the case be admitted, the Bog-sprite must be ranked among the most mischievous and malevolent of their gloomy tribes. The Water-Sheerrie is thought to wave a wisp of lighted straw in his hand, and hence the popular application to his first name. Some think he is a disembodied spirit, and the guardian of concealed treasures. Sometimes he flits about in every variety of maze, and frequently he stands still. Often he seems extinct, but only to shine again. Sometimes he appears in churchyards, and oftentimes to mariners out at sea. When observed about the masts, spars, or sails of a hooker or ship, it is thought by sailors that a wreck is imminent; yet, when two or more of those phosphoric lights appear, they regard such apparitions as a favourable portent.

An amusing story is told by Carleton regarding a notorious and an incorrigible scamp, called Billy Dawson, who lived a riotous and drunken life. This caused his nose to become very inflammable; and when an arch-enemy seized it with a red-hot tongs, a flame at once burst forth. This continued to burn on, winter and summer; while a bushy beard, which he wore, helped to feed the fuel. Hence, the northern country people say that Billy Dawson had been christened Will o' the Wisp, and that he plunges into the coldest quagmires and pools of water to quench the flames emitted from his burning nose. It is a remnant of his mischievous disposition, however, to lead unthinking and tipsy night-travellers into bogs, where they are likely to be drowned.

We have heard, in a few instances, related by friends

and acquaintances living in the midland counties of Ireland, most covered with bogs, that globes of fire are often known to appear suddenly near the marshy ground, and instantly to explode, scattering flashes of light around to a considerable distance; then these flames altogether vanish. Horses harnessed to vehicles, or under the saddle, are with difficulty restrained from running away on such occasions. It is a common belief, that those animals see a spirit when the latter is quite invisible either to the rider or driver.

Among our earliest recollections of objects noticed on the Irish bogs by night, luminous flashes of fire, and generally of a shifting appearance, may be mentioned. These were we taught to regard as the Bog-spirit, or Water-Sheerrie; and a natural fear of unpleasant consequences prevented a very close or dangerous inspection of Jack o' the Lantern and Will o' the Wisp. We do not remember, however, a single instance of any person having been tempted to follow this lure and find a watery grave. Such appearances, notwithstanding, created strange apprehensions in the minds of children, and even in those of grown people.

CHAPTER XXII.

THE FOMORIAN WARRIOR, BALOR OF THE EVIL EYE.

> " No magicke arts hereof had any might,
> Nor bloody wordes of bold enchanter's call;
> But all that was not such as seemed in sight
> Before that shield did fade, and suddeine fall.
> And, when him list the raskall routes appall,
> Men into stones therewith he could transmew,
> And stones to dust, and dust to naught at all:
> And, when him list the prouder lookes subdew,
> He would them gazing blind, or turne to other hew."
>
> SPENSER.

FAR back in the mists of time, according to the chronology of the Septuagint, the Four Masters have placed the landing of Parthalon in Ireland, A. M. 2520. During his time, the Fomorians, or pirates, first made a descent on our shores; and we obtain occasional records of their depredations in the days of yore, until the Tuatha de Dananns arrived as fresh invaders about A. M. 3303, and these conferred the sovereignty on Bress Mac Elathan. The Fomorians and Tuatha de Dananns, however, seem to have intermarried. Thus, Bress Mac Elathan, king of Ireland, belonged to the former race on the father's side, and to the latter by maternal descent.

Some of our historians consider the Fomorians to have been Scandinavians, and others of Asiatic or of African origin. One of their chief leaders, known as Balor of the Evil Eye, or Balor of the Mighty Blows, was regarded as a renowned champion of gigantic size and strength. He was also a magician. Throughout the northern and western parts of Ireland the old natives have vivid recollections of traditional tales in which he figures. In some places mothers frighten children by his name. That he was a ruthless tyrant, and richly merited his fate, would appear from the following popular account regarding his special connection with the north of Ireland.

Tory Island was thus denominated because it presented a towering appearance from the continent of Tir Connell, and owing to its many prominent rocks rising towards the heavens. Those were called *tors* by the natives. The famous warrior, Balor, ruled over this island. He had only one eye in the middle of his forehead, and another, directly opposite to it, in the back of his skull. A glance of this "evil eye" is said to have blasted the bleak islands lying to the west of Scotland. With its foul distorted glances, its piercing beams, and venomous properties, like those of the basilisk, this eye in the back of his skull would strike people dead. For that very reason, Balor kept it constantly covered, except whenever he wished to get the better of enemies, by petrifying them with his awe-inspiring looks. Hence the Irish, to this day, call an "evil," or "overlooking eye," Suil Bhaloir.

Though possessed of such powers for self-defence, it had been revealed to a Druid that Balor should be killed by his own grandson. At this time, Balor had an only child, his daughter Ethnea by name. Seeing that she was the only medium through which his destruction could be wrought, Balor shut her up in an impregnable tower, which he, or some of his ancestors, had previously built on the summit of Tor-more. This was a lofty and almost an inaccessible rock, which, shooting into the blue sky, breaks the roaring waves, and confronts the storms, at the eastern extremity of Tory Island. Here he also placed a company of twelve matrons, to whom he gave the strictest charge not to allow any man near her, not even to give her any idea regarding the existence or nature of man. The fair

Ethnea remained a long time imprisoned and within this donjon; but though confined within the limits of a tower, tradition says that she expanded into bloom and beauty. Though her female attendants never expressed the word "man" in her presence, still would she often question them about the manner in which she had received existence. She often inquired concerning the nature of those beings she saw passing up and down the sea in currachs. Often did she relate to her servants dreams about other beings, other places, and other enjoyments, which her imagination or dreams portrayed while locked up within her tower, and in a tranquil state of repose. But the matrons, faithful to their trust, never offered a single word in explanation of those fantasies or mysteries which enchanted her, even during her waking moments. In the meantime, Balor, now secure in his existence, and regardless of the Druid's prediction, continued his business of war and rapine. He achieved many a deed of fame, captured many a vessel, subdued and cast in chains many an adventurous band of sea rovers, and made many a descent upon the opposite continent, carrying with him to that island men and property.

Three brothers, named Gavida, Mac Samhthiann, and Mac Kineely, lived in the northern part of Ulster at this time, and near the shore opposite Tory Island. The first of these worthies was a distinguished smith, who held his forge at Drumnatinne, a place in the parish of Rath Finan. The spot where he wrought derived its name from that circumstance, for the Irish nomenclature signifies "ridge of the fire" in English, and it alludes to Gavida's furnace. Mac Kineely was lord of that district, comprising the parishes of Rath Finan and Tullaghobegly, and he was possessed of a cow called Glas Gaivlen, or Glas Gaibhnenn, and she was so lactiferous as to be coveted by all his neighbours. So many attempts had been made at stealing her, that he found it necessary to watch the animal constantly. Balor's ambition could never be satiated, however, until he should get possession of that most valuable cow. To obtain her, the magician chief directed all his powers of strength and stratagem.

One day, Mac Kineely, the chief of that tract of country opposit the island, had repaired to his brother's forge in order to get some swords fashioned. The chieftain took with him the invaluable Glas Galvin, which he constantly held in his own hand by a halter during the day. With this rope she was tied and secured each night. When he arrived at the forge, Mac Kineely intrusted the cow to the care of his brother Mac Samhthainn, who, it appears, was there too on some business connected with war. Mac Kineely entered the forge himself to see the sword properly shaped and steeled. But while he was within, assuming the form of a red-headed little boy, Balor came to Mac Samhthainn, and told him that he heard his two brothers, Gavida and Mac Kineely, saying within at the furnace, that they would use all Mac Samhthainn's steel in making Mac Kineely's swords, while they intended to make his own solely of iron. "By the *Seomh*, then," says Mac Samhthainn, "I'll let them know that I am not to be humbugged so easily; but hold this cow, my red-headed little friend, and you shall see how soon I'll make them alter their intention." With that he rushed into the forge in a passion. He swore by all the powers above and below, that he would make his two brothers pay for their dishonesty. So soon as he got the halter into his hand, Balor carried off the Glas Gaivlin, with the rapidity of lightning, to Tory Island. That place, where he dragged her in by the tail, to this day has been called Port-na-Glaise, or "the harbour of the green cow," in memory of this transaction.

When Mac Kineely heard his brother's exclamations, he

knew immediately that Balor had effected his purpose. Running out of the forge, he perceived Balor with his cow in the middle of the Sound of Tory. Being soon made sensible of Balor's scheme, Mac Samhthainn got a few cuffs on the head from his enraged brother; these the sufferer thought he deserved, and accordingly he bore them with impunity.

Mac Kineely wandered about distracted for several hours, before he could be brought to any deliberate consideration regarding what was best to be done in order to recover the cow. But after he had given full vent to his passion, this chief sought the lonely habitation of a hoary Druid, who lived not far from the place. Mac Kineely consulted him upon the matter. The Druid told him that the cow could never be recovered, so long as Balor was living; for, in order to keep her, the frightful monster would never close his basilisk eye, but petrify every man that should venture to approach the animal.

Mac Kineely, however, had a *Leanan-Sidhe*, or familiar sprite, called "Biroge of the Mountain." This friendly double undertook to put him in the way of bringing about Balor's destruction. After having dressed him in the ladies' clothes of that age, she wafted him on the whirlwind's wings across the sound, and to the airy top of Tormore. There, knocking at the turret door, she demanded admittance for a noble lady, whom she rescued from the cruel hands of a tyrant, who had attempted to abduct her by force from the protection of her people. Fearing to disoblige this Banshee, the attendant matrons admitted both into the tower. So soon as Balor's daughter beheld the noble lady thus introduced, the fair Ethnea recognized a countenance like that of one who had frequently appeared during her dreams. She had become enamoured with the ideal; and tradition says, that she immediately fell in love with the veritable prototype, who was really her noble guest. Shortly after this occurrence, by her supernatural influence over human nature, the Banshee lulled the twelve attending matrons to sleep. The chief wooed and won this fair daughter of Balor. With her he remained for some time, until at last he was invisibly carried back by his friendly sprite to his territory of Drumnatinne. When the matrons awoke, they persuaded Ethnea that the fancied appearance of Biroge of the Mountain, and her *protégé*, the chieftain, could only have been a dream. Still, they told her never to mention the circumstance to her father Balor.

Thus did matters remain until the daughter of Balor brought forth three sons at a birth. When Balor discovered this, he immediately secured the offspring, and sent them, rolled up in a sheet, which had been fastened with a *delg*, or pin. The children he had ordered to be cast into a certain whirlpool; but as they were being carried across the sound, through a small harbour on the way to it, the *delg* fell out of the sheet, and one of those children dropped into the water. However, the other two were temporarily secured, yet were only recovered to be drowned in the intended whirlpool. That child who had fallen into the harbour, though apparently he sank to the bottom, was, nevertheless, invisibly carried away by the Banshee, who had been instrumental in procuring his birth. To this very day, the harbour is called *Port-a-Deilg*, or "the Harbour of the Pin." Biroge of the Mountain next wafted across the Sound that child, who, it appears, had been the first of his brothers in seeing the light of this world. Safely was he received by his father, who sent him to be fostered with the brother Gavida. This smith brought him up to his own trade, which then ranked among the artistic professions. It was deemed so respectable, that Brighit, the goddess of the poets, thought it not beneath her dignity to preside likewise over the smiths.

Thinking he had thus baffled the fates by drowning his daughter's three children, Balor yet learned from his Druid that Mac Kineely was the man who had made such an effort to set the wheel of his destiny in rapid motion. The Warrior of the Evil Eye again crossed the Sound; and landing on that part of the continent called Ballyconnell, after some more recent possessor, with a band of his fierce associates, Balor seized upon Mac Kineely. Laying this chieftain's head upon a large white stone, one of the executioners holding him down by the long hair, while others held his hands and legs, Balor decapitated him with a single stroke of his ponderous sword. The blood flowed around in warm floods, and crimsoned the stone to its very centre. This rock, with its red veins, still traditionally testifies to this deed of cruelty; it even gives name to a district now comprehending two parishes. In 1794, it was elevated on a pillar 16 feet high, by Wyby More Olpherts, Esq., and by his wife. These persons had carefully collected all the local traditions connected with the giant Balor. It is shown to the curious traveller as Clogh-an-Neely, into which it has been Anglicized. This incorrect name, which Wyby More has unluckily committed to the durability of marble, differs from that given by the Four Masters. At the years 1284 and 1554 they more correctly term it Cloch Chinnfaeladh. It certainly forms a very conspicuous object in that neighbourhood, and near the small village of Cross Roads. It is situated in the north-western part of Kilmacrenan barony, in the County of Donegal.

Notwithstanding all these efforts of Balor to avert his destiny, the Banshee had executed the fated decree; for, after the decollation of Mac Kineely, Balor, now secure of his own existence, as he thought, and triumphant over the fates, frequented the continent without fear of opposition. Meanwhile, he employed or compelled Gavida to make all his military weapons. But, by degrees, the heir of Mac Kineely grew up to be a robust man; and becoming an excellent smith, the Warrior of the Evil Eye—who knew nothing concerning his birth—became greatly attached to him. Mac Kineely's son, however, was aware of his father's fate, and well acquainted with the history of his own birth, and informed about his escape from destruction. He was observed to indulge in gloomy fits of despondency, to visit often the blood-stained stone, and to return from it with a sullen brow, which nothing could smooth. One day Balor came to the forge to have some spears made for his use. It happened, as Gavida was from home upon some private business, all of that day's work was executed by his young foster-son. While speaking, during the course of the day, Balor happened to mention with pride his conquest of Mac Kineely, and the circumstances of his death. But this boastful speech resulted in his own great misfortune. The young smith watched his opportunity, and taking a glowing rod from the furnace, he thrust it through the basilisk eye of Balor. The burning bar ran out even through the other side of the tyrant's head. Thus the heir of Mac Kineely avenged the death of his father, by slaying his wicked grandfather, and executing the fatal decree.

Some say that this event took place at Knocknafola, or Bloody Foreland; but others place the scene of Balor's death at Drumnatinne. These latter account for the name of Knocknafola, by making it the scene of a bloody battle between the Irish and the Danes. Tradition errs, however, as to the place of Balor's death; for, according to O'Flaherty, he was killed by his grandson, Lughaidh Lamhfhada, or Lewy of the Long Hand, in the second battle of Meagh Tuireadh, or Moytura, which was fought within the parish of Kilmactranny, in the barony of Tirerril, and county of Sligo. Here several curious sepulchral monuments are yet to be seen on the field of battle. Balor is said to have fallen by a stone cast at him from a machine called a *tabhall*,—believed to have been a sling. His wife, Kethleen, fought with desperation by his side, and performed prodigies of valour. History or tradition, however, does not inform us, whether this heroine survived the death of her renowned warrior-husband.

Amongst the myths of Irish fable may be included the following, which has probably some connection with the Fomorian Balor. A superstition prevailed amongst the peasantry, that certain people are born with an *evil eye*, through some mysterious and magic influence. It is supposed that the possessor has power to injure those against whom a glance may be directed. The victims of this baneful influence usually pine away and die, if no counteracting charm be provided to remove this threatened danger. Rather than meet an *evil eye*, people were accustomed to turn back or diverge from the course of their journey, and especially to avoid the possessor's habitation.

In Turkey and Egypt, ignorant mothers use talismans to prevent all injurious effects owing to the *evil eye* of some envious person, who is supposed to have bewitched their emaciated or diseased children. In certain parts of Hindostan, likewise, the women are especially desirous to touch the garments of a widow about to devote herself to death on the funeral pyre of her deceased husband. They consider this act a sufficient protection from the *evil eye*, and one, in its own nature, highly meritorious.

It appears, such a superstition prevailed amongst the Greeks in the time of St. Chrysostom, who tells us, that in order to divert the *evil eye*, some persons wrote on their hands the names of several rivers, whilst others used salt, tallow, and ashes, for a like purpose. We are also assured, that modern Greeks employ a combination of garlic, cloves, talismans, and other charms, which are hung round the necks of their infants, to effect a similar object. Alluding to this *evil eye* superstition in the West of Ireland, Lady Morgan, in her interesting novel, *The Wild Irish Girl*, erroneously supposed that the priests suspend a *gospel*, which she calls a *consecrated charm*, around the necks of children, to frustrate its dangerous effects. But what is called *a gospel* is not specially used for such a purpose. It is to be regretted, that many writers on our peasantry's superstitions, social habits and usages, do not take the trouble to be better informed, when they only hazard assertions, which are calculated to lead their readers astray. Especially in what concerns the religious feelings and practices of the people, several absurd fictions have been circulated; and they are, as a consequence, believed, but not on those grounds which ought to produce reliance on the statements advanced, nor on the authority of persons who are pleased only to imagine what they asseverate as facts.

CHAPTER XXIII.

ANCIENT PLANETARY, ELEMENTARY, AND IDOLATROUS WORSHIP OF THE PAGAN IRISH.

> "That proud exception to all nature's laws,
> To invert the world, and counteract its cause.
> Force first made conquest, and that conquest law,
> Till superstition taught the tyrant awe.
> Then shar'd the tyranny, then lent it aid,
> The gods of conquerors, slaves of subjects made:
> She, midst the lightning's blaze, and thunder's sound,
> When rock'd the mountains, and when groan'd the ground,
> She taught the weak to bend, the proud to pray,
> To pow'r unseen, and mightier far than they;
> She, from the rending earth and bursting skies,
> Saw gods descend, and fiends infernal rise :1
> Here fix'd the dreadful, there the blest abodes ;
> Fear made her devils, and weak hope her gods."—POPE.

OUR Irish Gentile worship seems to have chiefly consisted in a certain reverence for invocations of the most striking heavenly bodies, or natural objects—such as the sun, moon, stars, air, and water; and idols were likewise objects of their adoration. By such elements and matters, our Pagan monarchs often swore, and pledged themselves for the more solemn observance of their engagements or treaties. It is likely, the forces and properties of nature were in some measure personified by certain diagrams, or idols, known to our heathen forefathers.

An ancient tradition has connected Nimrod, "the mighty hunter," with the first adoption of fire worship. The bright luminaries of heaven, whose motions were so enveloped in mystery, soon became symbols, or bodies, which occupied the Orientals' imagination, and taught them to venerate, in the leafy groves, or on the open hill sides. Thus, those starry orbs were visible and virtual objects of adoration; and the planetary fires were beheld with a submissive reverence, by a pastoral and sensuous people, who interpreted the decrees and resolutions of deities, or who predicted a fated futurity from their various changes and aspects. Holy Job, who lived in the land of Hus, following the law of nature and of grace, was simple and upright, fearing the true God, and avoiding evil. Doubtless, he had recognized the seductive influence of the fire, or Sabean worship, over the Orientals, when he said,—" If I beheld the sun when it shined, and the moon going in brightness; and my heart in secret hath rejoiced, and I have kissed my hand with my mouth: which is a very great iniquity, and a denial against the most high God" (Job xxxi. 26, 27, 28). While such faithful and pure-minded men had been preserved from error and idolatry, the sun worship of Egypt, the Sabeanism of Chaldea and Assyria, with the later Grecian and Roman deification of images, soon became developed into the strange compound of mystic, aërial, and festive mythology, which generally prevailed on earth before the introduction of Christianity.

Milton, whose varied learning and sound judgment almost equal his imaginative perceptions as a poet, when delineating the array of Satan's host, in the First Book of *Paradise Lost*, brings forward those Pagan deities—

> "who, from the bordering flood
> Of old Euphrates, to the brook that parts
> Egypt from Syrian grounds, had general names
> Of Baälim and Ashtaroth; those male,
> These feminine."

And again, he introduces the last-named evil spirit as being conspicuous among the other rebellious partizans of the fallen angel.

> "With these in troop
> Came Ashtoreth, whom the Phœnicians call'd
> Astarte, queen of heaven, with crescent horns,
> To whose bright image, nightly by the moon,
> Sidonian virgins paid their vows and songs;
> In Sion also not unsung, where stood
> Her temple on th' offensive mountain, built
> By that uxorious king, whose heart, though large,
> Beguiled by fair idolatresses, fell
> To idols foul."

Oriental nations worshipped the planets and the whole sidereal array of the heavens. The sun is said to have been propitiated, in nearly all the Eastern countries, by sacrifices of fire. The Egyptians and Assyrians are thought to have adopted this type of the deity's spiritual attributes at an early date. Moloch and his fires, Baal, with his groves and prophets, are frequently alluded to in the sacred Scriptures. One of these celebrations was held about the first of May, to obtain a blessing on seed previously sown. In the Irish language, the first of May is called La Beal-tine—said to signify the day of Beal's fire. It is stated by Vossius, on the authority of Herodian and of an inscription (*Appollini Belino*) at Aquileia, that Apollo had been called Belinus. Baal, or Baalim, in Phenicia, like the Irish Beal, or Bealin, denoted the sun. The moon, designated Astarte, Ashtoroth, or Ashtoreth, and other planetary bodies, were subsequently additional objects which formed the Sabeanism, or varied planetary and star worship, of Tyre and Sidon. Many places in Ireland, compounded with Bel, are said to have been connected with fire-god adoration.

Bel, Beal, Bal, or Baal, is supposed to have been derived from Belus, the first king of Assyria. A grand temple had been erected to his honour in the city of Babylon. His name is said to bear a Babylonish title, applicable to the sun. It was used by the Amonians in other countries; especially in Syria and Canaan. It is often found compounded with other terms—as in Bel-on, Baal-phegor, or Beel-zebub. From this designation came the Roman goddess Bellona, it is thought, and Baal-shamaim, or the great Lord of the heaven, as Eusebius tells us he was called by the Assyrians. These people cultivated astronomical science at an early period. Through all the Oriental countries, this branch of investigation seems to have been followed. There, the priests of the sun were greatly reverenced.

In some respects, the Pagan Irish seem to have conformed to practices and observances in use among the Egyptians, Phœnicians, and people of Eastern Asia; in other respects, we detect many divergences. The great privileges and immunities of the priests—these being regarded as depositaries of science and religion; their Sabean worship, feasts of lights, processions, general convocations, and sacrifices; their doctrine of metempsychosis; their adoration of Baal, or Osiris, thought to personify the sun, and of Astarte, Isis, Celestis, or Urania, supposed to represent the moon, with the veneration of many other strange idols; their auguries, omens, and divinations; their sacred books, and recognition of a divine power in natural objects and forces; the passing of men, women, and children through Moloch's fires; the invocation of idols, *genii*, demons, the sun, moon, earth, waters, meads, and rivers, as a guarantee for the stability of treaties,—all such customs appear not unlike what we may discover in the social life and usages of the Gentile Irish. But, regarding these latter, we cannot obtain evidences sufficient to establish a full conclusion, that the king united the sacerdotal with the regal character; that human sacrifices were permitted; that divine honours were paid to living animals, pulse, or roots; or that some animals were reverenced as gods, while others were held in abomination as demons. There can hardly exist a doubt, however, that many of our habits, customs, and superstitions, may be compared with Eastern usages and opinions, and found coincident with an early colonization and traditions derived from that cradle of our race.

To the Tuatha De Danaans may be ascribed the erection of several great sepulchral mounds, so many of which yet remain in this island. Eochaidh Ollathair, also called Daghda Mor, or "the Great Good Fire"—it is thought, owing to his military ardour—ruled for eighty years over Ireland, when he died, A. M. 3450, at Brugh-na-Boinne. Here, as a monument over himself and his three sons, Aengus, Aedh, and Cermad, the great mound, Sidh na Bhrogha, was raised, near the river Boyne. Aengus-an-Bhrogha was considered the presiding fairy of this locality by the people, until a recent period. This name is still mentioned by the old inhabitants of Meath.

The three last kings of the Tuatha-De-Danaan colony began their reign A. M. 3471, and were killed in battle by the Milesians, A. M. 3500. The real names of those kings were—Eathur, who was denominated Mac Cuill, because, it is said, he worshipped the hazel tree; Teathur, called Mac Ceacht, because he worshipped the plough, and probably desired to promote agriculture; while the third, Ceathur, was known as Mac Griene, because he adored the sun as his god. Such is the account we find extracted from an old Irish poem, quoted in Haliday's edition of Keating's *History of Ireland*.

The Cruthneans, or Picts, are said to have arrived in Ireland about A. M. 3502. They soon emigrated to Scotland, however; and previously they gave both sun and moon as their securities, that the kingly power in Pictland, or Alba, should be held perpetually, through right of the women, married by them in Ireland, rather than through that of the male progeny. Their wives are said to have been the widows of Milesian chieftains, who were drowned during the expedition they had undertaken, when coming from Spain into Ireland.

Even to Christian times, adoration of the great planetary bodies seems to have continued. We can furnish one peculiar incident, by way of illustration. In the introduction to M'Dermott's *History of Ireland*, we are told how a MS. Life of St. Columba mentions that, in his days, there existed in the north of Ireland a famous druidical temple of exquisite workmanship. On its altar, which was very superb, were painted in glass beautiful representations of the sun, moon, and stars—these being regarded as among the Irish Gentile deities.

In O'Mahony's Keating's *History of Ireland*, allusion is made to this temple, which would seem to have been erected by some Magus, who had set up in it images representing the sun and moon. Shortly afterwards, a great swoon came on that Magus, and a demon bore him off through the air. But, while both passed over the head of Columbkille, this saint made the sign of a cross in the air above him. Instantly the magician fell to earth at his feet. In remembrance of such rescue from the demon's power, and in gratitude to Columba, this Gentile priest is said to have dedicated his temple to the saint. Afterwards this Magus became a monk, and thenceforth he lived a holy and pious life. Such a legend concerning the heathen priest's miraculous rescue from the fiend's fangs may have reference to St. Columbkille's strenuous efforts to suppress idolatrous worship. In his time, it appears not to have been entirely extirpated from this land.

In the south-western parts of Ireland, a usual form of salutation prevails, *Grian an t-sonais leat*, "The sun of prosperity to you!" and the following malediction is sometimes employed, *Grian na tobaiste*, "The sun of misfortune to you!" These sayings are probably derived from Pagan times.

The bonfires, yet kindled in various parts of Ireland, are assumed to have been remnants of our ancestors' sun or fire worship. The Irish people, probably, have little idea of this connection, while enjoying the sports connected with such festive rejoicings. The use of fire or light with them has quite a different signification at present. When lighting a candle in the dark, many persons are accustomed religiously to exclaim, "May the Lord send us the light of heaven!" When putting it out, they say, "May the Lord renew for us the light of heaven!" Our altars blaze with lights now; but only to commemorate the Christian's great sacrifice. Popular rejoicings are also manifested, on special occasions, by the kindling of bonfires.

In the Irish language, *Ré* and *Luan* signify "the moon," and *Dia luain* corresponds with "Monday," according to O'Reilly. We seem to have fewer records remaining, and which regard popular opinion, concerning the place this planet held in public estimation, than on other objects held in reverence. Yet many think, in the customs and expressions of our people at the present time, we may trace some remnants of a moon worship among the more ancient Irish.

The moon was adored, it is said, under the name of *Samhain*, which is pronounced Sabbin, or Samin. This is thought to have corresponded with the Astarte, Ashtaroth, or Asturoth of the Phœnicians. Some curious practices still remain in various parts of Ireland. Thus, on the first day of the new moon, it is customary to borrow a piece of silver. This is cheerfully given, and, without inquiry as to its intended use, it was considered to omen plenty during the ensuing month.

The following places are mentioned as having been

derived from Irish moon worship:—*Lough-rea*, said to signify "lake sacred to the moon;" *Athlone*, or *Ath Luan*, "ford sacred to the moon;" and *Castlerea*, "castle sacred to the moon." These places, according to certain theorists, were devoted to the worship of Samhain, whose chief festival time fell on the first of November.

Irish records state, that Solomon, the son of King David, laid the foundation of his temple, A. M. 2933— 480 years after the going out of the Israelites. This temple, it is mentioned, was consecrated by Sadoc, the tenth high priest after Aaron, the brother of Moses. They further state, how all our historians of veracity unite in affirming that the Scots, or Scythians, arrived in Ireland, from Spain, during the reign of Solomon. Such statement is said, furthermore, to be confirmed by the genealogical accounts of the Milesians and of the high priest Sadoc.

This arrival is described as having taken place in the fifth year of the reign of Solomon—A. M. 2934—the solar cycle 2, and lunar 12, the dominical letter E. A very ancient Irish Christian author, named Achy O'Floinn, who had access to many old MSS., which have perished amid time's wreck, gives in his Irish poem concerning the different invasions of Ireland, a rann or verse, commemorative of those events. The verse has been thus translated:—

"On the seventh of the Moon, on Thursday's sacred light,
The Fenian heroes finished their adventurous expedition;
They landed, forceful to possess the soil,
On the Calends of the world, the beautifying month of May."

Superstitions connected with the increase and wane of the moon are very prevalent. It was formerly believed, that if pigs were killed when the moon was increasing, the bacon must prove the better in boiling. Tusser, in his *Five Hundred Points of Husbandry*, under the article "February," writes—

> "Sowe peason and beans in the wane of the moon,
> Who soweth them sooner, he soweth too soon;
> That they with the planet may rest and rise,
> And flourish with bearing most plentiful wise."

The foregoing lines, however, savour more of Saxon than of Irish land. But many Irish peculiarities were, doubtless, imported into Britain by the Irish; so that it is not easy to determine what wise saws, or popular opinions, were distinctive, or common, among the primitive inhabitants of these islands.

It was, and still is, a popular idea in Ireland, that to have the hair cut in the wane of the moon injures it very much, by causing it to grow thinly, and to fall away; and this should only be had done when the hair becomes too thick. To make the hair grow thicker, its cutting should take place, it was thought, just after the new moon.

Ancient Pagan salutations, when persons met one another, were linked with their favourite objects of worship. One of these is said to have been—"The blessing of Samen and Baal be with you." Another form of salutation was—*Gnuis Gealaigh sothaimh chugat*, "The countenance of a placid moon to you." Such expressions were usually addressed to young and amiable females. On the contrary, when it was customary to bann any person, whether intentionally or otherwise, this form was employed—*Guasacht Gealaigh chugat*, "Moon affliction to you." In Christian times, however, they assumed a very different turn. On many a country road in Ireland you still find persons going different ways, who will thus salute each other—"God save you," or "God save you kindly," "The blessing of God on you." At parting many exclaim—" God be with you," when the answer will be returned—" And with you too." Another Irish form of blessing or salutation is—*Dia 's Muire agus naom Padraig leat*, " God, and Mary, and St. Patrick, be with you." These little kindly sayings may, probably, be traced from the first dawn of Christianity in Ireland.

For aught we can tell, some of those words marked by inverted commas, may have fallen from the lips of the great St. Patrick, who was fond of retaining the sites of places formerly dedicated to Pagan worship, as so many centres for the rites of that religion, by which idolatry was to have been overthrown. Perhaps, also, he desired to rectify Pagan salutes and exclamations.

Good, an English priest residing in Ireland during the sixteenth century, declares that he knew not whether the Irish then worshipped the moon; but when they saw her after a change, the common country people fell down on their knees, repeating the Lord's Prayer. Near the wane, they addressed themselves to the moon, with a loud voice, saying, " Leave us as well as thou hast found us !" Duchesne, in his *Histoire d'Angleterre*, page 18, and Vallancey, tell us the same thing in substance; but their information had been derived, probably, from Good's account. This exclamation, however, may mark that transition period in Irish society, when the triumphs of Christianity had been established over the errors of Paganism.

In Galway a salutation to the new moon was, and perhaps is still, made, by the person kneeling down, reciting a Pater and Ave, and then saying, " O Moon! may thou leave us safe, as thou hast found us !" Another form of salutation used in Galway, and which might be applied to any phase of the moon, was to make a sign of the Cross, and to say in an under-tone, " God and the holy Virgin be about me!" Then followed this verse—

> "I see the moon, and the moon sees me;
> God bless the moon, and God bless me!"

Another Galway version, and a mode for females saluting the new moon, are tripping to the nearest stile, or gate, and looking over it thrice. Then the person looks up to the moon, and exclaims—

> "All hail to thee, moon! all hail to thee!
> I prithee, good moon, reveal to me
> This night, who my husband shall be."

Great honour used to be paid to the full moon; and it was the witching time for young girls to pry into futurity, with a hope of obtaining, in their dreams, a sight of husbands in store for them. The invocation used at this period, as related by a Kildare woman, runs in this form:—

> "Good morrow, Full Moon!
> Good morrow to thee!
> Tell, ere this time to-morrow,
> Who my true love will be—
> The colour of his hair,
> The clothes he will wear,
> And the day he'll be married to me."

Regarding the wind worship of the ancient Irish, we have only been able to obtain a few probable traces in the popular form of friendly salutation—*Gasch an t-sonais leat!* "The wind of prosperity to you!" It is much used among mariners. In English we find the following verse often recited as an adage:—

> "A wind that blows from the north-east
> Is neither good for man nor beast,"

Another tells us that

"A wet April and a windy May
Will fill the haggard with corn and hay."

Both of these aphorisms, however, may have been founded more on observation and experience of results generally produced in our ever-varying climate, under certain conditions of the atmosphere. Yet, those versed in old traditions maintain that the ancient Irish worshipped a god of the winds.

Idols were considered certain forms, or representations, of the elements as adored in Ireland. Many of those possibly referred to *genii* presiding over particular occupations or professions. They commemorated, in this case, as we may suppose, former living and traditionary personages. Thus, Ruad-Rofhessa, or "Lord of great knowledge," was a king of the Tuatha Dé Danann, A. M. 2804. In the *Book of Leinster*, "Aisiu" is called the son of Dan, "Poetry," son of Osmenta, "Scrutiny," son of Imrádud, "Cogitation," son of Rofhis, "Great knowledge," son of Fochmarc, "Inquiry," son of Rochmarc, "Research," son of Rofhis, "Great knowledge," son of Rochond, "Great sense," son of Ergna, "Cognition," son of Ecna, "Wisdom," son of the three gods of Poetry, three sons of Bresse, son of Elathan and Brigit the poetess, daughter of the Dagdæ Mór, who was called the Ruad-rofhessa, or "son of all the sciences."

Manahan Mac Lir, the British and Irish sea-god, is said, by Cormac Mac Cuillionain, to have been a celebrated Isle of Man merchant. By his study of the heavens, he was able to predict all changes from fair to foul weather. The disposal of good or bad atmospheric influences was his presumed attribute. He was the son of Allot, one of the Tuatha Dé Danann chieftains; and he was otherwise called Orbsen. This name was formerly applied to the present Lough Corrib. According to traditions prevailing in the Isle of Man, and in the eastern counties of

Leinster, this Manahan rolled like a wheel, on three legs, through the mist. Hence that three-legged figure on the Manx halfpenny, and its peculiar motto. This has been supposed to represent the three great strides of the sun— its rising, its culmination, and its setting. Throughout the mountainous districts of Derry and Donegal, Manahan Mac Lir is still remembered, and he is said to have an enchanted castle under the waters of Lough Foyle.

Ana is said, in Cormac's *Glossary*, to have been mother of the Irish gods, whom she nursed. She was usually called Danann. Her sons—Brian, Iuchar, and Iucharbu —were accounted gods for their feats of necromancy. The two-peaked mountain called, from her, *Da chich Anainne*, is situated in the barony of Magunihy, county of Kerry. Buanann is said to have been nurse of the heroes—*i. e.*, a good mother for teaching them feats of arms.

Neit, or Neid, was regarded as the god of battles among our Gaelic Pagans, and Nemon was his wife. Dian-cécht—a name for the god, or sage, of health—it is said, possessed wonderful leech-craft powers. Thus may we account for his deification in process of time.

Brigit, daughter of Dagda, was a poetess, and a female sage, or wise woman. She is considered as the goddess of song, having been adored by the poets, because her protecting care over them was very celebrated. She had two other sisters bearing a similar name—Brigit the female physician, and Brigit the female smith. From these, a goddess was known to the ancient Irish. The name is interpreted "a fiery arrow" in Cormac's *Glossary*. Again, Bridh, or Bride, was considered daughter to the fire-god, while she was regarded as the goddess of wisdom, art, and song. Hence, the Filleas and Olamhs worshipped her. Her blessing and inspiration were considered the richest and most valuable gifts men could receive from a superior power. Badhbh was likewise a goddess of war, and notable among the Tuatha De Dananns.

Remarkable persons, likewise, appear to have been deified by our Pagan fathers. It is said the chief druid and magician, opposed by St. Patrick at Tara, in presence of King Laoghaire and his nobility, had been named Luachra. He was considered by the Pagan Irish as a deity; and from him Tara has been called Teamair Luachra. Local *genii*, as in Oriental countries at the present day, are said to have been venerated by our ancestors.

Idolatry followed this sort of hero-worship. Thus we are told Maghsleaght—a place situated in the barony of Tullyhaw and county of Cavan—was so called from an idol of the Irish, named Crom-Cruaith. *Cruith* is possibly derived from the word *Cruithain*, which signifies "to form," or "to create." Hence the Irish word *Cruitheoir*, which means "the Creator." That, their great idol, was formed of a stone, capped with gold, and about it were set twelve other rough stones. It stood near a river called Gathand. All the colonists living in Ireland, down to the Irish apostle's time, worshipped this unknown deity; and afterwards St. Patrick erected a church, called Domnachmor, in the immediate vicinity of the place where it stood. Our Pagan ancestors sacrificed firstlings of animals, while they made other offerings to it. Tighernmas M'Folleigh, king of Ireland, who reigned from A. M. 3580 to A. M. 3656, first commanded sacrifices to this idol, on the day of Saman; and he ordained, that both men and women should adore it prostrate on the ground, until blood flowed from their noses, foreheads, knees, and elbows. As many died from the severity of this demoralizing and barbarous worship, the place was afterwards called Maghsleacht. Such, according to Vallancey, is an account found in the ancient MS. entitled *Duan Seancas.* On the very night of Samhain, A. M. 3656, Tighernmas died, with three-fourths of the men of Ireland about him, while worshipping Crom Cruach, at Magh-slecht.

In the county of Clare there is an elevation known as Tullagh na Greine, or "Hill of the Sun." On this is said to have stood the altar of Crom Dubh, or Duagh, which latter words, according as they are made applicable, may mean "black" or "sacrifice." This is thought to have been a local deity, with whom the idea of a worship had been associated, but altogether distinct from Crom Cruaith of Magh-sleaght. The people living around Slieve Callan are said to have sacrificed to their tutelary divinity on the 1st of August, during the Pagan period; and such traditions still survive in their neighbourhood.

According to certain writers, Crom, or Crom-eacha, was the title bestowed on their fire-god by the Pagan Irish. He was regarded as the dispenser of vital heat, of fecundity, and of prosperity. This term is said to have been derived from the Egyptian word Chrom, meaning "fire," because it was the only visible object of worship considered reasonable, and which served for a most suitable symbol of the Supreme Being. The Irish Crom-Cruith is thought to express an idea of "God the Creator;" and for many centuries before the birth of Christ, Zoroaster and the Persians are said to have adored him in a philosophic sense. Zoroaster is stated to have been the first inventor of the Magi doctrines and mysteries, while he was distinguished for his astronomical researches, and for his knowledge of cosmogony and other branches of natural philosophy.

When mankind began to degenerate from the purity of a first faith in the great Author of all created things, certain writers suppose that an astronomical basis had then been taken for the errors of early heathens. Others seek to demonstrate, that their irreligious ideas must be referred to phenomena of a purely terrestrial nature. A deification of nature's forces seems to have been practised among the first forms of Paganism; and from such abstract ideas, it is probable men passed to a worship of concrete representations. These were known as idols in the mythology of our benighted ancestors. Yet, it would be found a matter of difficulty, to determine such questions for the perfect satisfaction of those interested in such recondite subjects for investigation.

CHAPTER XXIV.

ANCIENT FESTIVAL CELEBRATIONS IN IRELAND.

> " One fair May eve, when by the lake
>   Our Bealtine fires all redly burn'd,
> And all the hills and distant cliffs,
>   From crag and height the blaze return'd,
> In answering signals, fast and bright,
> Like red stars glittering through the night,
> And, gathering round the ruddy flame
> In laughing groups, the neighbours came,
> With song and jest, and wondrous tales
>   Of Belfires in the olden time,
> When Formors met, by hills and dales,
>   In worship at the fire-god's shrine,
> Ere yet the blessed saint had trod,
> To save and bless our Irish sod."
> *The Monks of Kilcrea.*—"The Rapparee's Tale," § viii.

It would not be possible to enumerate and describe exactly the different festivities and rites, with their associated sports and ceremonials, that prevailed, from remote to modern times, throughout the various districts of Ireland. Premising the accounts contained in former chapters, it will only be necessary to classify some of them, chiefly in the order of annual commemoration. In his *Glossary*, Cormac says the four great Druidic fires were kindled in the beginning of February, May, August, and November. These, doubtless, had connection with Pagan ceremonies. But the Irish were still more attached to their religious rites and observances, when Christianity had supplanted Gentile errors. It will not be expedient to place upon record those festivals which were celebrated by them, in common with the people of other nations, during the ages of faith. Those only of a distinctive character we deem worthy of notice.

In Sir Henry Piers's "Description of the County of Westmeath," written A. D. 1682, and to be found published in General Vallancey's *Collectanea de Rebus Hibernicis*,* we are informed that it was customary, about that time, for the people to set up a sieve of oats as high as they could, on twelfth day eve after Christmas. In its centre, a large candle was placed, and a dozen of smaller candles lighted around it. This was done in honour of our Saviour and his apostles, who were regarded as the true lights of the world.

The old homely household rann, which runs thus—

> "Whenever cometh Candlemas day,
> Throw candles and candlesticks all away"—

has ancient and holy recollections connected with it. The Israelites called this period of the year the "Feast of Lights," which was said to have been instituted by Judas Maccabeus, in order to celebrate a victory over the Assyrians. This festival lasted for eight days. Even in these islands, the lights used on Candlemas day were often denominated Judas Candles.

The procession with lighted tapers on the Feast of the Purification is mentioned by Pope Galasius I. and St. Cyril of Alexandria, so early as the fifth century. By some writers it is said, however, that Pope Sergius, in the seventh century, commanded the Roman people to go in procession on Candlemas day, with lights burning in their hands. This procession has been described by St. Bernard; and he says, it was first made by the Holy Virgin Mother, St. Joseph, St. Simeon, and St. Anne; then in all places, and by every nation, was it observed in honour of our Blessed Lady's purification. This fes-

* Vol. i., No. i., page 124.

tival of lights was intended likewise to represent Christ as the great spiritual Light of the world, and to signify that fire of Divine love with which our hearts should be influenced. Some writers maintain this Feast of the Purification had been instituted to abrogate a Pagan celebration. On the 2d night of February, the Romans had been accustomed to go about the city of Rome with torches and candles burning in honour of Februa, who was regarded as mother to the Pagan god Mars. Many persons believe the month of February had been called after this goddess. Candlemas was formerly observed throughout Britain in much the same way, and about the same annual period at which the ancient Greeks celebrated their "Feast of Lights," in honour of Ceres. Pope Innocent III. explains the circumstance. Because the heathens dedicated the month of February to the Infernal gods, and at its beginning, as Pluto stole away Proserpine, and as her mother Ceres sought for her in the night with lighted torches; so, in the beginning of this month, those idolaters walked about the city with lighted candles. And since the holy fathers could not wholly extirpate such a custom, these ordained that Christians should carry about candles in honour of the Virgin Mary. Thus, what had been observed before in honour of Ceres, was afterwards done to venerate the Blessed Virgin.

There appear to have been some old superstitious practices connected with this period of the year, before the institution of Candlemas day. The following lines are found in Herrick's *Hesperides*,* and they seem to have reference to such usages:—

> " Down with the *Rosemary*, and so
> Down with the *Baies* and *Mistletoe;*
> Down with the *Holly, Ivie—all*
> *Wherewith ye dress the Christmas hall;*

* See page 361.

> That so the superstitious find
> *Not one least branch there left behind.*
> *For, look how many leaves there be*
> Neglected there! (maids, trust to me!)
> *So many goblins you shall see."*

Subsequently, instructions are given to kindle the "Christmas brand," and then to let it burn until sundown. Afterwards, it was to be quenched, and laid up for the return of the succeeding Christmas. Part of it was to be kept for the purpose of lighting the next Christmas log. The observance of such ceremonies, it was supposed, would keep fiends from doing any mischief in that particular place where they were practised. The Christmas sports were expected to cease about this time.

If the sun shone on Candlemas day, an ensuing cold winter was prognosticated, in most countries of Europe; and this opinion appears to have come down from remote times. There is a husbandman's proverb yet known in England—"Sow or set beans on Candlemas waddle." This latter word signifies "wane of the moon."

We are told by the poet Spenser, that towards the close of the sixteenth century, when the Irish went to battle on St. Patrick's day, they addressed certain charms, or invocations, to their swords. With these, they made a cross on the earth, and thrust the points of their blades into the ground. Thereby, it was supposed, better success must attend them in the fight, or during their campaign.

On St. Patrick's day—the great national festival of Irishmen—Patrick's crosses are worn by females over the breast or shoulder. These are usually composed of a card-paper, cut round, and covered with white silk or satin. Stripes of gay and party-coloured silk ribbon are crossed over this underwork, and elegantly fringed or tasselled, according to the wearer's taste or fancy. The males wore shamrocks in their hats, to commemorate St. Patrick's having used this trefoil to illustrate the doctrine of the Holy Trinity, while preaching to the Pagan Irish. General Vallancey, who is so fond of deriving every existing habit from our Gentile ancestors, tells us, the ancient druids and bards have an extraordinary veneration for the number three; and hence the mistletoe was held to be sacred, because, not only its berries, but its leaves, grow in clusters of three, united on one stock. For this same reason, he says, the Christian Irish held their seamrog sacred, because of three leaves united on one stalk. The famine-stricken Irish, in Spenser's day, were glad to feed on water-cresses or shamrocks, when their country was made desolate through war and rapine. Between May and harvest, butter, new cheese, curds, and sham-roots, or shamrocks, were the food of the humble classes of Irish, in the seventeenth century. Samuel Lover's beautiful song of the "Four-leaved Shamrock" is deservedly admired; and whoever happens to find one may, by wishing it, obtain the gratification of that object dearest to his heart.

The whitewashing of cabins and houses was pretty generally practised by the people, on the near approach of the Feast of our Lord's Resurrection. It would seem, there used formerly to be a general clipping of the hair, and head ablutions, in Ireland at Easter time, to prepare for this solemnity. It was called *Cend-lá*, in honour of our Lord's Supper; and those cleanly habits had the mystic meaning of a purification, to anticipate the incoming feast of Christ and his apostles.

On the Vigil of Easter, known as Holy Saturday, more than usual cleaning and purification for the following great festival formerly took place in many districts of Ireland. Gentle and simple contrived something in advance of their usual family fare for Easter day. Many a nicely-striped piece of well-cured bacon, with a fat hen or pullet, was put in the pot, even by cottiers' wives or daughters, before midnight on Holy Saturday. This was cooked after the witching hour, and at twelve o'clock all clapped their hands, with a joyous laugh. They then cried out, in an Irish phrase signifying that Lent was over, and afterwards a feast followed, in which Easter eggs were generally introduced. All felt anxious about cock-crow, or day-dawning, to watch for the sun dancing on the water, in honour of our Lord's resurrection.

On the feasts of Easter and Whitsuntide, as also on those of patron saints, in several Irish parishes, about 1682, as we are told by Sir Henry Piers, the meaner sort of people assembled in the evening on some spot of ground convenient to an alehouse. Here they danced for a cake provided by the landlady. It was placed on a board, fastened to a pike or pole, and about ten feet in height over the ground. From the board hung a garland, set round with meadow-flowers, if it were early summer time; but apples, fastened on pegs, were stuck around the garland, if it happened to be late in the year. A piper was usually in attendance; and while he played for them, the whole number of dancers formed in a ring. A man and woman were told off as partners, while all danced about the bush—as the garland was called—and around the piper. The couple holding out longest—

"The gentle pair that simply sought renown,
By holding out to tire each other down"—

then were declared winners of the cake and apples. Thus the alewife plied her business very briskly, before the assembled dancers departed for the night.

Belltaine, or May-day, is said, in Cormac's *Glossary*, to have been derived from *bil-tene*—i.e., "lucky fire." This consisted of two fires, which the druids kindled with great incantations. Each year they used to drive cattle between those fires, as a safeguard against disease. The Fiann Militia also lived by hunting and the chase, from Beltane to Samhain, and in performing those duties required of them by the Irish kings.

Before undertaking his great warlike expeditions, Dathi, the last Pagan monarch of Ireland, convoked a grand assembly of the states of the nation, to meet him at Tara, at an approaching feast of Belltaine, or May-day. This was always considered as one of the chief festivals of the Irish Gentile kings and people; so that it formed a sort of periodical epoch each year, for the celebration of their mythic sacrifices.

An informant, named Good, ordained a priest, and living as a schoolmaster by profession at Limerick, in 1566, had been educated at Oxford. He furnished Camden with an account of Irish manners, to be found in Gough's edition of his *Britannica*.* But, most assuredly, this information abounds with many most prejudiced and false statements. The Irish accounted every woman who fetched fire on May-day as a witch, he tells us; nor would they give it to any, but only to sick persons, and that with an imprecation; for they believed she would steal all the butter next summer. On May-day, they killed all hares found among their cattle; because they supposed them to be women, who had designs on their butter. They imagined butter so stolen might be recovered, if they took some of the thatch hanging over the door and burned it. They fancied that a green bough, taken from a tree and fastened against the house on May-day, would produce plenty of milk that summer. It must be remarked, the information thus conveyed, if reliable, might easily be rendered in more intelligible terms.

In 1682, the Irish, on the 1st of May, are said to

* See pages 665-669.

have had a custom to place their meal on a formal dish, whatever other provisions they might happen to possess. They boiled flour with milk, and made it thick. This was called stirabout, or hasty-pudding. This mess was regarded as an evidence of the goodwife's thrifty housekeeping; because she had made her corn last, so as to begin the summer with such substantial fare. If they could keep meal for bread to this time, the family, it was thought, might easily subsist until harvest, on milk, butter, new cheese, and curds, with shamrocks, which even the poor used all this season. The Irish were so habituated to this mess, that they failed not serving it up on May-day, in their greatest and most plentiful houses, where they had bread in abundance. Even those, who wanted bread for a month previous, were anxious to have the stirabout on this day.

Churning before sunrise upon May-day morning is an especial object with the "gudewife;" and to accomplish this matter, it is necessary to rise at an early hour. An ass's old shoe is sometimes nailed to the bottom of a churn-dash; coals of fire and some salt are placed under the churn; a scrap of charmed writing is also inserted between the hoops and staves. A branch or sapling or rowan tree, or mountain ash—called *crankeeran* by the Irish, and considered to have been endowed with miraculous properties—was cut on May eve, and twisted round the churn before the labour of churning commenced. These usages were supposed to influence favourably the product of a large quantity of butter. Lads and lasses alternately toiled with patient good-humoured perseverance, and great bodily energy, to bring the first lumps of butter through the lid-opening. This operation was always regarded as a sort of domestic festivity, and as a healthful, inspiriting exercise.

In Dr. O'Brien's *Irish Dictionary*, he explains how

Bel-tein was so called, from its being a festival where fire had been lighted in honour of an Asiatic god, called Belus. He says, that on the 1st of May, the druids were accustomed to light large fires on the summits of hills, and that into those they drove four-footed beasts. These ceremonies were used to expiate the people's sins. But the ceremony of lighting the fires in honour of the sun gave name to the month of May—which is called Beal-tine, and May-day is known as the Beal-tine. On this day, we are told, all the inhabitants of Ireland quenched their fires, and again renewed them from some portion of the sacred fire. Until lately, fires of straw were kindled on the 1st of May in the milking yards, throughout many parts of Ireland. Men, women, and children, passed through, or leaped over their flames, while cattle were driven through them. Pennant describes certain very curious ceremonies and practices of the Hebride islanders on the 1st of May. A sort of rural libation and incantation accompanied an entertainment, while the fires were kindled as in Ireland.

Although we never remember to have seen fires thus lighted in May, yet, at a later period of the summer, we have often witnessed men and boys tie a bundle of blazing fagots to long poles at bonfires. These torches were waved in the air, while the bearers ran about in different directions. In one particular case, we remember having beheld some young men running around the bonfires in circles, while small glass ink-bottles had been fastened over the leaf of each one's hat. These had been filled with some inflammable oil and wick, which continued to burn during the progress of their eccentric courses. Whooping and hallooing were not spared by the runners and the urchins who followed them.

In the south-western parts of Ireland, many persons yet living remember to have seen fire asked from a priest's house when any disease or epidemic broke out in the country. With this fire other fires, first quenched, were afterwards rekindled in the peasants' houses. Such practice was thought to avert the pestilence. But if the priest refused the fire—as he usually did, to discountenance an old superstition ; the people then sought it from the "happiest man"—supposed to be the best-living person in the parish. This curious custom is worthy of being recorded, for it seems to have come down from a very remote period.

The following practices, or superstitions, are probably referable to Pagan times. An Irish custom of dressing the May bush with garlands and wild flowers, whilst placing it on a dung heap, or before their doors, once so universal, is now rarely seen. The poet Furlong, before his last tranquil rest in the old haunted graveyard of Drumcondra, used to visit the more distant suburban village of Finglas, to witness the "May sports." This, he tells us, in an ably conducted periodical, to the pages of which he was a pretty constant contributor. These sports usually prevailed only in the districts of Fingal, Meath, and other detached localities, brought under English domination at an early period. In the north of Ireland, such amusements were also common, and they appear to have been introduced by English or Scotch settlers.

In the south-eastern district of Ireland, and probably in many other parts of our island, it was customary to elect a May Queen for twelve months each May-day. On such occasions, the young people of both sexes, with many old persons, collected in their various towns or parishes. Then they selected the most beautiful and amiable girl that could be found, and between the ages of eighteen to twenty-one years. She was crowned with a garland of wild flowers, while feasting, dancing, and rural sports succeeded. This was closed by a grand procession in the evening. The Queen of May was expected to preside over the young people at dances or merry-making assemblies. The most implicit obedience was paid to her directions, as she always swayed the willing hearts of her subjects. If not married during the twelve months of her reign, she enjoyed the privilege of re-election. This latter contingency, however, seldom happened. Some other candidate was in request, on the ensuing May Day, when a successor for crown and throne was selected.

In another very remote part of Ireland, the "May Sports" were conducted, with very eccentric peculiarities, during the last century. The people of Tralee were accustomed to ludicrous and grotesque games, more creditable to them in the "breach than the observance." Males and females, grinning for snuff and tobacco, with a running in sacks, and such like buffoonery and horseplay, were not calculated to improve the morals or manners of the commonalty, however absurdly promoted by the wealthier class of their townsmen and women. Even in 1856, as we learn from that interesting periodical, *The Kerry Magazine*, some remnants of former May-day customs were still observed. Idleness, drinking, and dissipation characterized, too often, these celebrations.

On the Vigil of St. John the Baptist's Nativity, and on the Eve of St. Peter's and St. Paul's Day, bonfires are still kindled in many of the towns, villages, and country districts throughout Ireland. Often were those fires seen blazing on elevated sites, within the fields, or on hilltops. By several writers, these are thought to have been originally kindled in honour of Baal or Beal, personifying the sun and the chief god of the Gentile Irish. In Clare and Kerry, down to the present century, the people carried fire about, and sometimes bundles of reeds, which were tied fast together and lighted; when waved about, these had an uncommon and wild effect. They hoped, by such a practice, to purify the air, to procure a good harvest, and to ward off all sorts of disasters. The custom is a supposed relic of Druidic or Pagan celebrations.

Music and dancing were continued for the greater part of the night around those fires. It is said that, even so late as the last century, the people ran through the fire with their sons, daughters, and cattle. They also ran along the streets and fields with wisps of straw blazing on long poles. This, it is thought, was intended to purify the infectious air from devils, hobgoblins, and spirits, which flew about on this night to hurt mankind. Yet, these customs and opinions were not confined to Ireland alone; it would seem that they came down from early Paganism, and various divinations were prevalent in most European countries on Midsummer Eve.

During the earlier period of the thirteenth century, it was customary to kindle fires on every elevated place around Cremona, as we read in that most interesting *Histoire de Sainte Elizabeth de Hongrie*,* written in his usual lustrous vein of composition, by the Count de Montalembert, whose pencil seems to adorn whatever subject it touches, like that rich colouring and floridness of tracery to be found so profusely distributed over our most genuine and most ancient Irish MSS.

On the first Sunday of August, in the seventeenth century, the Irish drove their cattle into some pool or river to swim them. This practice, it was thought, would cause them to live through the year. Somewhere about this time, Garland Sunday used to be observed in certain Irish-speaking districts of the country. According to the information of old persons,

* See chap. xiv.

consulted by the writer, it has been asserted by some, that it fell on the last Sunday of July, while others maintained it had been kept on the first Sunday of August. This divergence of statement may be reconciled, however, when we take into account the difference between the old and new styles in computation. The first Sunday of August was regarded as the true Garland Sunday. It appears to have been observed as a day of special devotion.

The games and ceremonies of Tailteen, now Telltown, in the county of Meath, are said to have been instituted over one thousand years before the Christian religion had been preached in Ireland. Lughaidh, or Lugh Lamh-fadha, or Lewy of the Long Hands, King of the Tuatha De Danaan, first established them in honour of Taillte, daughter to the King of Spain. There she had been buried, and an immense mound had been erected over her grave. This annual game—called likewise the festival or game of Lugh Mac Ethne, or Ethlenn—took place about the 1st day of August, or Lammas Day, called Lughnasa in Irish. This word signified Lugh's fair, games or sports. These continued to be observed down to the twelfth century. In the time of King Dathi, the fires of Tailteen were lighted, while the sports and rites were celebrated with more than their usual solemnity and magnificence.

Some remains of a large earthen rath, traces of three artificial lakes, with other antiquities, are still to be seen at Telltown, near the river Boyne. The Market Hill, or Hill of Buying, was formerly noted at this spot. As the traveller proceeds from Kells to Donaghpatrick, on the left side of the road, he may perceive a depression, called Lagan-aonaigh. In this hollow, according to tradition, marriages were solemnized in Pagan times. The people vividly retain legendary reminiscences, regarding the ancient fair of Telltown, while the Meath men were accustomed to practise hurling, wrestling, and other manly exercises there, to a comparatively recent period.

In Ireland, a sheep used to be killed, by every family that could afford it, on the anniversary of St. Michael's Day. It was ordained by law that a part of the animal should be given to the poor. This is said to have been done, in order to perpetuate the memory of a miracle wrought by St. Patrick, through the assistance of that Archangel. In commemoration of such an event, Michaelmas was instituted as a festal day of universal plenty, benevolence, and joy.

From Good's account, Camden, in his *Ancient and Modern Manners of the Irish*, tells us, that the married women and girls kept a fast every Wednesday and Saturday throughout the year, and some of them, likewise, on St. Catherine's Day, November 25th, in order that the girls might get good helpmates, and that the women might get better ones, after the death of their present husbands; or at least, that they might procure an alteration in their living husband's manners. It is very certain, that the ancient discipline of the Irish Church required a strict fast from men and women capable of fasting, on particular days and at stated times. But if, in special cases, individuals practised extravagant and unauthorized customs of their own selection, this must be attributed to their ignorance. The better instructed people are not likely to have followed such illusions. Nor does it appear, so many or such absurd incantations, as the English practised on St. Catherine's Day, had ever prevailed in the Irish-speaking districts of our island. At present, however, all such habits are not only obsolete, but they have almost faded away from popular recollection.

CHAPTER XXV.

ALL-HALLOWS' EVE, WITH ITS VARIOUS DIVINATIONS AND FESTIVE CUSTOMS.

"Some merry, friendly, countra folks
  Together did convene,
To burn their nits, an' pou' their stocks,
An' haud their Halloween,
    Fu' blithe that night."—BURNS.

"They've laughed round many an apple, they've burned the nuts in glee,
"And some will soon get married, and some will sail the sea!
They've danced for th' ancient piper, they've joked and sung between,
And told their wondrous legends, each rattling, gay spalpeen!"
                                            R. D. JOYCE.

THROUGHOUT these islands a great similarity appears to have prevailed, regarding the sports and incantations practised among our peasantry, on the Eve of All-Hallows. Many of those customs are fast disappearing. But, in former times, we can scarcely doubt, they had a connection with certain Pagan festivals. At present they are partially continued, as affording occasion for social and convivial amusements, especially amongst our young people.

Oidhche Shamhna is rendered by "All-Saints' Eve," in O'Brien's *Irish Dictionary;* and in O'Reilly's, *Samhain* is translated "All-Hallows' Tide," "All-Saints' Tide." We are told by General Vallancey that the Mi-Saman of the ancient Irish fell on the month of November. It was said to have been named Mi Du, or Dubh, *the month of mourning,* because it was a season appointed by the

Druids for a solemn intercession of the living, and for the souls of dead persons who departed life within the previous year. Samhain is said, by Dr. O'Donovan, to have been compounded from the Irish words *Sam*, meaning "summer," and *fuin*, "end."

We are next informed, that the Druids taught the Pythagorean doctrine, regarding a transmigration of souls. These were called to judgment at this season by Baal Samhan. According to their merits or demerits in past life, souls were assigned to enter bodies of the human or brute species. There were they to be proportionately happy or miserable during their next term of abode on this sublunary globe. But the punishment of wicked persons might be alleviated by the employment of charms and magic arts, or through means of sacrifices made by their friends to Baal. Hence the Eve of All-Hallows was called the Night or Eve of Samhan. The day following was a great festival, when sacrifices of black sheep[*] are said to have been offered for departed spirits; while the Druids exhibited every possible description of charms or natural magic. This great festival of the Druids is said to have continued until the beginning of December.

About a century before the Christian era lived Eochaidh Aireamh, Monarch of Ireland. In the *Sluaghid Dathi Co Sliabh n-Ealpa*, or Expedition of Dathi to the Alpine Mountains—a story in the Book of Leinster—this prince was told by a Druid, named Finnchaemh, that the ancient palace of Cruachain, in Roscommon, had been built by the first-named Monarch. After it was erected on the lands of the Feara Cul of Teffia, and on the following feast of Samhain, or November Eve, their king, Mormael, invited the Monarch of Ireland to assist

---

[*] Compare Virgil in his Georgics, lib. iv., line 547:—
"Et nigram mactabis ovem, lucumque revises."

at this great solemnity. Complying with his request, Eochaidh Aireamh was treacherously murdered in the night, and was found dead next morning, by his own people. The murderers escaped detection, and contrived, moreover, to charge their crime on the Tuatha De Danaans' secret agency.

The celebrated King Dathy went from Tara to Ballyshannon, close upon this great Gentile solemnity of November, as we are told by Professor O'Curry. On this Eve of the great Samhain festival, he desired his Druids might ascertain for him, by their incantations, whatever incident should occur from that time until another such eve came round, regarding his own and the destiny of his country. In compliance with such instructions, his Druids left the camp in secret with the king, and all arrived in due time at Rath Archaill plain, where Druids' altars and idols stood. Dathi's queen, Ruadh, had a palace in this neighbourhood, and at a place still known under such name, in the Parish of Screene, and County of Sligo. Here the king slept for the night, while Doghra, the Druid, repaired to Dumha na n-Druadh, or the Druid's Mound, not far distant. After the exercise of his art, and at the sun's rising on the following morning, the Druid repaired to the king's bedchamber. Doghra then announced his having consulted the clouds of the men of Erinn. He found that the king must soon return to Tara, when he would invite all the provincial kings and chiefs to a great feast. Then should Dathi decide with them to undertake an expedition into Albain, Britain, and France, following in the conquering footsteps of Niall of the Nine Hostages.

It has been recorded that the ancient militia of Ireland went into winter quarters *o oidhche Shamhna go Beilteine;* *i. e.*, from All-Hallows' Eve until May-day. *Mi-gam* is said to mean the month of November; and it is thought .

marriages were then more common in Ireland, than during any other month. At the great periodical feast of Samhain, we find it stated, that poets and professors of all arts assembled. They brought tablets with them, likewise; and it is probable, these had been employed for the purpose of recording, in verse or prose, various ceremonies or incidents which passed under their observation.

How far the modern festivities or incantations of All-Hallows' Eve have been derived from ancient Gentile rites or ceremonies would prove a question difficult to determine. But this time of year formed a sort of era, remarkable for its peculiar observances among our ancestors.

Alluding to All-Hallows' Eve, or Vigil of Saman, General Vallancey makes mention of prevailing usages in vogue amongst the Irish peasantry during the last century. One of their practices was to assemble with sticks and clubs, going about from one house to another, collecting money, bread-cake, butter, cheese, eggs, &c., for a feast. They demanded such viands in the name of St. Columbkille, desiring their patrons to lay aside the fatted calf, and to bring forth the black sheep. Verses were repeated in honour of this solemnity. The good women were employed in kneading, in baking the griddle-cake, and in making candles. The latter were sent from house to house in the neighbourhood. They were lighted up on the next day, which was dedicated to Saman. Before these candles the recipients prayed, or were supposed to pray, for the donor.

Every cottage or farm-house abounded in the best viands its owners could afford. Apples and nuts were devoured in abundance. The nut-shells were burned on a clean part of the hearth, and many strange predictions were announced from the appearance of the ashes. Cabbages were torn up from the root by boys and girls blindfolded, about the hour of twelve o'clock at midnight.

Their heads and stalks were supposed to indicate some physical or mental peculiarities, such as tidiness, slovenliness, &c., of a future husband or wife. Hemp seed was sown by the maidens, and they believed that an apparition would be seen, if they looked behind at a man, intended to be their future spouse. They hung a *chemise* before the fire at the close of these ceremonies. They sat up as watches during the night, but concealed in the corner of a room, or more usually looking through the key-hole of a closed door. They supposed that an apparition of the man intended for a future husband would come down through the chimney, and be seen turning the garment. They used to throw a ball of yarn out through a window, and then wind it on to a reel kept inside of the house. They supposed, by repeating a *Pater Noster* backwards, and looking out of the window, that they would see his sith or apparition. Boys, and sometimes girls, would dive head and shoulders into a tub filled with water, endeavouring to bring up with their mouth an apple or money cast therein. Apples and lighted candles were stuck on cross sticks, suspended by cords from the roof or couples, and the former swung round in rapid motion by an unwinding of the line. During this motion the peasant endeavoured to catch an apple with his mouth, avoiding the flame, if possible. These and many other playful or superstitious ceremonies, which are said to have been relics of Druidic rites, were observed at this time. Vallancey thought they could never be eradicated whilst the name of Saman should be permitted to remain; but this name and their ceremonies are already fast falling into oblivion.

Sometimes girls take a riddle and collect a quantity of thrashed grain, which they winnow, believing they shall see a future spouse before their work is ended. It was also customary to place three plates before a person blindfolded, who was led towards them. One of the plates contained water, another earth, and the third meal. If the person put his hand in the water, it indicated that he should live longer than a year; if in the earth, it was thought he must die before the close of a year; if in the meal, it betokened the attainment of wealth. Collcannon is prepared at this time, by washing and boiling potatoes, cabbages, carrots, turnips, and parsnips, sprinkled with salt and pepper. A lump of melted butter is placed on the top of this dish, and the mess is eaten without any other condiment. Young females go out at midnight, and cast a ball of yarn into the bottom of a lime-kiln, whilst holding on by a thread. If the girl wind on, and if nothing hold the yarn, it is a sign the winder will die unmarried. If she feel it pulled from her, she asks, "Who pulls my yarn?" when it is supposed her future husband will give his name or appear to her. Sometimes a demon will appear instead; and this latter event indicates that her death is not far distant. These customs are almost entirely extinct; and they were considered too closely allied with *diablerie* and magic, to be used by any except the most reckless and unchristian practitioners.

It is customary on All-Hallows' Eve for young women and their friends to place on a well-heated and smooth stone of the hearth, or on the level bars of a grate, two or more hazel nuts. These are called after the names of supposed lovers; and they are watched with great anxiety, while burning before the fire. A popular belief in various contingencies, which may result from the process, has been thus versified, in a collection of poems published by Charles Graydon, in Dublin, about the beginning of the present century. The lines are extracted from a piece which is headed, "On Nuts' Burning, All-Hallows' Eve;" and they run as follows:—

"These glowing nuts are emblems true
Of what in human life we view:
The ill-matched couple fret and fume,
And thus in strife themselves consume;
Or from each other wildly start,
And with a noise for ever part.
But see the happy, happy pair,
Of genuine love and truth sincere;
With mutual fondness while they burn,
Still to each other kindly turn;
And as the vital sparks decay,
Together gently sink away:
Till life's fierce ordeal being past,
Their mingled ashes rest at last."

Bonfires were formerly kindled at this time, as well as at Midsummer. When the embers had partially burned out, those who assembled were accustomed to cast them about in various directions, or sometimes at each other, with no slight danger to those who were not skilful in parrying or escaping from the burning brands. Among men and boys this was regarded as an amusement only, however dangerous it might prove to individuals; but it is thought to have been connected with former Druidic or Gentile incantations. The high streets or market squares of towns and villages, or fairy-greens and cross-roads in the country places, were usually selected for kindling this Samhan pile. It is supposed the Druids delivered or distributed the brands of this November fire to the people, who were expected to light their household fires with them on the day following.

Melting lead in a greasepot, and then pouring it through the wards of a door-key, into a basin or tub of water, was a source of great amusement. From the fantastic shapes it assumed afterwards, when sufficiently cooled, various prognostics were drawn respecting the fortunes of that person who held the key during the previous process. Castles, shops, farm-houses, and offices, ships, and various implements of trade, were imagined, in the residuum of the lead. These grotesque objects were supposed to bear a certain relationship with the young diviners, in their subsequent journey through life.

On Hallow Eve, in the Highlands of Scotland, a bunch of broom was fastened round a pole, and this combustible material was set on fire after dusk. The bearer, attended by a great crowd, ran through or round the village. Afterwards, flinging his burden down, a great quantity of fagots and inflammatory matter was heaped on the burning embers, until a large bonfire was kindled, which illuminated the surrounding place. This practice is a supposed relic of Druidism; for the old Gallic Councils forbid Christians to carry torches about, whilst the *accensores facularum* were condemned to capital punishment—this being esteemed as a sort of demoniacal sacrifice. Similar customs seem to have prevailed in Ireland; and it is probable enough that, in times far remote, additional incantations were used.

It is considered that, on All-Hallows' Eve, hobgoblins, evil spirits, and fairies, hold high revel, and that they are travelling abroad in great numbers. The dark and sullen Phooka is then particularly mischievous, and many mortals are abducted to fairy land. Those persons taken away to the raths are often seen at this time by their living friends, and usually accompanying a fairy cavalcade. If you meet the fairies, it is said, on All-Hallows' Eve, and throw the dust taken from under your feet at them, they will be obliged to surrender any captive human being belonging to their company. Although this evening was kept as a merry one in farmsteads, yet those who assembled together wished to go and return in company with others; for in numbers a tolerable guarantee, they thought, was obtained from malign influences and practices of the evil spirits.

CHAPTER XXVI.

MEMORIALS OF REDWOOD CASTLE.

"Oh! come for awhile among us, and give us the friendly hand,
And you'll see that old Tipperary is a loving and gladsome land;
From Upper to Lower Ormond bright welcomes and smiles will spring,—
On the plains of Tipperary the stranger is like a king!"
Miss Mary Eva Kelly.

"Soon on the waves the curraghs tossed,
From land to land they safely crossed;
But just as half the shattered ranks
Had landed on the further banks,
Upon the yet remaining few,
The Sheriff's savage party flew.
Bloody and brief the fight that sped,
Ere back the beaten Palesmen fled,
And the light curraghs onward bore
The victors to the Galway shore."—T. D. Sullivan.

"In felon chains they hung the dead,—
    The noble dead, in glory lying;
Before whose living face they fled,
    Like chaff before the tempest flying."
Hercules Ellis.

The Mac Egans were formerly celebrated for their knowledge of Brehon law throughout the provinces of Connaught and Munster. Many learned ollavs of the name are noted in our annals during the middle ages. The Munster Mac Egans were settled on lands which they held in right of their profession,—having been, for many centuries, hereditary Brehons to the O'Kennedys of Lower Ormond, and professors of the Brehon laws for all Ireland. Besides being learned in the laws, certain members of this family were distinguished for their poetic abilities, and their skill in music. Many of them were likewise eminent for keeping a house of general hospitality,—thus securing very great esteem, and at a time when this characteristic of a chieftain's house served to render the owner extremely popular.

Down to the time of Queen Elizabeth, this family was considered highly respectable, so far as worldly wealth and possessions were concerned; but towards the close of her reign, some of them appear to have chosen the stronger side, and to have been in league with the English against O'Niell's and O'Donnell's confederacy. The cause assumed by them, however, was sealed with their blood. Gradually their estates passed away, and little property now remains in the possession of those bearing the name. The old castle of Redwood, rising on a green hillock, high over the Shannon, was once their ancient mansion; but it lies in ruins at present. Here they lived, studied, and kept a celebrated law school, while they supplied good cheer for their students and guests. But while honourable reminiscences attach to this old castle and its chiefs, there are base actions to be recorded, likewise, and which are memorable at two distinct periods of our history.

The fortress—for such it must be called—was of immense strength; and, though roofless, it is still in a good state of preservation. The keep, or centre building, about 50 feet in length, by 30 in breadth, was flanked with square turrets, and entered through the usual low and narrow door-case. This leads by a short passage into what was once the great hall. Over it, a noble and lofty vaulted stone ceiling yet remains, and protects the interior from rainfall. The eye can scarcely reach its coved details, as the light penetrates but dimly through the narrow windows. Near the top of this dome, a gallery or passage may yet be perceived running round three sides of the building's interior; but this offset from the higher wall is scarcely as many feet in width. Over this a small chamber or cell lies bedded in the walls. Neither can it be conveniently reached from the spiral stone stairs, so common in nearly all old castles. At the end of this gallery, on one side, there is no apparent protection; and few persons would have the nerve to traverse its slippery flagway, for the least false step must entail certain destruction. Such is the existing condition in which the Mac Egans' Castle may be found.

Their ancient stronghold was built on a limestone rock, which is elevated in some degree, amid an extensive ridge of green meadow land. Between it and Ireland's greatest river, a level callow plain extends, and along its margin the sluggish but deep waters wind around many large and flat islands, just below the old abbey and village of Meelick, on the Connaught side. Near this point, three of our Irish provinces have their lines of boundary defined.

When his fortress of Dunboy had been taken, and its brave defenders put to the sword, or executed by their English conquerors, in the summer of 1602, O'Sullivan More and his confederates were dispersed through the mountains near Glengariff. After having maintained themselves with a desperate energy and courage for some months, it was at length deemed advisable to retreat, with their available forces, towards Ulster. Here it was supposed the northern chiefs were in arms. But the intervening route was beset by hostile bands, timid sympathizers, and doubtful adherents, in the forlorn state of their fortunes. This resolution was taken in the middle of a very severe winter, and over a route, rugged and destitute of good roads, for the conveyance of their scanty commissariat. Every hope of successfully maintaining a partizan warfare in the mountains was lost, when this desperate but heroic resolve had been made.

However, under the leadership of Donnell O'Sullivan

Beare, about 400 armed men assembled, with a crowd of women and children, forming altogether a body of above 1,000 persons. A scanty supply of horses and baggage was obtained. On the last day of December, 1602, this harassed and starving band set out from Glengariff to Aghers,—thus accomplishing a march of six-and-twenty miles. The Mac Carthies, then taken under English protection, skirmished with those fugitives along the Muskerry mountains, and lives were sacrificed on both sides; but the onward course of the brave Donnell and his devoted clan could not be stayed.

On the day following, January 1st, 1603, they reached Ballyvourney, where they prayed and offered gifts at the shrine of St. Gobnata, to obtain a prosperous issue for their adventurous journey. Protected in some measure by the woods and mountains, they fought their way on to the O'Keefes' and Mac Auliffs' territories, where they encamped. Again on the wing at morning's dawn, the O'Sullivans fled through a rush-grown valley to Liscarroll, while the Barrys fell on their rear at the ford of Bellaghan. After an hour's severe engagement, the Barrys' more numerous forces retired. Burying their dead, and collecting their wounded, the fugitive band entered the fastnesses of Aharlow, where they lay down, wearied and almost starved to death. Once more their camp was raised, and after bearing the brunt of a continuous action for eight hours, while frozen and famished, they reached Kilnamanagh woods. Then, kindling their fires, some roots and the leaves of trees furnished their sole miserable means of subsistence.

From Donhill, they face upwards the steep sides of Slieve Felim mountains, and driving the Bulters from their passes, until the war-wasted band reached Latteragh. Next day the O'Sullivans fled to Baile-Achadidh-Caoin, in the barony of Lower Ormond. During all this time, not a single day or night passed without an engagement taking place between themselves and their pursuers; but the fighting contingent, on retreat, bore every danger, privation, and adversity, with manly fortitude and indomitable courage. Whenever the O'Sullivans drew up in order of battle, their enemies fled; but when the march was resumed, a cloud of pursuers hung on their rear and flanks.

Finally, on the ninth night of this extraordinary retreat, —not surpassed in address and endurance by that of the ten thousand Greeks, as recorded in Xenophon's *Anabasis*,— the O'Sullivans reached Coillfhine forest, not far from the Little Brosnach river, which enters the Shannon nearly opposite Meelick. Here they lurked in the woods for two nights and a day, while the Shannon's waters ran past in a flood. There the sheriff of Tipperary County came upon them in force. Nor could they find boats or curraghs to waft them across the swollen river; for these had been removed by order of the authorities. No ferryman dare ply his craft to secure their passage, under pain of death. To render matters still more desperate, Donough Mac Egan, of Redwood Castle, either through zeal for the royalist cause, or through fear of incurring governmental displeasure, drew out his followers to molest the fugitives. Despair of escaping the toils now woven around them began to seize on their minds. Sadly, too, were their numbers thinned, since they left Glengariff's wild solitudes.

In this state of anguish and uncertainty, Dermot O'Sullivan, father to the historian who has detailed this eventful expedition, declared he would extricate the clan from what seemed inevitable destruction, and secure food for his people at the same time. He advised them to fell trees in the depths of Coill-fhine forest, and to arrange those in a defensible position, throwing up earthworks against them for greater protection. Then, cutting down large osiers, their thickest ends were to be stuck in the earth, and twigs well woven through them, to a height of nearly 5 feet. The prow, however, was to be somewhat more elevated, in order better to resist the action of the waves.* Then the upright rods must be lapped over and secured, so as to form a basket-shaped keel, all the interstices being interwoven with smaller twigs, while over these eleven horse-skins were to be sewed together firmly, thus completely covering the bottom and sides. This advice was immediately adopted. The framework of a flat-bottomed vessel, 26 feet in length, by 6 in breadth, was at once constructed. Scantlings, stakes, and boards, were laid along the bottom and sides, while cross-benches secured seats for the rowers, and served to strengthen the framework. Oars and a rudder were provided. The mounted horsemen of the O'Malleys were satisfied with a much smaller and ruder boat-model,—for a single horse-hide they thought sufficient to cover its rounded keel. The sides were deeper, in proportion to the size of this frail vessel, than might be deemed necessary, and its form was nearly circular; while it unfortunately happened, the sides had not been protected by placing planks across, to strengthen the slightly cohesive and elastic osiers.

For the first time, since their retreat from Glengariff, its scattered clan obtained a full and not unwholesome meal,—for they all fed on the flesh of those twelve horses that had been killed, with the exception of their leader, Donnell O'Sullivan, his relative Dermot, and Dermot O'Houlaghan. Their devoted followers had probably procured more delicate meats for these noble chiefs. Meantime, the two osier-wrought curraghs having been finished, were brought on men's shoulders by night to the

* See *Historiæ Catholicæ Iberniæ Compendium*, a Philippo O'Sullivano Bearro, Tomus III., Lib. vii., cap. vi., vii., viii., ix., x., xi., xii.

Shannon's banks. Philip O'Sullivan appears to have written from memory, or from some imperfect notes or narratives taken from his father's or cousin's dictation, and without a correct map of this place before him. He tells us these cots were launched at Portland, whence Donnell O'Sullivan began to embark his men for the purpose of secretly passing over the Shannon.

The townland surrounding Redwood Castle still bears the name of Killaroe; but in the time of O'Sullivan Beare, it was denominated Cuillthe Rua, or Coilte Ruadh. From the Mac Egans' castle an old road, leading down to the Shannon, may be seen, and it is called the Togher of Redwood, because elevated considerably over the callow meadows and pastures on either side. It terminates near the edge of the great river. The Four Masters state that the O'Sullivans crossed the Shannon at Ath-Coille-Ruidhe; and this, undoubtedly, must have been very close to the Togher's end. At present, a light boat, and a very civil ferryman, are in waiting, at all times, to convey travellers up the stream towards Meelick. Leaving Lehinch and Coorinch islets, the boatman directs the wherry's course between two very considerable insular tracts, known as the Big Island, and Friar's Island. Waving bulrushes and long water-grasses gracefully bend, as if to salute you, when stirred by the oarsman's stroke, while the boat skims along over the placid surface. Waterfowl in abundance float on the stream, or take refuge among the reeds.

Lower down on the Shannon, Bally-Mac-Egan, Long, and Portland Islands, barely rise above the waters. Below the last of these islets, the ancient Castle of Portland has a picturesque appearance on the Tipperary side; and Portland House, with its fine woods, is delightfully situated near the ruins. At this point there is a ford across the Shannon. It would seem, that from Portland to Kiltaroe, dense woods formerly extended along the river's margin. But a mile or two above Portland, the poor hunted outlaws from Glengariff seem to have formed their lair in the recesses of these wooded slopes and river bottoms.

Donnell O'Sullivan had taken the wise precaution to place some twenty of his musketeers, and as many pikemen, in ambuscade, to cover the retreat of his people. Thomas Burke commanded this rear-guard. Soon Donough Mac Egan began to attack the baggage-drivers, and to plunder their stores. Some of these sutlers were killed, and many poor terrified women then rushed forward into the very waters. Immediately, indeed, was this cowardly act avenged; for the men in ambush fell upon the Mac Egans, who fled away with the loss of their leader, Donough, and fifteen men slain, besides a still larger number badly wounded. The shots exchanged between those combatants, however, aroused the inhabitants on either bank of the Shannon, and they collected in numbers to ascertain the actual results of this encounter.

Meantime, the larger vessel had safely conveyed thirty armed men across the river, and had returned for as many more passengers. The horses swam behind this vessel, while their owners guided them by reins from the poop. Unfortunately, the smaller and less manageable cot was swamped in the middle of the swollen stream, and ten of O'Malley's soldiers, who had embarked in it, were drowned. While the large osier vessel was prepared to receive its last contingent of voyagers from the Tipperary side, great confusion and a panic ensued, in consequence of the Mac Egans' attack. Men, women, and children, rushing towards it, the unwieldy vessel capsized, when many persons fell into the water. They were near the bank, however, and no lives were then sacrificed. At length, their vessel having been put to rights, the rear-guard embarked, while some of the camp-followers, left behind, plunged into the river, with a hope of crossing it by swimming. Others fled into the woods, endeavouring to hide from the anticipated vengeance of their pursuers. When the O'Sullivans landed on the opposite shore, their vessel was torn into fragments, lest it might be used by the enemy. Their line of march was then resumed.

Their heroic retreat was not even yet safely effected. The Earl of Clanrickard's son, and several of the Burkes, the Mac Coughlans, the O'Maddens, the O'Kellys, with many others, collected in overwhelming numbers on and around the O'Sullivans' movements, through Galway County. Greater danger now impended. But when they had reached Aughrim, in Hy Many, Donnell O'Sullivan, choosing the most favourable position he could find, drew up in order of battle, with less than 300 men. He addressed these in a few spirit-stirring words, and told them they must then conquer or perish. Nerved for action, the O'Sullivans, bravely led, rushed on their foes, and after a few irresistible charges, the English, Anglo-Irish, and Irish enemies, fled in confusion, with the loss of their choicest captains, and nearly 100 slain. Their foes were scattered before the small but resolute spirits, who secured the victory. Fourteen men fell on the O'Sullivans' side. Without stay or rest, the victors were obliged to press onward, amid many hair-breadth escapes. Reduced to eighteen armed men, sixteen suttlers, and one woman, at last they reached O'Roorke's castle, in Leitrim. This was the miserable remnant of over 1,000, who had left Glengariff in company. Death, wounds, accidents, cold, hunger, and desertion, told fearfully on the wretched but gallant fugitives, during their two weeks' memorable retreat.

We shall now pass over a considerable interval, and then revert to another memorial connected with Redwood

Castle. James Meaney, commonly called "the bold captain," was a celebrated character in the south-west of Ireland, towards the close of last century. His name is well remembered by the peasantry of the surrounding district, in which he chiefly figured. He was born about the year 1770, at Tenescragh, in the county of Galway. His father had been a respectable farmer; but having had a large family, James removed to a place called Kilnacross, near Redwood, in the county of Tipperary. There he rented about thirty acres of land. In this place he lived quietly for some years,—his principal feats having been performed at the country hurlings, so common about that period. At these gatherings, he distinguished himself so much, that he acquired a considerable share of popularity, with no small amount of admiration, bestowed by the country people of those days on such accomplishments. In this way, Meaney secured a great and widespread influence amongst them. To it must mainly be attributed the poor fellow's celebrity, and, indeed, his ultimate ruin. Meaney, who was fairly educated, possessed besides a rare intelligence, very much superior to that of his companions. Sensitive and of an ardent temperament, he easily discerned, and keenly felt, the many wrongs under which his country laboured at that time. In consequence, he eagerly enlisted under the United Irishmen's banners, when their organization spread. For many reasons, he was soon selected as one of their captains in his district. Of almost gigantic stature, combined with great physical strength, wonderful agility, and swiftness of foot, Meany was immediately welcomed as a most desirable acquisition to their confederation, by the leaders of that society. His zeal and earnestness were appreciated, and he was taken a good deal into the confidence of their directory. Under his local leadership, a large number hailed him in his assumed capacity of captain. But after the premature outbreak of 1798, poor Meaney was at once marked for vengeance by the authorities. Having been publicly summoned to surrender, and knowing the punishment that most probably awaited him, he refused to comply with so kind a request. Then he was immediately outlawed, and orders were given that he should be taken, either alive or dead. Meaney, thus driven to extremity, determined on fighting to the last. He took refuge in the picturesque old castle of Redwood. He was well acquainted with the people of this neighbourhood, and loved the more by them for his courage and misfortunes. These, united with that unshaken fidelity manifested by him in the brief but unsuccessful struggle, in which he had been so lately engaged, furnished claims on the sympathies and assistance of his neighbours, so far as they could be secretly rendered.

The small chamber, or cell, where Meaney lay for so long a time concealed, was approached by the perilous flagway or gallery already described. The dimly-lighted cell is called after his name to the present time. There he was surrounded, and secretly fed by faithful followers. Whenever danger loomed in the distance, he had timely notice, through watchful and intelligent friends. Some outlaws, like himself, gathered around their forlorn captain, and under his leadership they levied black-mail from many of the loyalist gentry, who had been most distinguished for their insolent behaviour and cruelties to the harassed peasants, during and after the memorable year of Rebellion.

Elevated from earth, like an eagle in his eyry, Meaney called a council of war in his narrow chamber one stormy night, towards the close of 1799. It was then proposed by a member of the company, as they could exist no longer without having recourse to extreme means, that for the purpose of procuring supplies they should attack the mansion of a gentleman named O'Carroll. This popular resident's house was about seven or eight miles away, at a place called Kilfadda. "Now," said the rascal who made this proposal, "begorra, I am courting the cook myself, and I can give the crathur a whishper not to bar the doore, for she is morthial fond of me, an' resave the ha'porth we'll have to do in this earthly world, but jist rise the latch. Thin the matther is done, boys, in a jiffy, and we can keep our powdher for the yeomin. Now, yez see, there'll be no throuble at all at all." To this dishonourable proposal Meaney stoutly demurred for some time, because he particularly shrunk from attacking this old gentleman, who was beloved in the neighbourhood. Moreover, in O'Carroll's younger days he had been one of the most deadly shots, and a very expert swordsman. He was regarded as a celebrated duellist in the province to which he belonged; and the terror he inspired caused many of the Cromwellians in Tipperary to lower their haughty pretensions. Such an exercise of his qualifications was much admired by the peasantry of that period, especially when O'Carroll was known to sympathise warmly in the cause of their country. The outlaw's remonstrances were overruled by the majority of his band, and he was obliged to yield an unwilling assent to their project. Accordingly the night was fixed, and Kilfadda Castle fell an easy prey to those raiders, as had been anticipated. Meaney, indeed, did all he could to save whatever property was exposed, and to prevent any personal injury from being done to the inmates. But the country people never forgave this outrage, as O'Carroll was a universal favourite. He was one of the old stock, and almost regarded as a chieftain, by his dependants and friends.

Meaney was obliged to quit his hitherto safe retreat

at Redwood soon after this occurrence. He was now haunted with a fear, that should any information be given to Government, he would be surrounded by the military. However successfully he might prevent their approach, he must be starved out ultimately, and thus captured. Consequently, he then thought of seeking refuge in Lusmagh parish, King's County; and thither he fled for further protection. Here, returning alone from a friend's house to his night lair, Meaney encountered a body of yeomen, known as Colohan's Corps. Espying these from a distance, and coming towards him, his resolution was at once formed; for he knew Captain Colohan's yeomen to be the most bloodthirsty of all the dogs of war then let loose on this unfortunate country. As generally happens with ruffians of base instincts, they were likewise the greatest cowards that ever disgraced a uniform. They would, indeed, slaughter without mercy those who were defenceless; but they usually ran away on scenting the slightest danger. Trusting to good-luck, poor Meaney lay down behind a hedge bordering the road. This also inclosed a small plantation. On the yeomen coming near, he stood boldly up, and at the same time he ordered pretended companions to be quiet, but to be ready. He then deliberately fired at Colohan, who was in front. The gallant captain immediately turned his horse and fled, followed by the brave company. Meaney still shouted, and fired shots in quick succession—for he was well armed—until the yeomen scampered out of sight.

But this rencounter proved very unfortunate for him. Now it became known that he lay lurking in the neighbourhood, and a large body of troops was ordered from Banagher to scour the country. At this time, Meaney was concealed in a cave, surrounded by woods, and situated not far from Cloughan Castle, at that time the seat of the well-known Colonel O'Moore, so often mentioned in the life of our national poet Goldsmith. Here, probably, he might have remained concealed for many a day; but, however, he was betrayed, either through fear or jealousy—people say the latter—of a girl, who brought him food from a neighbouring farmer's house. Through whatever motive actuated, certain it is, this damsel gave information to the authorities, while soldiers came direct to the place she pointed out; and on Meaney appearing to learn what was the matter, a dozen muskets were levelled. Immediately, as many bullets passed through his body. His mangled remains were carried into Banagher town, and there hung up in chains at the market-place. Such a spectacle had been deemed an example for the people, subjected to similar civilizing influences, according to the custom of the "good old times." But it teaches other lessons, which are long perpetuated in the memory of an outraged race. Sensitive to every injury and insult heaped upon a proscribed people, and keenly detesting tyranny on the part of a dominant power or faction then swaying the destinies of this nation, we need scarcely feel surprised if local traditions are yet well preserved, and if the hostile passions or prejudices of many survive such bloodstained eras in our annals.

CHAPTER XXVII.

IRISH MARRIAGE CUSTOMS.

> "The face of my love has the changeful light
> That gladdens the sparkling sky of spring;
> The voice of my love is a strange delight,
> As when birds in the May-time sing.
> Oh, hope of my heart! oh, light of my life!
> Oh, come to me, darling, with peace and rest!
> Oh, come like the summer, my own sweet wife,
> To your home in my longing breast!"
>
> CHARLES GAVAN DUFFY.

INNOCENT merriment is practised at Irish weddings, but nothing indecorous is ever allowed. The bride's and bridegroom's stockings were sometimes removed, and thrown amongst young unmarried people. It was prognosticated, that the persons on whose heads those articles fell should be married before that day twelvemonths.

So late as the seventeenth century, before an Irish marriage took place—especially in districts where cattle abounded—the parents and friends of the parties about to contract were accustomed to meet on a hill-side, or, if the weather were cold, at some sheltered place, midway between the dwellings of those parties concerned. If satisfactory arrangements ensued, the people there assembled drank what was called the bottle of agreement, which was filled with strong usquebagh, or whiskey. The marriage portion was usually a determinate number of kine. It was borrowed by the bride's father, or next kinsman, and from friends or neighbours in many cases. Each one of the latter lent a cow or heifer, security being taken from the bridegroom on the day of delivery, that the cattle he received should be restored, if his bride died childless within a certain time, limited by this agreement. In such case, every man's own beast was restored. Thus, care was taken that, by frequent marriages, no man should grow over-rich. On the day of bringing home his bride, the bridegroom and his friends rode out and met herself and friends at the place of treaty. It was customary, in approaching each other, to cast darts at the bride's company; yet at such a distance, that no hurt usually ensued. Still, it was known to people living in 1682, that Lord Howth lost an eye on a similar occasion.

In Sampson's *Statistical Survey of Londonderry*, published A.D. 1802, we are told, how at Scotch descendants' weddings in that county, the groom and his party vie with other youngsters, as to the man who shall gallop first to the bride's house. Nor is this feat of gallantry always accomplished without danger; for in every village through which they are expected, pistol and gun shots salute them. These discharges are intended to honour the parties, yet often promote their disgrace, if a tumble in the dirt may be so considered. At the bride's house a bowl of broth is prepared. This was intended to be a reward for the victor in the race. Hence it was called running for the *brose*.

In the mountainous districts especially, Irish wedding customs were somewhat different. There the groom must first affect to run away with the bride. After a few days' carousal among the groom's friends, the *weddingers* moved towards the bride's country. On this occasion, not only every relative, but every well-wisher of either party brought with him a bottle of whiskey, or the price of a bottle, to the place of rendezvous. After this hilarious matrimonial escapade, the bride and groom proceeded quietly to their designed home. Then, forgetting frolic, they settled down to their ordinary occupations.

On coming home to her new dwelling, the bride must not step over the bridegroom's threshold, but her nearest relations were required to lift her over it, by locking their hands together, when she sat over their arms and leant upon their shoulders. This practice of carrying is known as the play of *shough-sollaghawn,* so merrily enjoyed by little Irish boys and girls, who thus coach one another about, until tired with the performance.

Lavish expenditure and unlimited hospitality characterized marriage feasts in the olden time, especially within the houses of respectable farmers. Family pride and a natural generosity of disposition urged them to indulge in outlay for creature comforts and other objects, admittedly in excess of what the occasion and their social position naturally warranted. Not alone near and distant relations of the contracting parties, but even all neighbours and acquaintances, considered suitable as guests, had invitations to a real Irish country wedding. The humblest labourers or cottiers, and also strolling mendicants, who assembled there, were bountifully regaled; while to each comer was vouchsafed, not only the word, but also the look and feeling of welcome.

CHAPTER XXVIII.

THE SOLITARY FAIRIES.

"Stranger sight than I can tell—oh! a little merry fellow,
With nose and cheek most mellow, is seated all alone,
O'er a broken shoe low bending, mirth with business deftly blending,
Its heel he's neatly mending—his stool, a mossy stone—
And his voice has mirth and music in its tone—
    Music such as fairy voices own."—J. L. FORREST.

"Wouldst know what tricks, by the pale moonlight,
Are played by me, the merry little sprite,
Who wing through air from the camp to the court,
From king to clown, and of all make sport;
    Singing, I am the sprite
    Of the merry midnight,
Who laugh at weak mortals, and love the moonlight."—MOORE.

BY many writers on Irish superstitions, the following individuals of our elfin tribes have been confounded. All of them, indeed, belong to the *solitaire* species of sprites, but they have distinct peculiarities and callings. In the traditions and ideas of our peasantry, they are likewise constantly distinguished. How nearly or distantly they claim relationship with the social denizens of the raths may admit of various explanations.

The Luricaune, Lurigadawne, or Leprechawn, is an elf essentially to be discriminated from the wandering *sighes*, or trooping fairies. His lonely habits and love of solitude are remarkable characteristics; for he is always found alone, and never in any company. He is regarded also as being more material and less richly clad than the ordinary *sighe*. During day-time, the Leprechawn appears as a little wrinkled old fellow, usually dressed in a three-cornered cocked hat, with a leathern apron over a green coat of antique cut, having large buttons. He wears shorts and white stockings, with great silver buckles upon his old-fashioned shoes. His countenance is grotesquely deformed, and his features very irregular. He has piercing black eyes, always twinkling with mischief or dry humour; his nose is hooked; his mouth grins from ear to ear; his jagged teeth are of a yellowish-white colour; and his face altogether covered with wrinkles. In Ulster he is known as the Logheryman.

The Leprechawn knows where all hidden treasures lie; but he will not reveal them unless compelled by some resolute person who captures him, while engaged at the shoemaking trade. This he pursues under some shady hedgerow, or within a clump of hazels. As Mab is the fairies' midwife, so the Leprechawn appears to be the fairies' shoemaker. The odds-and-ends of his work are sometimes gathered after he decamps from the *gite*, where his open-air workshop had been placed. These are supposed to furnish an indication of where he may again be found; and Leprechawn-hunters keep on the watch for his reappearance, especially towards the close of a warm summer's day.

His love for evil-doing makes him an object of suspicion; and he is feared by all the peasantry. He is often seen tapping his little hammer, and working away at a pair of shoes, while whistling some tune or other. A lapstone is on his knee. Thus, it is possible to catch him when you steal upon him, his attention being otherwise engaged; but it is necessary to keep your eye steadily on him, for he is a great rogue, and a skilful deceiver. He ever possesses a power of becoming invisible; and he can easily escape from the hands of those whose glance he succeeds in diverting from him for a single instant.

To effect this object, when captured, he uses every possible artifice. No matter how quick-witted or persevering the mortal may prove, the Leprechawn has so many devices, that he generally throws a captor off his guard, diverts attention by some alarm, and then disappears, to the great annoyance, mortification, and disappointment of the treasure-seeker. Hoarse, cackling laughter is generally heard from the Leprechawn, when he has safely escaped from a person's grasp.

By premeditation or design, mortals have been known to surprise him. This opportunity being afforded, they must pounce on him with a sudden spring, and grasp him firmly with both hands. Then it is thought requisite to threaten him with death, unless he will deliver the money of which he is guardian. He first endeavours to treat the matter as a joke; he next urges various excuses to create delay. When pressed to deliver, he points out some spot where the treasure lies concealed, if only a pick or spade were to be had for digging. Sometimes the captor will consent to have this place marked, by putting up a stake, or the branch of a tree, over it; but on returning with the instrument required, he will find several similar objects multiplied and scattered all around the former sign. Meanwhile, the Leprechawn may be laughing in his sleeve at the simplicity of the disappointed man. He seems to be in great terror while under arrest. Women have alighted on him betimes; but he fears them less than men,—for he knows how to put the oil of flattery on his tongue, and turn the poor creatures' heads with pleasant allusions to, and delusive promises regarding, some happy matrimonial engagement nearly affecting them. Sometimes he affects to espy their husbands or sweethearts approaching at a distance, and then he calls the supposed comers by name. This word, pronounced by him, usually diverts attention to some quarter indicated by the wily Leprechawn; the female takes her eye off him for a moment, and the next he has escaped from her hands.

He carries two purses, for the sake of deceiving a person by whom he may happen to be surprised. In one there is a magical shilling. This coin invisibly returns to his purse after having been expended, so that the Leprechawn can pay out large sums without growing the poorer on this account. In the other purse, he puts a common shilling, or a copper coin, which he gives to any one who has attempted to make him surrender his magic treasures. If the latter be not accepted as a legal tender, the Leprechawn presents the former to his captor; and while the mortal thinks he has secured a prize, yet, on searching a pocket-book, or purse, he finds that the coin has most unaccountably vanished.

The Cluricaune is an idly-inclined, a mischievous, and a busy little sprite. His pleasures are smoking and tippling. He sometimes attaches himself to certain families; and he is found to prove rather partial towards their wine-cellars. He dwells with his favourites, so long as any of the family members exist,—indeed, they cannot fairly get rid of him. He is usually dressed in a red coat, und he wears a red cáp; so that, owing to these circumstances, he gets the name of Fir Darrig. Some, however, distinguish this latter fairy from the Cluricaune. He plays all sorts of tricks and practical jokes; but, if not thwarted, he is hardly ever malevolent. However, the Cluricaune is a great disturber of order and quietness in a household. He makes every sort of noise by day and by night. Whenever seen, he is usually engaged in vaulting, tumbling, or playing at hop-step-and-leap. He is thought to take special care of his selected family's house, property, or life, and to ward off coming danger or accidents,—provided he be left to the bent of his own sportive humours, and not molested.

THE SOLITARY FAIRIES.

Another sort of sprite, distinct from either of the former, must here be noticed. Notwithstanding his bad or sullen dispositions, the house fairy respects the head of a family, and renders him many a service, when he becomes attached; yet, he is very choleric, and he gets huffed if neglected, or his food be forgotten, or not placed in the spot he has indicated by some peculiar token. He is industriously inclined, and will do handy turns about that house he frequents. His visits are always made during the night, and when all members of the family are presumed to be in bed. The house fairy is lubberly and uncouth in his motions,—his figure is less accurately defined than that of other *sighes*, and all his labour is silently performed. Sometimes, however, he is heard stumping about the room he enters, or his approach and exit may be discovered by a slamming of doors or windows. All our information leads us to state, that the old castles, or mansions, and their generous occupants, were alone favoured with his visits. The farm-houses and peasants' cabins were not frequented by the house fairy.

CHAPTER XXIX.

DIVINATIONS, ENCHANTMENTS, ASTROLOGY, AND NOSTRUMS.

> "Cold, weak and cold,
> Is earth's vain language, piercing not one fold
> Of our deep being! Oh, for gifts more high!
> For a seer's glance to read mortality!
> For a charmed rod, to cull from each dark shrine
> The oracles divine!"—MRS. HEMANS.

> "But o'er the elements
>   One hand alone—
>   One hand has sway.
> What influence, day by day,
>   In straiter belt prevents
>   The impious ocean, thrown
> Alternate o'er the ever-sounding shore?
>   Or who has eye to trace
>   How the Plague came?
> Forerun the doublings of the Tempest's race?
>   Or the Air's weight and flame
>   On a set scale explore?"
>   VERY REV. JOHN HENRY NEWMAN, D.D.

IN the fantasies of men's imaginations, astronomy and astrology seem to have been strangely confounded in past ages; and the speculations of various dabblers in mysticism were opposed alike to true experiment, to reason, and to revelation. Soothsayings, lots, divinations, oracles, fortune-telling, calling up demons, shapes and phantoms, demoniacal sacrifices, rites and ceremonies, pretending to a knowledge regarding dead or departed persons, marking nativities, witchcrafts, enchantments, mummeries, casting figures or diagrams, consulting astrologers' tables or almanacs, guessing by signs or objects to arrive at conclusions with which they have no natural relation, were formerly very prevalent. At present they have greatly disappeared, and they must soon become almost extinct, as popular intelligence keeps pace with modern enlightenment.

Since the century of Christianity's first introduction to our country, magic, demonology, and witchcraft seem to have nearly died out; and our earlier sorcerers' arts have been almost forgotten. In the parts of Ireland, settled by the English or Scotch, more traces of a popular belief in magic practices and in the wizards' or witches' profession remain, than in our purely Celtic districts. In the latter, such necromantic habits and usages are called *pisheogs;* and this term has a contemptuous meaning attached to it, in the apprehension and estimation of the better classes among our people.

Notwithstanding those various attempts made by a Eugenius Philalethes, in 1650, to trace the distinctive characteristics of magic, from the days of Adam to our own; or of a Servatius Gallæus to illustrate by dissertations and engravings the history of the Sybils and their oracles;[*] or of a Martinus Debrio, in the folio volume, *Disquisitionum Magicarum Libri Sex,* with similar efforts to describe or expound different occult sciences,—it is doubtful enough, if our real knowledge on such subjects can be materially or usefully increased.

In former times, there was a certain formula of Irish incantation, called *Imbas forosnai,* which enabled the poet or seer to discover anything he desired to know, or

---

[*] His work, *Dissertationes de Sibyllis earumque Oraculis cum figuris Aeneis,* was published at Antwerp in 4to shape, A.D. 1688. At Paris, in 1818, appeared a work by Jules Garivet, having for its title, *Histoire de la Magie en France depuis le commencement de la Monarchie jusqu'à nos jours.*

wished to manifest. He first chewed a piece of flesh, taken from a red pig, or from a dog or cat, and then put this meat on the flag behind the door. Afterwards, he pronounced an incantation over it, and offered it to gods or idols. These he called to his aid, and if the seer did not obtain his desire on the day following, he pronounced incantations on his two palms. Then he called on the idols, that his sleep might not be disturbed. Next he placed his two palms on his two cheeks, and in this manner he fell asleep. He was watched, so that no one might arouse or disturb him, until everything wished for had been revealed to him. A minute, or two, or three, had been allowed to elapse, or so long as he was supposed to be engaged at the offering. This form of incantation is said by Cormac Mac Cuillionain to have had its name from the circumstance of the two palms being employed; one of these being placed over, and the other under, his cheeks. St. Patrick abolished this practice, and another known as the *teinm lægda*. About the latter we know very little. Finn hua Baiscni is represented, however, as putting his thumb in his mouth, and speaking through *teinm læghdha*. St. Patrick declared, that whoever would be guilty of either incantation should possess neither earth nor heaven, because it was regarded as a renouncing of baptism. He left a *dichedul do chenduibh*, or "an extempore recital," to be composed in right of their art. This, it would appear, required no offering to demons. Yet in it, we are told, there was an immediate revelation from the fingers' ends of the poet.

The ancient Irish bards believed, that there were fountains at the heads of our chief Irish rivers, over each of which grew nine hazels. At certain times of the year, these hazels produced beautiful red nuts, which fell on the surface of their respective springs. Salmon or trout of the rivers came up and ate them, and this is said to have caused red speckles to appear on their bodies. It was thought, whosoever could catch and eat one of those fish must become endued with a sublime and poetic inspiration.

Lugad, the blind poet, once came to Bangor, as we read, and his people went to the strand of Inver Béce, an ancient name for Drogheda. There they found a small bare skull, and they brought it to Lugad, asking whose head it was. He desired them to put the end of the poet's wand upon it. This being done, he said that the tempestuous weather, and the waters of Coire Breccain's whirlpool, had destroyed Breccain, grandson to Niall of the "Nine Hostages," with his mariners and ships. He declared the head was that of Breccain's drowned dog. This whirlpool appears to differ from that mentioned as the Corrivreckin, in Scott's "Lord of the Isles," in Leyden's ballad, and in Campbell's "Gertrude of Wyoming." The latter one was situated between Jura and Scarba; while, according to the Rev. William Reeves, the Irish Coire Breccain whirlpool lay between the coast of Ireland and Rathlin Island.

It is said by Solinus, the ancient Irish were so given to war, that after the birth of male children their mothers were accustomed to put the first meat into their infants' mouths, on the points of their fathers' swords. With heathenish imprecations, they wished their sons might die no otherwise than in war or by the sword. It is yet customary for Irish mothers, first to feed their female infants with apple juice, which they suppose will have the effect of producing a clear articulation or a melodious voice. Giraldus Cambrensis tells us, that the wild Irish would not suffer the right arms of their infants to be immersed in water, at the time of their baptism. By avoiding this, it was thought, their right arms must give a more deep and an incurable blow.

From earliest times, it would appear, the ancient Irish thought, when a person's two ears burned or were very warm, some one else had been speaking or engaged in some enterprise about that person. Thus, in Cormac's *Glossary*, we are told of a poetess, the daughter of Ua Dulsaine of Mus-Craige Liac Thuill, in the south-west of Limerick County, who went on a circuit of Ireland and Scotland. She fell into a state of great poverty, and was found on the strand of Mann, cutting sea-weed, but famished almost, and without suitable raiment. She felt her ears burning, when Senchán, a poet of Ireland, discovered her, and she accompanied him to Ireland, when he put noble raiment on her. There she saw an enchanted young man, beautiful in form and dress, who was formerly most ill-favoured in visage, and covered with rags. This strange companion sailed over with Senchán and his retinue of poets and students. When all had returned to Ireland, the enchanted young man went sunwise round Senchán and his people. After that, he was never more seen; but scarcely a doubt existed, that he was the spirit of Poetry. His being ill-visaged, at first, was supposed to represent the difficulty of this art to a beginner; and his subsequent comeliness the exquisite beauty of Poetry, when one has been rendered more familiar with its spirit. This Senchán Torpeist was regarded as chief poet of Ireland, when Guaire Aidne reigned over Connaught, from A.D. 649 to 662.

In the sixteenth century, as Good mentions, when any entered upon a public office in an Irish town, women through the streets, and girls from the windows, sprinkled them and their attendants with salt and wheat. Before seed had been put into the ground, the mistress of the family sent salt into the field. To prevent kites from stealing their chickens, the people hung up in their houses those shells, in which they had been hatched. It was thought unlawful to rub a horse's heels, or to dress him with a curry-comb, or to gather grass for him on Saturdays. If they never sent fire out of their houses to serve their neighbours' use, the people fancied their horses would live longer and be more healthy. If the owners of horses ate eggs, it was insisted they must eat an even number; otherwise some mischief must betide the horses. Grooms were not allowed eggs; and riders were obliged to wash their hands after eating them. When a horse died, his feet and legs were hung up in the house. Even the hoofs were accounted sacred.

It was by no means allowable to praise a horse, or any other animal, without spitting upon him, or sáying, "God save him." If any mischance befell the horse in three days after, they found out the person who commended him, that he might whisper the Lord's Prayer in the animal's right ear. It was believed, some men's eyes had a power of bewitching horses; and then the owners sent for certain old women. These restored the horses to health, by muttering some short prayers. Their horses' feet were subject to a worm, which gradually crept upwards, and produced others of its species. It corrupted the animal's body; and to heal this distemper they called in a witch, who must come to the horse on two Mondays, and on one Thursday. She breathed over the place, where the worm had lodged; and after repeating a charm, it was supposed the animal must recover. After first swearing certain persons to secrecy, this charm was taught to the uninitiated for a sum of money.

The Irish, as Good continues, thought that particular women had effectual charms against all complaints divided and distributed amongst them. To these persons certain people applied, according to their several disorders. The wise women constantly began and ended their charms with *Pater noster* and *Ave Maria.*

Diviners formerly looked through the bare blade-bone of a sheep; and if they saw a spot in it darker than ordinary, they foretold that somebody would be buried out of that particular house. The howling of dogs, or the croaking of ravens, at night, is supposed to indicate the near approach of some person's death in a dwelling, where it may happen to be heard.

When the Irishman of that day happened to fall, he sprang up again, turning round three times to the right. He then took a sword or knife, and dug the soil, taking up some turf, because it was through the earth his shadow was reflected to him. This strange action was owing to the belief of a spirit dwelling in the earth. If the man fell sick within two or three days afterwards, a woman skilled in those matters was sent to the spot, when she said,—" I call thee P. from the east, west, south, and north; from the groves, woods, rivers, marshes, fairies white, red, black," &c. After uttering certain short prayers, she returned home to the sick person to discover if he were afflicted with a sickness called the *esane*, which was supposed to be inflicted on him by the fairies. She whispered in his ear a short prayer, with the *Pater noster*, and put some burning coals into a cup of clear water. We are told, that she then formed a better judgment regarding the cause of this disorder than most physicians.*

When speaking of our people, in his work called *The Glory of England*, Gainsford tells us that, in 1619, the Irish used incantations and spells, wearing girdles of women's hair, and locks of their lovers. They were also curious about their horses tending to witchcraft. This information he seems to have drawn from Good's account. But while decrying these practices, in giving a description of the many excellent prerogatives and remarkable

* See Gough's *Camden*, vol. iii., page 668, &c. Edition, 1789.

blessings whereby England triumphed over all nations of the world, the writer already quoted seems altogether to overlook several much more offensive forms of superstition, and which prevailed in the country he so much glorified.

The Irish game of Shec Shona, or Jack Stones, played by the youth of both sexes, comes from an old custom of divination at the time of marriage, if we are to credit Vallancey. Then the sorcerers sought to learn the fortunes of a married couple from the success or failure of the cast. The five small round stones were taken up, one by one, tossed in the air, and then caught in succession, on the back of the hand. Sleeping on bride-cake, it was thought, would call up in a dream the apparition of a future wife or husband.

During the continuance of a well-known astronomical phenomenon, known as the harvest moon, it was customary with young women to place a prayer-book, a pack of cards, and many other emblematic objects, under their pillows. Then lying down to rest, and before falling asleep, they recited some invocation verses to the moon. Afterwards, if dreams succeeded, and had reference to those special objects placed under the pillow, it was thought their future fortunes might be derived from its connection with those articles beneath their heads.

The old Irish had some acquaintance with astrology. There is yet extant an anonymous poem of twenty-eight verses, describing the natural qualities of persons, born on each day of the week. It was written apparently by an ancient poet. Dr. Whaley, a notorious and professional astrologer, lived in Dublin, over one hundred years ago, and he became quite as celebrated there, as elsewhere Wharton, who wrote various works on astrology in the sister kingdom. These were published in 1683. Dr. Whalley was held in esteem, and extensively patronized by the middle classes.

The following old rann, still in common use through Ireland—

> "One magpie is sorrow, and two is mirth,
> And three is a wedding, and four is a birth"—

bears in its lines probable traces of some ancient Roman mode for auguring future events by the flight of birds.

A singular and very revolting event occurred in the northern part of Normandy, towards the close of 1864. The *Courrier du Havre* related the following extraordinary affair, which caused great excitement in that town and neighbourhood:—"As a sportsman named Lemonnier was out shooting in a small wood not far from the cemetery of St. Adresse, he found the dead body of an old woman wrapped up in a shroud. He immediately informed the authorities; and the body was recognized as that of a Mme. Allain, aged eighty-two, buried at St. Adresse on the 24th of October. It was at first supposed the corpse had been disinterred, for the purpose of stealing any jewellery that might have been buried with it; but a closer examination having shown that the corpse had been in part deprived of the skin, and that the chest and abdomen had been cut open, it was concluded some believer in witchcraft had taken the skin and fat to use as charms in his incantations. It appears, that a belief in the magical virtues of human remains is prevalent in that neighbourhood; for only a few months previously, a young mason dug up a body in the same cemetery, cut off one hand, and burned it to ashes, which he mixed with gunpowder, in the belief that he should then be able to shoot game, without his gun making any report to attract the notice of the *garde champêtre*." Such ideas and practices occurring are almost incredible at the present time; but superstition has extraordinary demoralizing influences over its votaries.

As in certain parts of northern France, at the present

day, it was supposed the possession of a dead hand, in Ireland, when burned and reduced to ashes, would produce certain effects. Such charms or witchcrafts appear to have had some superstitious power over the imaginations of our peasantry. This dead hand was usually kept for the practice of peculiar incantations, grossly repugnant as well to reason as to religion.

At Rathdangan, in the County of Wicklow, there is a well called Tubber Rowan, or "Well of the Ash Tree," formerly visited by mothers who suspected fairies for having made to them an unsatisfactory exchange of children. The mode of operation employed was to dip a supposed changeling three times in the well. If their own child was there, it would at once thrive and flourish after this dipping; if not, it was thought death must immediately ensue. The water of this well used to be brought away to distant parts of the country in order to cure fairy-stricken cattle, such animals being rather large and unwieldy for the plunge bath.

In the fine ballad of Samuel Ferguson, "The Fairy Well of Lagnanay," the following superstitious opinion, with other magic arts, is found, and thus rendered into verse:—

> "Una, I've heard wise women say—
> (Hearken to my tale of woe)—
> That if before the dews arise,
> True maiden in its icy flow
> With pure hand bathe her bosom thrice,
> Three lady-brackens pluck likewise,
> And three times round the fountain go,
> She straight forgets her tears and sighs."

The Yarrow, or *Achillea millefolium*, is supposed to represent Fame. Its botanic name was conferred in honour of Achilles, who is said to have discovered its virtues. With such a little herb, that warrior's earthly greatness is strangely consorted. This renowned hero of antiquity, although celebrated in the poets' songs and fables, should hardly be recognizable in the emblematic name or properties of this humble divining weed. A Wicklow woman gave us another version of the Kildare woman's lines, quoted in a former chapter of this work, in reference to the full moon, as a form used at Hallow Eve by girls, when pulling the mystic yarrow. The only change introduced is found in the first line, where "Good-morrow, good yarrow," &c., has been substituted for "Good-morrow, full moon," &c. On pulling the yarrow, and repeating these lines, a person using the invocation was obliged to retire for the night, without speaking. Should a single word be said, this invocation was pronounced in vain; and a great deal of the evening's fun arose from parties trying to engage in talk those they suspected of making the invocation.

In her beautiful poem of "The Indian Bride," where Zaide sets her flower-decked lantern afloat upon the river Ganges, to divine by its course if her love will have a prosperous termination, L. E. L. thus gracefully and leniently speaks concerning such youthful follies:—

> Oh, it is not for those whose feelings are cold,
> Wither'd by care, or blunted by gold,
> Whose brows have darken'd with many years,
> To feel again youth's hopes and fears;—
> What they now might blush to confess,
> Yet what made their spring-day's happiness."

Among the MSS. of the Royal Irish Academy are some tracts, which embody a good many recipes in furtherance of the fairy doctor's art. One of these is an herb preparation against the evil eye or fairy cast; another contains a remedy for cows overlooked or otherwise injured by necromantic agency; another nostrum is intended for a fairy stroke; while we find one for the recovery of a child, who has received a fairy touch or start during sleep. It would prove an endless task to enumerate all those prescriptions, which are administered by adepts in the use of simples, throughout the country parts of Ireland.

CHAPTER XXX.

DUNGAL THE RECLUSE, A LEARNED IRISHMAN OF THE NINTH CENTURY.

> "Philosophy, as it before us lies,
> Seems to have borrow'd some ungrateful taste
> Of doubts, impertinence, and niceties
> From every age through which it pass'd,
> But always with a stronger relish of the last.
>
> . . . . . .
>
> "Yet shall the traces of your wit remain,
> Like a just map, to tell the vast extent
> Of conquest in your short and happy reign:
> And to all future mankind show,
> How strange a paradox is true,
> That men who liv'd and died without a name,
> Are the chief heroes in the sacred lists of fame."
>
> DEAN SWIFT.

THIS erudite man is better known to us through his writings, than from any recorded particulars of his life. Dungal was born in Ireland, and probably towards the middle of the eighth century. About this period, also, the illustrious St. Virgil, afterwards Bishop of Saltzburg, is known to have studied in Ireland, of which country he was a native. He taught the sphericity of the earth— a theory not then generally understood, except by the most learned philosophic investigators. The exact place of Dungal's birth cannot be discovered; but Dr. Lanigan conjectures, that before leaving Ireland he belonged to the religious community of Bangor, and was obliged to quit this retreat in consequence of hostile incursions of the Danes. This he supposes possible from the opinion of Muratori, that the *Antiphonarium Benchorense*, in the library at Bobbio, had been presented by Dungal. Yet such a matter is rather doubtful; nor does it appear the Danes devastated Bangor before A.D. 811, when Dungal lived in France. The particulars of his early life are but imperfectly known; however, it appears certain, that he was versed in the liberal sciences, and particularly in the knowledge of astronomy, such as it was then understood. The Holy Scriptures were the constant books of his study.

With an amount of learning which might enable him to push his fortunes to advancement in almost any temporal station, he went over to France, possibly towards the close of the eighth century. Although certain writers state, that he had attained the rank of deacon;[*] yet his own words only warrant the assumption, that he was a subject of the French king, and his *orator* or lecturer. But, as this pious servant of God desired chiefly his progress in perfection, he led the life of a recluse, either in the Abbey of St. Dennis, or in its immediate neighbourhood. The fame of his learning, however, reached the ears of Charlemagne, then Emperor of the French, and a munificent patron for men of letters. That double eclipse of the sun, which is said to have occurred in 810, strongly excited the scientific curiosity of the Emperor, who applied to the Abbot Waldo, Valdo, or Valton, requesting him to obtain a reply from his disciple, Dungal, to certain questions sent for solution. If he were not a monk living under the rule of Abbot Waldo, near Paris, at least this ecclesiastic seems to have been his intimate friend and confidant. In obedience to the wishes of the Emperor and of his superior, Dungal returned

---

[*] He was advanced to the rank of Deacon, according to the opinions of MM. Cave and Du Pin. See Article "Dungal," in Moreri's *Grande Dictionnaire Historique*.

the following epistle, which certainly displays an acquaintance with the writings of the ancient classical and learned authors, even although it do not prove in all respects conformable to the received doctrines of modern philosophy. It would appear, especially, that the theories of the ancient astronomers, Hipparchus and Ptolemy,* had been well studied by this erudite Irishman; and, in all probability, those were the most generally received opinions of the philosophers living in his time.

Epistle of Dungal, Recluse, to Charlemagne, on the Double Eclipse of the Sun, in the year DCCCX.

In the name of the Father, and of the Son, and of the Holy Ghost. Length of days, uninterrupted health, constant good wishes, peace, an incorruptible crown, and glory without end, to our most illustrious Prince, to our most serene Emperor Charles, excelling all preceding Roman Potentates, in the noble and honourable endowments and exercises of regal virtues. Whereas, dearly-beloved Prince, I, Dungal, your faithful servant and lecturer,† have heard that, not unmindful of me, you addressed an epistle to the Abbot Waldo, that, according to your own words, you would have me interrogated concerning the reasons for that double eclipse of the sun, which you discovered, from the relation of many, to have occurred during the past year 810, from the Incarnation of our Lord; and which, as you remember to have read, not only the ancient Pagan philosophers, but even a certain bishop of Constantinople, predicted how it might take place, through the natural effect of a usual concursion

---

* The studious reader will find an exposition of their astronomical knowledge in Delambre's *Histoire de l'Astronomie Ancienne*, 2 vols., 4to. Published at Paris, 1817.

† The term in Latin is "orator."

of elements, and be known by the experience of certain inquiry.

Wherefore, it pleased your gracious and serene Highness to require, that I, as a follower and lover of science, should be asked for my opinion, on the aforesaid reasons, that I might confess what I knew and thought on the subject, and after that, in reply, the result of my conclusions should be written, and the writing be conveyed to you. Wherefore, I shall neither hesitate nor dissemble, in obeying your most felicitous and useful precept, according to the extent of my ability: and I wish I were able to procure for you the object of your desire, in as satisfactory and competent a manner as my will inclines me, although to the Supreme Ruler be referred that sincere and earnest affection of my mind, for the thing to be effected and fulfilled.

Since therefore, my Lord, the investigation and science of this question specially and exclusively appertain to philosophers, who treat on the laws of nature, as your shelves furnish many authors, whose books are elegantly and accurately written, although they are out of my reach, and as they have treated on these and like subjects in a more finished style and laboured expression, I believe I should be able to reply to your inquiries, in a more lengthy and erudite manner, by having access to them. Although the books which I now possess are simple, elementary,* and compendious, I shall, nevertheless, through their means, reply as best I can, and inasmuch as the torpor of a penitential breast, and an intellect scarcely exercising itself, and acting by slow progress and impotent endeavour, can discuss the matter, lest according to the vulgar proverb, like the wolf in the fable, I might seem to be oppressed by a timid and stupid silence; knowing, however, most undoubtingly, that your indulgent

* The Latin word is "leves," in the original.

clemency of serene and pious forbearance will easily accord me pardon, if I shall fail in my literary attempt, and correct me in a paternal manner, if through frailty or infirmity of intellect I seem deficient, either in industry or study.

The origin of this question, as is usual in all other dissertations, must be sought in its commencement—the reason to be explained proceeding through a certain order, that a proper answer may be given to the interrogatory. Wherefore Macrobius, Ambrosius,* in his exposition of Cicero, among other subjects, treats regarding the nine circles that surround the "aplane"†—namely, the great visible sphere, in which the twelve signs are contained, and subject to which are seven other spheres, through which two luminaries run, the sun and moon, and five which are moving. The first of these orbs, or of the aforesaid circle, is the galaxy or milky way, Lacteus, as it is rendered in Latin, which is alone visible; the other circles being comprehended, rather by conception than by vision. The second circle is the zodiac or the sign-bearer, so called on account of bearing and containing the signs—namely, the stars and constellations. The five other circles are called parallel, since in all *respects* they are neither equal nor unequal. Concerning these, Virgil treats in his Georgics.

Besides these, there are two Coluri, to which an imperfect conversion has given name; two superadded to the former number, the Meridian and Horizon, which are not described on the sphere, because they can have no determined place, but are varied with respect to the difference of situation of those observing from or inhabiting a certain place; all which, named and numbered in

---

* Recte, "Aurelius."
† "Aplanen" is the Latin word in the original. "Aplanes" signifies "the firmament," from the Greek word ἀπλανής, "non erraticus."

a cursory manner, we have no occasion to exhibit in this instance. Wherefore, the two former luminaries—to wit, the sun and moon,—with five stars, which are called erratic, divide the seven subjective spheres, containing the twelve signs of the great sphere called the "aplane," and in the void which they occupy, all have possession of peculiar and special positions.

But, in the first of the seven spheres is the star of Saturn; in the second, that of Jupiter; in the third, that of Mars; in the fourth, or middle one, is the Sun; in the fifth, lies the star of Venus; in the sixth, that of Mercury; while the Moon occupies the seventh sphere, which is the lowest and most extreme of all. Such is the description of Cicero, with whose opinion the reasoning of Archimedes and of the Chaldeans agrees. But Plato asserts, that the sun holds a position the second above the moon, that is, the sixth place amongst the seven spheres; thus following the Egyptians, who are the masters of all branches of philosophy, and who will have it, that the sun is placed between the moon and Mercury. Yet, although this persuasion—founded upon certain dogmata and credible reasons of Tullius and of its abettors—prevailed and has been generally received; however, the clearer observation of Plato seems to have detected a truer arrangement, which also this reason, independent of ocular demonstration, recommends, that the moon, which wants intrinsic light, and borrows it from the sun, should of necessity be subjected to the fount of his illumination. For this reason does not cause the moon to have a peculiar light to illuminate all the other stars by her own, because they are placed beyond the sun in that most pure ether, in which everything—that I might use the words of a philosopher—has a natural and peculiar light, which so entirely covers the sphere of the sun with its fire, that the zones of heaven removed from the sun are oppressed with perpetual cold; but the moon cannot shine, because she alone is under the sun, and next to a region of shadows, void of inherent light. In fine, because the earth is the inferior part of the whole universe, and the moon the inferior part of ether, they have named the moon an etherial earth. Yet, like the earth, she cannot be immovable, because in the sphere, which is rolled round, nothing remains immovable except the centre; but the earth is the centre of the mundane sphere, wherefore it alone remains immovable. Again, the earth, receiving the light of the sun, is only enlightened itself, and does not illuminate; but the moon, like a mirror, emits the light by which she is enlightened, although denser than all the other celestial bodies; however, as being much purer than the earth, she becomes penetrable to light received, so that she emits light again from herself, nevertheless producing no sense of heat, because the ray of light, when it comes to us from its source, which is the sun, draws with it the nature of the fire from which it is produced. But, when it is infused into the body of the moon, and is thence reflected, it produces brightness only, but no heat; for the mirror, when reflecting the brightness of fire opposed to it, only shows us the representation of fire, without the sense of heat.*

We must add to these an observation, that, unless the sun, moon, and five wandering stars, all the others are stationary in the firmament, and only move with it. There are writers, who more correctly assert, that these also have their peculiar movements, by which they are said to approach with the revolution of the heavens, but to require for one circuit of their course many centuries, exceeding a credible numeration, on account of the immensity of the extreme circle; and that, therefore, no

---

* This is like an indistinct perception of the distinction between luminous and obscure heat.

motion of theirs can be observed by man; for the course of human life, at most of short duration, is not sufficient to discover such a slow accession. It is asserted, with probable arguments, that the sun, moon, and five wandering stars advance, by their own motion, to the east from the west, besides the daily revolution of the heavens which draws from the east to the west; for both vision and reason assure us, that these move and are not stationary in the firmament, since at one time they are seen in this, at another time in that, region of the sky. And often, when two or more are found in conjunction, and when, from the place in which they were seen together, they are afterwards separated from one another—which occurs not to the fixed stars, always seen in the same place, and never parted from one another when in conjunction—it is evident, not only from undoubted reason, but from the laws of vision, that they are rolled in a contrary direction, from the orient to the occident, by a nearer motion.

For the consideration of the signs by which we see the zodiac divided or distinguished, I shall take my commencement from any one sign. When Aries appears, Taurus rises after it; the Gemini follow; after these, Cancer follows; and the remainder are found in order. Wherefore, if these advanced from the east towards the west, they ought not to revolve from Aries towards Taurus, which is placed behind, nor from Taurus to the Gemini, a posterior sign; but they should proceed from the Gemini towards Taurus, and from Taurus towards Aries, by a consonant accession of direct and universal revolution. But when they revolve from the first to the second sign, from the second to the third, and thence to other signs which are posterior, though the signs are borne in a stationary manner in the firmament, we unhesitatingly conclude, that those stars do not move with, but against, the firmament.* That this may plainly appear, I will prove when treating of the course of the moon, which is more remarkable for its lightness and velocity. On the second day, towards its setting, she is commonly seen as if accompanying the sun, which she lately left, after he had disappeared—she occupying the extremity of the heavens over the west, to the antecedent; on the third day she sets later than on the second; and thus, every day, she retires farther from the west; so that on the seventh day, at the setting of the sun, she is seen in the zenith; but after seven other days, when he sets, she rises; so that, in the middle of the month, by retiring from the west to the east, she measures half the firmament, that is, one hemisphere. Again, after seven other days, towards sunset, she occupies the vertex of the latent hemisphere, a proof of which is furnished, by her rising in the middle of the night. In fine, as many similar days having elapsed, adding two other days, more or less, she overtakes the sun, and a joint rising of both is seen, until, succeeding the sun, she moves again; and then retiring, she leaves the west by degrees, always moving back towards the east. The sun also moves in no other manner than from the west to the east; and again retiring by degrees, he always leaves the west, moving towards the east; the sun himself thus naturally moving from the west to the east. And although he retires more tardily than the moon—since he measures one sign during the time the moon describes the whole zodiac—however, he affords manifest evidence and ocular demonstration of a peculiar motion. I will then suppose him to be in Aries, which, because it is the equinoctial sign, makes equal day and night. When he sets in this sign, we see the Balance, that is, the scales of Scorpio, about to rise, and Taurus appears bordering on the west; for we see the Vergilian

* The Latin word is "cœlum."

and Hyadian parts of Taurus sinking in a brighter manner, a little after the sun. The following month, the sun retires into the latter sign—viz., into Taurus; and so it occurs, that neither the Vergilian nor the other part of Taurus is seen on that month; for the sign which sets together with the sun is always obscured, so that the neighbouring stars in connection with the sun are concealed; because then the Dog-star, which adjoins Taurus, is not seen, being covered by the propinquity of light. And to this Virgil alludes,* when he says,—

"Candidus auratis aperit cum cornibus annum
Taurus, et adverso cedens Canis occidit astro."†

For, he does not wish to be understood, Taurus with the sun being in the east, that at the same time the Dog-star should be in the west, it being near Taurus, but that Taurus with the accompanying sun oppresses it, as then the sun, being near, renders it invisible. However, the sun setting, the Balance is found in the ascendant to such a degree that, rising, the whole Scorpion may appear: the Gemini which are near are seen towards the west. Again, after the month of Taurus, the Gemini are not seen, which is an indication that the sun has migrated into them. After the Gemini, he returns into Cancer; and then, when he obscures it, the Balance is immediately seen in the vertical firmament. Hence, we must allow, that the sun, having passed three signs—viz., Aries, Taurus, and the Gemini—has receded to the middle of the hemisphere.

In fine, after the three following months, having illuminated the three signs which follow—I mean Cancer, Leo,

* *Georgicon*, lib. i., lines 217, 218.
† "When, with his golden horns, in full career,
The Bull beats down the barriers of the year,
And Argo and the Dog forsake the northern sphere."
DRYDEN'S *Translation*.

and Virgo—he is found in the Balance, which again brings the night equal to the day; and whilst he falls into that sign, Aries immediately rises, into which the sun passed six months previously. But on this account have we wished to propose the consideration of his setting to his rising, because the latter signs are seen after the setting; and whilst we have shown the sun's return to these signs into which he falls, we have certainly indicated his return by a contrary motion to that of the heavens. These observations, regarding the sun and moon, are also sufficient to establish the regression of the five stars; for, by migrating into the latter signs, through like reasons, they are always moved by a contrary mode of progression to that of the world, the courses and regressions of which are said to be regulated by the sun himself; for the certain definition of space is, when each receding erratic star has approached the sun, it is, so to say, not allowed a farther advance, and it seems to go back. Again, when, on retiring, it hath reached a certain part, it is recalled to the accustomed track of a direct course; so the laws of the sun, and the power of motion, in all the other luminaries, are moderated by fixed limits.

Wherefore, the course or circle is understood to be one entire and perfect revolution of each star; that is, a regression to the same place, from the same place, after measuring the sphere round which it moved. But here is a line surrounding the sphere, and making, as it were, a path through which the sun and moon run, and within which the legitimate course of the wandering stars is confined; which stars were said to wander * by the ancients, because they held a course of their own, and rolled by a contrary motion from the west to the east, against the impulse of the great sphere or firmament; all of them

* The Latin word is "errare."

having the like celerity, similar motion, that is, a mode of passing, but all of them not completing their circles and orbits in the same space of time. But the inequality of the spheres, under the same celerity, makes a differing space for the courses which the several stars pursue; because, from the sphere of Saturn, which is the first of the seven, to the sphere of Jupiter, the second from the highest, so great is the distance of intervening space, that the former finishes its circuit of the zodiac in thirty years, and the latter in twelve. Again, such is the distance of the sphere of Mars from Jupiter, that the same course is completed in two years. But Venus is so much lower than the region of Mars, that a year suffices her to complete the circuit of the zodiac.

But now the star of Mercury is so close to that of Venus, and the sun is so close to Mercury, that these three complete their circuit in an equal space of time, which is a year, more or less; and, therefore, Cicero called these the two concomitant courses of the sun, because, in equal space they never depart far from one another; yet the moon departs so much from these, that she completes *a circuit* in XXVIII. days that occupies them a year. But Cicero would station the sun in the fourth place among the seven, although it occupied not only about the fourth middle place, but becomes the exact middle. However, he does not say in the following words, in a positive manner, that the sun is exactly in the middle, but that it is almost there:—"*Deinde de septem mediam fere regionem sol obtinet.*" * Yet, the adjunct is uncalled for, by which this assertion is restricted; for the sun, holding the fourth place, obtains the middle region as to number, but not as to space; since the star of Saturn, which is highest, surrounds the zodiac in thirty years; the

---

* In English :—" Next, the sun occupies nearly a middle place among the seven."

sun, in the middle, *makes his circuit* in one year; while the moon, which is last, *accomplishes it* in one month, not entirely completed. The relation, therefore, between one and XXX. exists between the sun and Saturn, and between the sun and moon as between XII. and one; whence it appears, that a certain division out of the middle part of the whole space, from above to below, does not take place in the region of the sun. But, as relating to number among the seven, the fourth is considered the middle place; however, on account of the inequality of distances, an addition of the particle *fere* is required. Wherefore, the zodiacal circle is one of the eleven already named, and which only can derive its latitude in this manner related. The nature of celestial circles is incorporeal; and since a line is conceived, as having length alone without breadth, the capacity of the signs in the zodiac *only* require length. Wherefore, so much space, as the wide dimension of straggling stars occupies, requires limitation within two lines; while the third, drawn through the middle, is called the ecliptic; because, when the sun and moon equally describe their course in the same line, it becomes a matter of necessity that an eclipse of one or other should occur: of the sun, if the moon be under; or of the moon, if then it be adverse to the sun. Wherefore, we can only have an eclipse of the sun—which never fails us—on the thirtieth day of the moon; and on the fifteenth day of the sun's course, an eclipse of the moon only occurs; for it thus happens, that the cone of the earth is found opposed under the same line of the moon, placed opposite the sun, to borrow from him solid light; or she herself, coming under the sun, by such an object, his light is withdrawn from human vision. During an eclipse, the sun himself in no wise diminishes, but our vision is obstructed; yet the moon labours under a peculiar defect in not receiving the light of the sun, through whose influence she illuminates the night; from a knowledge of which, Virgil, skilled in all science, has said,*—

"Defectus solis varios lunæque labores."†

Although the describing of three lines, therefore, both incloses and divides the zodiac, antiquity, the authority for words, would only have them named one. However, according to some philosophers, the latitude of the zodiac is measured by twelve lines, of which, according to the nature of equal numbers, two must be considered the middle ones; they allow these to be enlightened by the sun, the moon passing through all. "Wherefore, on one side and the other, the wanderer does not permit an eclipse to take place every month. They allow, that every year, at stated days and hours, eclipses of either planet may take place, although they do not always appear, and because sometimes they are under the earth, in the part of the latent hemisphere, and sometimes above; yet, on account of the clouds, and the rotundity and convexity of the earth, they cannot be seen by all, everywhere and at the same time; when it is most certain, that eclipses take place oftener than they are seen, nor when they are seen, do they equally appear to all. Hence, the Orientals do not perceive the vespertine eclipses of the sun and moon, nor the Occidentals the morning eclipses—the convexity of the earth intervening, and not admitting vision. Wherefore, by probable reason and tradition, we learn that an eclipse of the moon occurs sometimes in the fifth month from the first; and that the sun, in the seventh, in like manner is concealed on the

---

* *Georgicon*, lib. ii., line 478.

† "Teach me the various labours of the moon,
And whence proceed the eclipses of the sun."
DRYDEN'S *Translation.*

earth twice in thirty days, and nevertheless is seen by others, since either planet has been eclipsed in twelve days."*

I have therefore answered, most revered Emperor, as appears to me, the inquiries in your letters; and I have explained, on the authority of those named, how the ancient philosophers both knew, and had a foreknowledge regarding the manner, in which an eclipse of the sun takes place, and when it must occur. For those were skilled in all kinds of science, and had a knowledge concerning every approved school of the ancients; they sought, with most unerring direction of unprejudiced and pure minds, and with most perspicuous and keen vision of internal perception, the nature, the reason, the cause, and origin for all things; by a searching and close rational investigation, most accurately and efficaciously, they discovered what was sought, through the aid of Him *from whom every good and perfect gift is received.* When *things were* discovered and brought before their minds, they observed with diligence and accuracy; whence, those philosophers, who made astronomy their chief study, through the same continued and studious diligence, most fully investigated the rising and setting of the stars by observation, from which they derived experience. They discovered, also, the advance and regress, the accession and retirement, of the sun, moon, and five wandering stars; and they knew undoubtingly, in like manner, by their investigation, how many lines of the zodiacal circle each wandering star traversed, and through which of these lines, properly and specially, its present course had been directed, and in what sign, or part of a sign, it was to be found. Therefore, they who know most certainly and accurately about the more intri-

---

* This passage here quoted is taken from Pliny, (lib. ii., cap. xiii.) But "quatuordecim" should be substituted for Dungal's "duodecim," towards the close.

cate, though true and natural, movements of other stars, why should they be ignorant concerning the courses of the sun and moon, which are plainer and more easily known? how could it escape their observation, in what manner and when, these should run through the same ecliptic line of the zodiacal circle, while traversing it in one and the same course? must they not coincide in one sign and at one part, and unite in the same part, the moon in the succession to the sun thus causing an eclipse of the sun?

Not only, therefore, the philosophers foreknew the eclipse or defect of the sun, and foreknowing it, they predicted how it must take place after one month, but they foretold also when it should take place within one year, or within twenty, one hundred, or one thousand years, owing to the same ingenious inquiry and diligent observation, derived from past experience. Yet, a subject of greater wonder is, how, by using like arguments, they have extended their foreknowledge to fifteen thousand years. Whence Cicero, relating the vision of Africanus, says:*—"Homines populariter annum tantummodo solis† unius astri reditum metiuntur; re autem recta cum ad idem unde semel profecta sunt, cuncta astra redierunt, eamdemque totius cæli descriptionem longis intervallis retulerunt: tunc ille vere vertens annus appellari potest, in quo vix dicere audeo quam multa hominum sæcula teneantur. Namque ut olim deficere sol hominibus extinguique visus est, cum Romuli animus hæc ipsa in templa penetravit, quandoque ab eadem parte sol eodemque tempore iterum defecerit, tum signis omnibus ad idem principium stellisque revocatis expletum annum

---

* There appear to be a few readings in this passage which are not conformable, in all respects, to the more modern versions of Cicero's works.

† In most versions, "id est" is here inserted.

habeto; cujus quidem anni nondum vicesimam partem scito esse conversam."*

Which words of Tullius, the Ambrosanian † exposition lays open and explains in this manner. The year is not that alone, which is so called, by common acceptation; but, the peculiar year of the several luminaries, of the sun, the moon, and stars, in their return to the same place from a certain place, after measuring the whole circuit of the heavens. Thus the year of the moon is that in which she traverses the circuit of the heavens; for the month is named from the moon, because, by a Greek name, the moon is called *mene*.

Wherefore Virgil, wishing to signify the year which is effected by the course of the sun, to distinguish it from the shorter lunar year, says,‡—

"Interea magnum sol circumvolvitur annum,"§

thus calling it the great year of the sun, by comparing it with the lunar; for the course of Venus and Mercury is nearly equal to that of the sun, but the year of Mars is almost equal to two, as in such a length of time he

---

* The following is an English translation of this passage, to be found in that fragment of Cicero known as *Somnium Scipionis*:— "Mankind ordinarily measure their year by the revolution of the sun—that is, of a single heavenly body. But, in reality, when all the planets shall return to the same position which they once had, and bring back, after a long rotation, the same aspect of the entire heavens, then the year may be said to be truly completed; in this I do not venture to say how many ages of men will be contained. For, as of old, when the spirit of Romulus entered those temples, the sun disappeared to mortals, and seemed to be extinguished; so, whenever the sun be eclipsed, at the same time, all the stars and constellations having been brought back to the identical starting-point, then you may consider the year to be complete. But be assured, that the twentieth part of such a year has not yet elapsed."

† *Recte*, "Aurelianian."   ‡ *Æneidos*, lib. iii., line 284.
§ "The sun had now fulfilled his annual course."

DRYDEN'S *Translation*.

revolves in the heavens. But the star of Jupiter takes twelve, and that of Saturn thirty years, in the same circuit.

These things are known already concerning the sun, moon, and erratic stars, as related; but the mundane year, which is revolving, because effected by the conversion of the whole universe, is explained from remote ages. The reason is as follows. All the stars and constellations, which are seen fixed in the heavens and whose peculiar motions human vision neither can perceive nor detect, nevertheless move. And besides the revolution of the heavens, in which they are always attracted, by their own advance, they also move so slow, that no man's life is sufficiently long to detect by continued observation the change of position made from the place in which . . . first he had seen.* Wherefore, the end of the mundane year takes place, when all the stars and constellations, which the "aplane" contains, have revolved from a certain place to the same place, so that not even one star of heaven can be in any other place than that in which it had first been. When all others have moved from that place, to which they afterwards returned, they have accomplished their year; so that the sun and moon, with the five erratic stars, will be in the same places and parts, in which they were at the commencement of the mundane year. But this, as philosophers say, takes place at the end of fifteen thousand years.

Wherefore, since the year of the moon is the month, and the year of the sun twelve months, and the above-named periods are the years of the other stars; so fifteen thousand years make the mundane year, as we now compute it. That indeed is truly the revolutionary year,

* A slight erasure seems to have occurred here in the original. Therefore, it is possible, the last four words in the text may have been mistranslated.

which not only measures the return of the sun, that is, of one star, but which includes the return of all the stars, which are in any part of the heavens, to the same place, under the same description of the whole firmament; whence it is called mundane, because the heaven is properly called "mundus." Wherefore, as we do not consider, from the kalends of January, to the same kalends, as the solar year only, but from the day following the kalends to the same day; so, in like manner, from any day of each month, to the return of the same day, is called its year. Hence the beginning of this mundane year each person may establish for himself. As for instance, Cicero named the beginning of the mundane year from that eclipse of the sun, which happened at the death of Romulus; and although many eclipses of the sun took place afterwards, these repeated eclipses are not said to have completed the mundane year. But it must be completed, when the sun himself, being eclipsed, shall be found in the same position and part, and all the stars and constellations shall be also found in like manner, as they were under Romulus; when after fifteen thousand years, as philosophers assert, the sun shall be so eclipsed, that it shall be found in the same sign and the same part, as in the time of Romulus, all the stars and constellations being in like manner brought to the same beginning.

Therefore, in the past year, from that of the Incarnation of our Lord, DCCCX., it does not appear strange, as your letters say, that an eclipse of the sun occurred on the seventh of the Ides of June,* the first moon then commencing, and again in the same year, the day before the kalends of December XXX., the moon commencing, and from the first eclipse seven months elapsing—viz., the

* The annals of Eginhard have "VIII. Idus Julii," which is supposed to be incorrect. We find "VIII. Idus Junias," in *Vita Karoli Magni*, and in other ancient chronicles.

month of December beginning. Thus this eclipse of the sun is known to have occurred during the first and last moon, and at the seventh month from the first eclipse; although sometimes the eclipse does not become apparent, when it undoubtedly takes place; or if it appear, it is not always seen in every place; or if it be visible, all do not equally see it at the same time, on account of the aforesaid reasons.

If, therefore, any person, even at the present time, were endowed with the same keenness of perception—if he would endeavour with the same laborious investigation—if he were diligent to the same degree, both in inquiry and observation, having the same leisure and curiosity, as those who lived in a former age—if he carefully loved in such measure the study of astronomy or any other science—ought we not in reason to believe, that he should acquire also the knowledge and prescience of the ancients? The will to act in such a manner is now wanting, and hence nature should not be blamed, since she is always one and the same; however, she makes men differ from one another to some extent, as we find that in the beginning of the world a greater strength of body and vigour of sense prevailed among our progenitors than among ourselves.

Here, then, shall I conclude on the subject of the solar eclipse; not perhaps because I have supposed enough to have been already said, but because at present the extent of my knowledge will not enable me to call to mind anything more in this place. I am in want of the second Pliny, and other books, with which I might be able to supply my deficiency, since of myself I neither should dare nor presume to dogmatize on such a subject. But I earnestly beseech you, O most pious Emperor, to whom God hath granted an abundance of wisdom and of all other virtues in excellent measure, that you would deign to instruct and direct, regarding what you may deem me to be ignorant of in this particular, or to apprehend in a false light.

For the foolish things of the world hath God chosen, and *there is no exception of persons with Him,* so that not only may the light of your pure and bright wisdom enlighten those that are near you, but those who are removed; and not only may the emitted ray of your bounteous splendour brighten those running through the open plain, but even may it search out the recluse in his cell and retirement. All of us are bound to entreat and beg, by constant and assiduous prayer, that our Lord and Saviour Jesus Christ would grant to His people for many years a prince and ruler, who is universally esteemed the chief master of all good works, virtues, and liberal sciences, and a perfect example—to rulers for the good government of their subjects—to soldiers in lawfully conducting warfare—to clerics in observing the duties of the Christian religion in a proper manner—to philosophers and scholastics, in justly acquiring philosophy and knowledge regarding human sciences, and in reverently weighing and believing, according to faith, those sciences that are divine. What more should I try to say, regarding the great virtues and excellencies of our Lord Emperor Charles, when, although I might wish to exalt each particular endowment, I cannot enumerate all those perfections? I shall only assert, with truth, what all allow, that within this land of which the Franks are rulers,[*] through God's permission, never from the beginning of the world was there seen, in like degree, a King or Prince, brave, wise, and religious, such as our Lord Emperor Charles. Regarding the future, however, perhaps on account of his just and exalted

---

[*] From this passage, Muratori infers, that Dungal wrote his astronomical epistle, not in Gaul, but in Italy. See *Antiquitates Italicæ Medii Ævi,* tome iii., dissertatio xliii., pages 117, 118.

merits, such another may arise from his seed. This alone remains, that all Christians should unanimously invoke and beseech the Lord, with urgent prayers and devout hearts, that He would multiply the triumphs of our most excellent Emperor Charles, that He would extend this empire, preserve his dear progeny, increase his health, and extend his life to many annual revolutions. Hear, hear, hear us, O Christ!

Since, therefore, revered and beloved Emperor, you have ordered your most faithful servant of God, the Abbot Waldo, that in calling my attention to the inquiries of your letter, he would ask and require a solution, as in obedience to you, he has earnestly and importunately, although gently, forced upon me an inquiry into this matter; so I send to you, through him, that your gratitude may be applied to him, for what I have solved, in a proper manner, whether willingly or unwillingly, at his urgent demand. But if, through my own neglect, anything has been improperly treated, I wish you graciously to impose on me whatever penance you think expedient. Most excellent Emperor, and not only excellent Emperor, but most pious and loving Father, I always wish you strength in our Lord.*

* The foregoing epistle of Dungal is found in D'Achery's *Spicilegium Veterum aliquot Scriptorum*—tomus x., pages 143 to 157. In the 4to edition, published at Paris, in thirteen volumes, A.D. 1655 to 1677, we are told that Mabillon collected it "e scripto codice Sanremigiano." According to D'Achery's confession, when he found some difficult passages in it, he consulted Ishmael Bouillaud, an excellent mathematician and a profound scholar, that the latter might pass his opinion on it. He wrote the following observations, which are found in D'Achery's note to the epistle in question:—

"Hæc epistola Dungali, quamvis nec perite, nec clare respondeat questioni ab imperatore propositæ, neque demonstret quæ ostendere oportuit, utilis nihilominus in eo est, quod arguat tunc temporis plures, ipsumque Imperatorum dubitasse de eo, quod a quibusdam temere et inani jactantia impulsis asserebatur, duas eclipses solis anno Christi DCCCX., factas et visas fuisse in nostra Europa, qui

According to a very prevalent opinion, this Dungal travelled into Italy after writing his epistle, and he was most graciously received by Lothaire I., who appointed him President over the University of Pavia. About this period, learning had greatly declined in Italy; but that enlightened ruler earnestly desired its revival, by establishing schools at convenient places, and by furnishing, even to poor scholars, opportunities for receiving instruction in the liberal arts and sciences. A knowledge of classical literature and science was thus afforded to scholastics. Previous to Dungal's appointment, Charlemagne had sent Joannes Albinus, an Irishman, to open

quidem ratione fulti dubitabant, cum possibile non fuerit hoc anno 810, VII. Id. Jun. Solem defecisse, aut defectum illius in Europa adnotatum fuisse. Optime ad hunc annum adnotavit Calvisius, et rectissime judicavit hanc eclipsim solis die VII. Id. Jun. ab aliquo, qui Kalendarium scripsit, prædictam fuisse, calculo ex tabulis astronomicis imperfectioribus deducto: sed non factam (addo et non visam Europæis nostris hominibus) Chronologi nihilominus, ursamque visam in suis Chronicis scripserunt, opinionem, vel potius errorem vulgi secunt. Addendum mihi videtur, calculatorem anni illius 810, in hoc hallucinatum fuisse, quod non monuerit illam eclipsim in locis lineæ æquinoctiali subjectis, aut meridionalibus apparituram fuisse, et visendam in hemisphærio australi. Non est enim possibile, ut in locis ab æquinoctiali linea paulo remotioribus intra semestre spatium linæ eclipses solæ cernantur, quod sub lineo æquinoctiali vel in locis subjacentibus parallelis ab ea non longe descriptis accidere potest: intra vero quinquemestre spatium in eodem hemisphæro boreali vel austrino binæ eclipses solares conspici quæunt; quæ omnia demonstrari possunt, utpote vera. Sed hujus Epistolæ Auctor Dungalus has differentias ignorasse videtur. Cumque pridie Kal. Decemb. ejusdem anni 810, eclipsis solis animadversa ab Europæis, priorem illam, VII. Id. Jun. factam ab Antoecis nostris et Antipodibus, aut saltem in hemisphærio australi visam fuisse asserere debuit, ut quæstioni plene satisfaceret." In the version of this epistle of Dungal, a literal translation has been chiefly adhered to; but to render it more intelligible, it has been judged necessary to depart occasionally from the obscure and prolonged continuation of too many among his sentences. The words in *italics* are for the most part superadded, to make the apparent meaning better understood.

a school or university at Pavia; and now Lothaire I., who was a nephew to that celebrated emperor, resolved to select Dungal, from the distant Scotia, to preside over his regal foundation. Lothaire had founded schools at Milan, Brescia, Bergamo, Novara, Vercelli, Genoa, with other places, and he gave the Irish scholar full jurisdiction over them.* He also published a Capitular, in which the name of Dungal occurs. Honourable mention is made of him, in connection with Pavia, and those subordinate schools. Mabillon, however, supposes the stranger, Dungal, known as the Recluse, to have spent his days in Gaul, and there to have penned a work against Claude's errors, regarding which we shall presently treat; while the learned Muratori, on the contrary, thinks the author of that controversial treatise passed the greater part of his life at Pavia, in Italy, having been engaged there in the work of educating youth.†

Claude, Bishop of Turin, having attacked the veneration due to images, in the beginning of the ninth century, an Irish writer, called Dungal, assumed his pen to defend the Catholic dogma. This defence, written in 827, was dedicated to the Emperors Louis and Lothaire.‡ The

---

* "Primum in Papia conveniant ad Dungallum de Mediolano, de Brixia, de Laude, de Bergamo, de Novaria, de Vercellis, de Artona, de Aquis, de Genua, de Haste, de Cuma." See the Capitulars of Lothaire I., as published by Muratori in his *Rerum Italicarum Scriptores*, tomus i., pars. ii., pages 151 to 153, published in twenty-five folio volumes, at Milan, A.D. 1723, *et seq.* to 1751. Muratori says, the reading "de Derthona," now *Tortona*, must probably be substituted for "de Artona." To most of the places above mentioned, he does not append further explanation, nor determine their modern denominations.

† See Muratori's *Antiquitates Italicæ Medii Ævi*, vol. iii., dissertatio xliii., pages 823, 824. This learned work, in six folio volumes, was printed at Milan, A.D. 1738 to 1742.

‡ A specimen of the Latinity of the controversial epistle, with the motives which engaged the author to write, is furnished in the opening sentence. "Hunc itaque libellum responsionis ex auctoritate ac

first editor of this tract made use of a codex, belonging to the monastery of St. Denis, on the Seine river, and which afterwards came into the possession of Paul Petavius, a Parisian senator. In this MS. the writer calls himself "a stranger," who had long before migrated to the place in which it had been written.*

This treatise, although sufficiently argumentative, while full of quotations and convincing proofs regarding the Christian practices of the early Church, and the testimonies of several ancient fathers, is yet rather diffuse, unpolished, and obscure in style.† The astronomical

doctrina sanctorum patrum defloratas et excerptas cotinentem subn, nomine et honore gloriosissimorum Principum, Christianissimorum Sanctæ Ecclesiæ rectorum, domini Hludouuici maximi et serenissimi Imperatoris, ejusque filij nobilissimi Augusti Hlotharij ego Dungalus in Dei et eorum obsequio esse dicandum componendumque deuoui, contra insanas blasphemasque Claudij Taurinensis Episcopi nænias, non quod ante jam dudum ex quo in hanc terram aduenerim, occasio mihi copiosa hac de re reclamandi conquerendique assidue non occurreret, dum dominicam vbique messem malignis zizaniis lolioque infelici horrere cernendo suspirarem, sed ne conatus nostri aërem ut dicitur verberando, incertaue pro certis adfirmando deluderentur, sub silentij diutina anxiaque observatione ora continui, mœrens dolensq; murmur multum, antiquamque contentionem de corpore Christi, hoc est Ecclesia, passim in turbis fieri, quæ quondam præcessit de capite." Dungali Responsa contra perversas Claudii (Tavrinensis Episcopi) sententias, page 903, col. 1. See *Avctarii Bibliothecæ Patrvm, Vetervm Auctorum Ecclesiasticorvm,* tomus ii., Parisiis, 1610, pages 897 to 948.

* See Mabillon's *Annales Ordinis S. Benedicti.* Tomus ii., lib. xxx., § iii., pages 508, 509. From intrinsic evidences in this tract, Mabillon shows that it was composed A.D. 827.

† This treatise was printed at Paris in 1608, by Papire Masson, and it may be found also inserted in *Bibliotheca Patruum,* tome xiv., page 199. That the work was written by Dungal, the monk of St. Denis, appears evident from an old catalogue of the books left by "Dungalus præcipuus Scottorum" to the monastery of Bobbio. Amongst the number is found, *Dungali contra perversas Claudii sententias.* From this inconclusive fact, however, some would infer a distinct Dungal to be the author of the above-named work. Again, it has been supposed that Dungal, *the Recluse,* was not likely to assume the public functions of a learned professor at Pavia. The

epistle, likewise, labours under the two latter defects. Notwithstanding an opposite opinion of the learned Italian author Muratori, most classical readers would be inclined to find fault with its style, even when approving the erudition and method of this controversial treatise. A poem, written in elegiac verses, and in praise of Dungal, was found on the manuscript from which the treatise against Claude had been printed. This has been published by Martene; and it contains the assurance, that Dungal had many disciples who were instructed by him in the Holy Scriptures. It appears to have been written by a contemporary author, and whilst Dungal was yet living.* Other poems, attributed by Martene to the Recluse, are published.† These are known with certainty to have been written at St. Denis, and under the reign of Charlemagne. In some of them the writer calls himself "the Irish stranger."

In his search among the archives of St. Remigius of Rheims, Mabillon also discovered an acrostic poem in manuscript, composed by Dungal, and in which he calls himself "the stranger." These lines were written in praise of Hildoard, Bishop of Cambray and Arras; but it is to be regretted they have not been published by the learned Benedictine.‡

We cannot find any authentic information regarding the year in which the death of Dungal occurred; nor is

latter, however, appears to have been for the most part regarded as author of the work written against Claude. This seems to be the opinion of Muratori. See *Rerum Italicarum Scriptores.* Tome i., part ii., page 152, n. 6.

* This elegiac Latin poem has been likewise published in Mabillon's *Annales Ordinis S. Benedicti.* Tomus ii., appendix L., page 726. See the folio edition of this learned work, in six tomes, published at Paris, A.D. 1703 to 1739.

† See Martene's *Amplissima Collectio.* Tome vi., page 811.

‡ See Mabillon's *Annales Ordinis S. Benedicti.* xxx., § iii., page 509.

there any certainty that he long survived A.D. 827. If, however, he must be identified with that recluse near Paris, and to whom Ebbon, Archbishop of Rheims, retired, after the restoration of Louis le Débonnaire, he must have survived to 834. Before his death, Dungal probably bequeathed a large collection of books to the monastery of Bobbio, founded by St. Columbanus. Indeed, the old index to the Bobbian MSS. states, that Dungal's collection had been presented to the blessed Columban.* The greater part of his MSS. were afterwards removed to the Ambrosian library of Milan by Cardinal Frederic Borromaeo. A catalogue of these books has been preserved by Muratori,† in his account of the contributors to the library of Bobbio.‡ This he has copied from the more ancient one, supposed to have been compiled in the tenth century.

Subsequent to the time of Dungal, the science of astronomy appears to have been cultivated by Irish scholars. A certain John has been denominated *de Sacro Bosco*,

* Referring to Dungal, Muratori says, that in his own time there was a codex kept in the Ambrosian library, but greatly worn, through age or neglect. It had been written over nine hundred years previously, "literis quadratis," and in it Dungal's name expressedly occurs, in these three hexameter lines:—

"*Sancte Columba, tibi Scotto tuus incola* DUNGAL
Tradidit hunc Librum, quo Fratrum corda beentur,
Qui legis ergo, Deus pretium sit muneris, ora.*"

Hence it would seem, that the book in question had been presented to St. Columba—that is, to his monastery at Bobbio—by a Scottish Dungal. From the foregoing lines, it has been inferred, he was a monk there living. This codex appears to have contained the lives of many holy fathers. See *Antiquitates Italicæ Medii Ævi.* Tomus iii., Dissertatio xliii., page 826.

† "Ex quo constat Monachorum certe opera et industria, non solum Sacros, sed et profanos Historicorum, Oratorum et Poetarum libros servatos fuisse." See Palma's *Prælectiones Historiæ Ecclesiasticæ,* Tomus ii., ch. xv., pages 110, 111.

‡ See *Antiquitates Italicæ,* Tom. iii., Dissertatio xliii., pages 817 to 823.

because he is regarded as having been either a native of Holywood, in the county of Down, or of Holywood, in the county of Dublin. It may be observed, there was a Jesuit writer, called Christophorus, *a Sacro Bosco*, on account of his having belonged to Holywood, in the diocese of Dublin. Such a place is known in the county of Wicklow. He died in 1626.* Joannes *de Sacro Bosco* was a philosopher, and he flourished early in the thirteenth century. By English and Continental writers, this learned man has been generally reputed as a native of Holywood, in Yorkshire, England, and a scholar of Oxford. He was also a professor of astronomy and mathematics in the University of Paris.† However, it will be seen, by referring to Harris Ware,‡ that Stanihurst and other writers state, Joannes *de Sacro Bosco* was born at Holywood, in the county of Dublin. His tract, *De Sphera*, has been often printed. Other treatises, on philosophical subjects, have been attributed to him. His *Tractatus de Sphera* formed a small quarto manuscript, as lately described in a London bookseller's catalogue. On application, with a view of purchasing it for an Irish library, the manuscript in question had been sold; nor can the purchaser be traced, even by the bibliopolist.§ It is probable, however, that many other copies of it may be extant.

There is a very curious astronomical treatise, written in the Irish language, and about the period of the fourteenth century. This imperfect manuscript forms

* Some notices of this Irish writer and of his works occur in the *Bibliotheca Scriptorum Societatis Jesu*, page 144. This folio volume was published at Rome, A.D. 1676.
† See Delambre's *Histoire de l'Astronomie du Moyen Age*, Livre ii., pages 241 to 247. Fabricius' *Bibliotheca Mediæ Ætatis;* also, *Histoire Littéraire de la France*, and M. le Dr. Hoefer's *Nouvelle Biographie Générale*, &c. Tome xxvi., page 556.
‡ See vol. ii., *Writers of Ireland*. Book i., ch. x., page 73.
§ Mr. Thomas Arthur, 45 Booksellers' Row, Strand.

only eight quarto vellum leaves; evidently only an inconsiderable portion of a very large and complete tract on the subject. Some of the leaves are so stained, that they are in part illegible; and the MS. had been written in double columns. It includes several very curious astronomical diagrams, elegantly drawn and coloured, serving, we may presume, for illustrations of the writer's descriptions. So far as a hasty examination may serve for apprehension, the present writer regards some of those diagrams as exhibiting the relative position of various planets to the earth, and especially of the sun and moon, in reference to their respective positions. Shadows are represented on the moon's surface. Altogether, this seems a most curious and learned treatise; and, fragmentary as it appears, there can hardly be a doubt, that its translation by a competent Irish scholar, with suitable comments by some accomplished man of science, must furnish exceedingly important information regarding Irish learning in the middle ages.* There is another short tract, likewise, on the time of sun and moon entering the different zodiacal signs. †

We find, in addition, a large quarto vellum MS. of forty-nine written folios, belonging to the Betham collection, in the Royal Irish Academy's library. ‡ Some tracts in it are referable to the fourteenth century. It appears, however, to have been written by various hands. It contains a *Treatise on Astronomy and on the Celestial*

* This MS. is to be found in the Royal Irish Academy's library. It is classed 23, F. 13.

† The MS. in which this brief extract is contained apparently refers to the fourteenth century. It is a small 4to vellum codex, comprising fifty-eight numbered pages, but one of these is blank. The contents are of a miscellaneous character, written by different hands, and probably at various periods of time. The ink is decayed or obliterated in several places, and many pages are almost quite illegible. This MS. is classed 23, O. 4.

‡ It is classed 23, Q. 10.

Bodies. This has been written in double columns, and on the first ten folios. Initial, traced, and coloured letters appear throughout, and to the concluding line, which leaves this treatise unfinished. It commences with a Latin opening, "Mundus ita que ut dicunt Mercurius dicitur tribus modis." Then follows an explanation in Irish, that, in a heavenly sense, the world was to be regarded in a triple point of view — viz., incorporeal, invisible, and accompanied by light. At the bottom of this page, but apparently in a different hand from that in the tract, there is a note which states, that this treatise had been written by Donnall Albanach, or "Donnell the Scotchman." But whether he was a native of Scotland, or an Irishman who resided there, may be reasonably questioned. The following ancient writers or books are mentioned in this treatise:—viz., Marsian, *De Libro Cœlo, De Mundo,* St. Augustine, St. Gregory, Bede, Ar—— (? Aristotle), Isiodorus, Basilinus, *Libro de Causis Elementorum,* Job, Faibili, Aristotle, Nisdomini, Alexander, *Exemeron,* Damascenus, Anasyagorat, Alafraganus, Albomaser or Albumazar, *Liber de Motionibus Astronomeorum* or *Astrologeorum,* Misahel, Boeta. The author thus seems to have been versed, not only in classical and patristic lore, but even to have studied some Arabic writers. The MS. treats concerning the composition of elements in a moral and in a philosophic sense; about the poles and two stars, situated in the upper and lower part of the heavens; regarding the nature of the firmament and the generation of fire; respecting the crystalline heaven above the firmament. It explains the transparency and rotundity of the firmament; views of philosophers regarding the opposite parts, and how they are compactly bound together; it distinguishes the first heaven or dwelling of the angels; the ether or fire; with the nature and form of the sphere. It describes the situation of the zodiacal signs, and especially in reference to astrology; it discusses, likewise, the double movements of planets, from the western point to the eastern point, and against the motion of the firmament, they being forcibly propelled from the time they rise in the east until they set in the west. Towards the imperfect ending, it is stated, that the Creator formed the world in a manner corresponding with the sphere, so that they should not attempt to conflict with each other. In the same MS., and on folio 34, there is a small tract, which says, that the nature of the seasons is not the same in all regions, and especially when the sun is in the quadrangular zodiac.

Even in the last century, our Irish hedge-school scribes were busily employed in preserving fragments regarding subjects of natural science. Some astronomical tables, with a tract, on the latter page of which there is a fanciful diagram representing the four elements, will be found in a MS., which at present belongs to the Royal Irish Academy.* This MS., in which it is contained, had been formerly procured by Sir William Betham. It is a folio paper volume, comprising matters of a miscellaneous character, and transcribed between the years 1789 and 1818, by James O'Horachaidh, or Hore — as he writes the name—and by James O'Farrell. It seems to have been written in the parish of Killtoome, and county of Roscommon. The name and date—"Edwd Hore, Berries, 178—" is found appended to this astronomical tract. The last figure of the date is cut from the page.

Dungal's holiness, and love for retirement, did not prevent him from prosecuting various sacred and profane studies; on the contrary, such qualities seem to have constituted a great impelling motive to urge him onward in the tranquil and earnest pursuit of science. The study of natural philosophy, and especially of that branch

---

* See pages 401 to 403. The MS. is classed 23, Q. 18.

known as astronomy, were then, and before that time, successfully cultivated in the schools of Ireland. As an astronomer, Dungal appears, in his age, to have enjoyed a well-known and justly appreciated reputation. Without desiring to parade his erudition, the humility of this devout man, and his established reputation for learning, merited the applause and recompense of a truly great prince. In Italy, no less than in France, his abilities were recognized and rewarded. Were his astronomical epistle illustrated by the comments of a competent man, possessing scientific attainments, no doubt such a task might afford him scope for remark and reflection. It may serve, also, to furnish a proof regarding the cultivation of science, and the knowledge of astronomy obtained in Irish schools, by our learned men of the eighth and ninth centuries. Early learning in any country is the test of its true civilization.

CHAPTER XXXI.

POPULAR NOTIONS CONCERNING GOOD AND ILL LUCK.

"And 'tis plased that I am, and why not, to be sure!
Since 'tis all for good luck, says bold Rory O'More."
SAMUEL LOVER.

"Your health, my friend!—till life shall end,
May no bad chance betide us."
THOMAS FURLONG.

THE observance of lucky and unlucky months, or days and nights, of omens and prognostications, of meteoric and elementary changes, of colours, dreams, and bodily sensations, the practice of sorcery and adjurations, form an almost endless concatenation of superstitions. It would be quite impossible to recollect or enumerate any very considerable portion of those various empiricisms, which have not wholly lost their influences over the opinions and acts of many foolish persons.

From the heathens are derived those vain and idle observations, which especially characterize the ignorant and superstitious. St. Paul cautions the Galatians against noticing in an unchristian sense "days, months, times, and years;"[*] while he specially inveighs against idolatry and witchcrafts, with other associated and degrading passions, which exclude from the kingdom of God.[†]

The ancients seem to have regarded some days as peculiarly lucky, and these were marked with a white stone or character in their calendars, to denote a day of good fortune; while other days were considered unlucky,

[*] Gal. iv. 10. [†] Gal. v. 19, 20, 21.

and these were noted with a black stone or mark, to signify their being destined for misfortune or mourning. Traffic, journeys, expeditions, plantings, field labours, enterprises, sailings, marriages, surgical operations, physicians' practices, were followed or suspended, according as the ancient diviners or astrologers laid down such old wives' decrees for a special day of the week or month, or for the moon's change or season.

The Irish, like the ancient Greeks and Romans, paid especial attention to lucky and unlucky days. Augustus, the pious, never went abroad on that day succeeding the *Nundinæ*, nor did he undertake any serious business on the *Nonæ*, in order to avoid an unlucky omen.* It was considered unlucky by the Irish to get married during the month of May. The ancient Romans had a like superstition against entering the matrimonial state at this period, as Ovid testifies.†

In the Highlands of Scotland, the 3d of May was called *La Sheachanna na bleanagh*, or "the dismal day." It was considered unlucky to begin any affair of consequence on that particular date.

A superstition prevailed that there were two days in the change of every moon, and which were peculiarly unlucky. These days were considered perilous for many issues, and they were regarded as being unpropitious for any undertaking then commenced. Although it would be possible to give the months and days of each month so designated, we prefer to leave many of our readers uninformed on this matter; for not only, as the poet Gray says,—

"Where ignorance is bliss, 'tis folly to be wise,"

but we consider it, moreover, as a very useless exer-

---

* See Suetonius, *Vita Augusti*, c. 92.
† " Hac quoque de causa, si te proverbia tangunt
    Mense malas *Maio* nubere vulgus ait."
                    Fastorum, lib. v.; *vv.* 489, 490.

cise of memory for either the learned or illiterate, when it cannot add to a stock of practical information.

Mariners feared to sail on Friday from their port of departure; but they always thought Sunday a lucky day for the commencement of a voyage. Whistling on board a vessel, they think, will raise or increase the violence of a gale. The Irish boatmen around our coasts show their religious faith and feeling by desiring a priest to bless every new boat or ship launched or about to sail out on the deep sea. They also ask their pastor's prayers for a safe return. They consider it a circumstance happy beyond their hopes, should a priest or religious person sail with them in their barks. This is very different in some other countries, where seamen think, if a clergyman of any persuasion embark with them, they are sure to encounter a storm or calamity.

In some places, Monday is thought to be an unlucky day, and Wednesday is not held much in popular esteem. January and May are not favourite months for the solemnization of marriage. Tuesdays and Thursdays, but especially the Sundays, are usually preferred or selected for the performance of this ceremony; and Shrove Tuesday was often remarkable, especially in the country districts, for the number of marriages taking place on that day. This may be accounted for because of Lent commencing on Ash-Wednesday, which followed; as, according to the Church's discipline, a solemn celebration of marriage had been forbidden during the seasons of Lent and Advent.

Some field-works or other occupations are supposed to be best done before the full moon; while others are regarded as only suitable for performance after its wane. Respecting this planet, the following lines are considered referable to the unlucky event of

> "Friday's moon,
> Come when it will, it comes too soon."

A growing moon and a flowing tide are considered lucky at the time of any marriage.

There are various social customs in Ireland, which are especially practised in country parts, and which are observed as a matter of courtesy and kindness. When a stranger comes into a farm-house, while churning takes place, if a hand be not given to the well-plied dash by this visitant, it is supposed the butter must be abstracted in some mysterious manner. Even the upper classes will not refuse a share in this labour, through a motive of kindliness and consideration towards the residents' feelings, and to prevent ill luck.

To pluck a fairy hawthorn tree is supposed to be extremely dangerous and rash, as it provokes elfin resentment, and bodes ill luck. Cairns and raths are respected for the very same reason; and probably to a fear of removing them, many now remain. Instances are often cited of evil consequences incurred by the leveller or desecrator of such objects.

Among the strange habits and observations of our peasantry, the following deserve to be noticed:—A horse shoe is nailed on the threshold of an Irish peasant's cabin, and cloves of wild garlick are planted on the thatch over the door, for good luck. House-leek is also thought a preservative against the destruction of a person or a cottage by fire. The throwing an old shoe after a person going out of doors, or about to undertake a journey, will insure a fortunate issue. The following couplet is often quoted, and much importance is attached to it by the country people:—

> "Happy is the bride that the sun shines on,
> Happy is the corpse that the rain rains on."

It is regarded as unlucky to find a pin with the point

turned towards you; but it is considered a lucky circumstance to find a crooked pin. A red-haired woman, if met first in the morning, betokens some unlucky accident happening during the day. It is considered lucky to see magpies in even numbers; but it is regarded as unlucky to find them in odd numbers. It is deemed unlucky to build a house on the usually travelled path, where *sheeoges* or fairies pass. The occupant of such a dwelling is said to merit their vengeance. It is thought he will suffer evil consequences, by the wreck of his property, or by the premature death of his stock. Disasters often happen to members of his family as a supposed result; and sometimes by his own maiming, or sudden decease, his children, or relatives, are deprived of necessary means wanting for their support.

Whoever breaks a looking-glass, is supposed to incur some future calamity. On this superstition, an appropriate ballad, called "The Doom of the Mirror," has been written by B. Simmons. And our greatest national poet, Thomas Moore, makes a playful allusion to the mirror, in his Irish melody on "ill omens," when the enraged beauty brushes away an insect from its surface, and moralizes on the result. Again, many remark that the upsetting of a salt-cellar, or of salt, indicates ill-luck to the person who has done it, even through accident. Many other such notices might be included; but as they are not of any real importance in extending the range of useful knowledge, our readers must be satisfied with the instances already produced.

CHAPTER XXXII.

TIR-NA-NOG.

> "Thou may'st rove
> O'er flower-painted plains at dewy morn,
> Where wave ripe meadows and the yellow corn,
> And 'mid the shades of dreamy even-tide,
> By the still waters of some wood-girt lake,
> Thy sweet contemplative repose may take,
> Watching the cygnets on its bosom glide.
> In the hot noon-tide thou canst seek the shade
> Of the cold grotto, or the sylvan glade;
> Where, through the interlacing forest trees,
> With not ungentle hand, some wandering breeze
> A moment puts aside their leafy hair,
> So that the fresh and flower-scented air
> Creeps in, and through the rich, umbrageous roof
> The gorgeous sun-rays fall upon the grass,
> Shattered by leaf and branches as they pass,
> Verdure and life inweaved like warp and woof."
>
> JOHN FRANCIS WALLER, LL.D.

BARDIC fictions, usually classed under the denomination of Ossianic or Fenian poems, are yet preserved in the Irish language; but, for the most part, these bear intrinsic evidence of their origin and composition referring to no very remote period. Doubtless, in many instances, they have been interpolated or amended by more modern Irish rhymers or transcribers. Numberless copies, with various readings, exist in MSS. belonging to individuals and to public institutions. Specimens of these compositions have been published by the Ossianic Society, founded in Dublin in the year 1853, by Mr. Hardiman, by Mr. O'Flanagan, and by other gentlemen. Most gracefully have many such fragments received English poetic expression and interpretation, through the versions of William Hamilton Drummond, D.D., M.R.I.A., Thomas Furlong, Miss Charlotte Brooke, with other writers. While illustrating a rude state of social habits, usages, and modes of thought, these remains oftentimes present interesting evidences of inventive power and graphic description. In the Irish language, such lengthened compositions were frequently repeated from memory, and transmitted in this manner from father to son, through many succeeding generations. Even in the wilds of Connemara, as likewise in the remote glens of Ulster, and through the mountain districts of Munster, such bardic fyttes are yet recited. Throughout the province of Leinster, however, these fireside poems have nearly fallen into desuetude, especially since the beginning of this present century.

The Irish, in the sixteenth century, supposed that departed souls went to the company of some heroes, living in enchanted places. Concerning those they had stories and songs. Among their heroes most commemorated were the giants Finn Mac Huyle, Osker, and Mac Oskin. These were often seen, as the people fancied. Such, at least, is the testimony of Good, the priest, who then lived in Limerick. There can hardly be a doubt, he made allusion to the fairy realms of Tir-na-nog, or the perpetual Land of Youth, supposed to lie out in the ocean, and far beyond the opening of the river Shannon. To it, the lines of Wordsworth are applicable, as seen by the peasants on our western coasts, in their visionary explorations:—

> " Yon azure ridge—
> Is it a perishable cloud? or there
> Do we behold the frame of Erin's coast?
> Land sometimes by the roving shepherd swain,
> Like the bright confines of another world,
> Not doubtfully perceived." *

* Poems—"View from the Top of Black Comb."

Mr. Bryan O'Looney has translated and edited an Irish poem on this subject, and it has been issued by the Ossianic Society's efforts.

One of the most charming English metrical descriptions, respecting this land of the immortals, is that presented in "The Gleeman's Tale," which may be found, as one of a series, in that truly exquisite poem, "The Monks of Kilcrea." Its author's modest and retiring nature has not hitherto allowed the publication of his name; but he deserves to rank foremost among the poets of his age, and, as time rolls onward, his reputation will not admit of decline. After describing the wondrous scenes to be met with in the Land of the Living, and in suitably harmonious versification, the chieftain and lady, who left earthly enjoyments and perils for those subaqueous regions of delight, are greeted thither with the strains of elfin music, and a chorus of sweet voices. How ravishing were the notes, we can have no means left us for an adequate conception; but the words of the fairies' song are glowing with fine imagery and sentiment:—

I.

" Come, dwell in our Island, come, live in those bowers,
   Which sorrow or care never gazed upon yet;
Where true love rears altars, encircled with flowers,
   The fairest and sweetest the eye ever met.
Whose skies are unclouded, whose fountains are flowing,
   With no icy chill on their soft gushings cast;
And hearts that inhabit, like the buds round them blowing,
   Bloom on in their freshness, unchanged as the past!

II.

" Here death never cometh!—here grief never enters!
   Age ne'er brings decay to the happy and young:
No time ever withers the pure joy that centres,
   In each twin-heart, roaming the rose glens among.
Here friendship ne'er changes!—here love is undying!
   And hope is still truthful, affection sincere;
Here falsehood ne'er lurks, and the summer breeze sighing,
   Ne'er kisses a cheek that is wet with a tear!

III.

" Leave to earth its frail joys—its perishing feelings—
   Its flowers that blossom one moment and fade;
Leave to earth its misgivings—its bitter revealings,
   That love is a folly, and friendship a shade!
Oh! who for such pleasures would e'er be repining?
Oh! who for such teachings a fond heart would cheer?
Leave such wisdom behind you—fresh rose-wreaths are twining,
   True lovers, to crown ye—come, dwell with us here!"

It is probable, indeed, that optical illusions may have frequently presented *mirages*, through the vapoury exhalations which are so often witnessed around our coasts. Like those appearances of water in the arid desert, and which delude the approaching traveller with hopes of immediate refreshment, the glittering city domes and pinnacles, with the coloured hills and plains of this floating island, disappear from ocean's surface, when the mariner desires to reach a harbour of safety and rest. While the Island Hy-Breasail was supposed to have been a large territory, inhabited by a race of human beings, the Island Tir-na-nog was generally regarded as the region of departed spirits, the heroes of ancient traditions. In the latter dominion, its inhabitants are hought to remain for ever young, to suffer no decay, and to enjoy lives of unalloyed happiness. It had a peculiarly bright atmosphere, and it exhibited vistas of surpassing loveliness. The old bards seem to exhaust all their powers of poetic delineation in describing its perpetual verdure, its vocal groves, its grand palaces, its soft and silent glades, its undulating hills and vales, with its lofty and majestic mountains.

This enchanting country has been described under other titles than Tir-na-nog, or Land of Youth. It has been denominated Oilean-na-m Beo, or Island of the Living; Tir-na-m Buadha, or Land of Virtues; Hy-na-Beatha, or Island of Life; Tir-na-m Beo, or Land of the

Living. Sometimes it is called the Land of Heroes, and the Land of Victories. All these terms indicate a felicity to which its inhabitants had attained; and along the western shores of Ireland various legends are yet current regarding this lovely region of the immortals.

During the twelfth century, a rumour was prevalent that, off the Irish coast, an island suddenly made its appearance one clear day, but when people approached, that moment it disappeared. At length a party went out in pursuit of it, and, having steered within bow-shot, —as Giraldus Cambrensis states—one of the voyagers struck it with a red-hot arrow, in consequence of which immediately it became stationary. This enchanted island long haunted the memory and imagination of fishermen and mariners,—especially living along the north-western coasts of Ireland,—and from the headlands of Donegal the inhabitants often assembled to discern its shadowy outlines. A general theory was held that the Fomorians, and Tuatha de Danaans, dwelt there under some magic thrall; and that adventurous or wrecked voyagers had been cast on that fabled land, where they found chieftains and warriors silent or somnambulant, being incapable of giving any information about their past, present, or future state.

CHAPTER XXXIII.

SAINT LEGENDS.

"When Patrick discoursed of the things to be,
When time gives way to eternity,—
Of kingdoms that cease, which are dreams, not things,
And the Kingdom built by the King of kings."
                                        AUBREY DE VERE.

"That tale, to me as yet untold,
Though far renown'd, do thou unfold,
In truths severely wise."
                        REV. WILLIAM H. DRUMMOND.

THERE are various legends current among our peasantry, living in the vicinity of old ruined churches and monasteries. Those usually have reference to celebrated miracles wrought by their patron saints. In many instances, such traditions have been found recorded in the yet extant acts or lives of saints. In other cases, no trace of a record has been discovered, serving to corroborate such local traditions. Many miracles, sayings, or prophecies of Irish saints have been likewise versified or related in the native language. Those, however, appear to have been clumsy and unaccountable inventions of the middle ages, or of periods far removed from the time when such saints flourished. As a specimen of once favourite popular traditions, the following have been extracted from rare works, or from yet unpublished MS. accounts. They refer chiefly to the great Irish Apostle St. Patrick, to St. Brigid, to St. Columbkille, and to other less celebrated saints.

The following legends are told of St. Patrick's infancy. While this holy child increased in years, he grew likewise in grace. His boyhood was rendered remarkable by the performance of very astonishing miracles. In Emptor Town, where he and his sister Lupita were brought up, under the care of an aunt, as Joceline, the monk of Furness, informs us, after the frost had disappeared, a certain pool or hollow swelled with water, so that it threatened the destruction of many houses. This inundation especially overwhelmed that habitation wherein the holy child lived. While all the household effects were overflowed with water, the blessed infant, being hungry, called to his nurse for bread; but she answered, that he was nearer drowning than getting anything to eat. On the instant, St. Patrick dipped his fingers in the swelling waters; and sprinkling them thrice over the spot, with a sign of the holy cross, he commanded the pool to recede in the name of the most holy Trinity. It was wonderful to see how soon the inundation ceased, while the pool or vault became suddenly dry. From his sacred fingers, to those standing by, it appeared that, instead of water-drops, sparkles of fire issued. These were thought to have dried up this inundation.

On a certain day in winter time, the holy child, being among a company of his playfellows, gathered up some pieces of ice. Carrying them home, he laid them upon the floor. His nurse then said to him, that it would have been better, and much more fitting for the season, to have brought wood for the fire than such silly play-toys. The sweet child answered wisely by saying, "It is easy for the Author of nature to dispense with its course, and to make even this frozen water serviceable for the fire." Then he laid those pieces of ice together, and after praying and making a sign of the cross over them, he blew upon them. They kindled into a fire, which cast out such flames and heat, that it yielded not only warmth, but also matter for excessive admiration to all that were present,

What else could this fire foreshow, but that the great saint should inflame the cold and frozen hearts of many, and with the word of God, breathed from his sacred soul, infuse into them the love of so potent a Lord?

One time, as Lupita, St. Patrick's sister, went to wean the lambkins from their dams, she fell upon the ground. In falling, her head struck against a sharp-edged flint, that wounded her cruelly. Many ran to see that great mischance, and among others the blessed Patrick. By making a sign of the cross on her forehead, he restored her to perfect health. In like manner did the holy child revive his uncle, after a sudden death, by making another sign of the cross over him, and by offering devout prayers for him.

St. Patrick was assigned the charge of keeping sheep by his aunt. One day, as he led them out to their pasture, a famished wolf rushed from a wood hard by, and carried away one of the sheep. His aunt, missing this animal, imputed the loss of it to her nephew's negligence, by not taking care of the flock. Patiently he supported her undeserved reproof, and he prayed to God most earnestly for the bringing back of his lost sheep. Behold, on the next morning, the wolf came and carried that sheep in his mouth! He laid this same sheep before the saint, and so went his way.

The holy child's nurse, during her sickness, had longed much for honey; but none being available, she grieved and lamented, when the holy child blessed a cup of cold water. This was instantly converted into honey. Then he gave it to his nurse. Whereupon she satisfied her longing, and perfectly recovered her health.

A nobleman who lived in Emptor Town forced St. Patrick's aunt to undergo the heavy yoke of servitude. He charged her to cleanse every day ordure from a great stable and ox-stall, where many oxen and horses had been stabled. The virtuous woman supported with great meekness this affliction, as coming from the hand of God. But St. Patrick offered his prayers to the Almighty for his aunt, when all the stalls were cleansed. So they continued for a long time, and even without any human help. This great miracle excited the admiration of all persons; and it was a chief cause why the woman was set at liberty, while the saint was held in great veneration.

The following stories are told regarding his escape from servitude in Ireland. After three days' sailing, and the winds being favourable, St. Patrick, with his companions, arrived safely on the coast of England. There going on shore, and while travelling through a solitary and barren country, some four-and-twenty days together, they began to feel greatly the extremity of hunger. St. Patrick, all this while, ceased not to preach the kingdom of heaven, and the faith of the most holy Trinity, to his heathen fellow-travellers; but they wilfully shut their eyes against the light of truth, until their very misfortunes—often the incentives to virtue—gave them understanding. Being sorely pinched with the implacable rage of famine, their leader broke out into these words,—"Thou seest, O worshipper of Christ, to what extremity we are brought; invocate then thy God, whose omnipotence thou hast so often vaunted, to the end that, tasting of His liberality, we may be incited to adore and acknowledge His Majesty." Then St. Patrick offered up his prayers to God in their behalf, when suddenly there appeared a herd of swine; and wild honey so plentifully abounded, that their present distress was at once relieved; while they were well provided against the recurrence of any future necessities. Though, for the present time, St. Patrick's companions thanked God, and held His saint in great reverence; yet this gale of prosperity and plenty was soon succeeded by an oblivion of their bountiful benefactor, and ingratitude for the singular benefit he obtained for them. While partaking of that miraculous provision, they offered victims and sacrifices to their idols, and afterwards they ate such viands. Yet of these idolatrous victims St. Patrick refused to taste, albeit he was earnestly entreated to do so; but by God's favour, he fasted twenty whole days without any kind of corporeal sustenance.

Lest the greatness of his miraculous signs or fasts should cause God's chosen vassal, St. Patrick, to be filled with pride, the Angel of Satan was permitted to buffet him. One night, the prince of darkness rushed upon the holy youth so fiercely, that he deprived him of the use and exercise of his limbs and senses. Thus did the foul fiend molest him for three whole days. The saint, in his distress, had recourse to God, his sure and sovereign refuge. Twice did he invoke, for his help, Elias, the prince of prophets. Being sent by our Lord, the holy Elias chased away that diabolical temptation, and restored the saint to the use of his senses and limbs. Both inwardly and outwardly, heavenly splendour irradiated his soul and body. Overcoming this assault of his adversary, together with some other difficulties met with during his journey, the blessed Patrick returned home to his native soil, and to the unspeakable joy of his parents. These earnestly requested him, with tears in their eyes, never to deprive them any more of that consolation which parents feel in their children's presence. Patrick, who was the mirror of obedience, of reverence, and of respect towards his parents, remained with them for awhile; but he was only undergoing a course of preparation for the great mission on which he afterwards engaged, when the Almighty called him to gather that wonderful harvest of souls, in the island of his former captivity.

In the third *Life of St. Brigid*, abbess of Kildare, as published by Colgan, we find the following recorded miracles. One of St. Brigid's nuns had been afflicted with a severe illness at a particular time, and this patient asked for a little milk; but Brigid's community had no cow to afford it, when the saint told a companion to fill her vessel with cold water, and give it to the sufferer. This order having been complied with, the vessel was found replenished with milk, and warm, as if it had been just drawn from the cow. When the sick nun tasted the beverage, she recovered. Two females, belonging to her own family, who were paralyzed, and who lived near Brigid, asked this holy abbess to visit and heal them. She complied with their request; and when she arrived, having blessed salt and water, of which those females partook, they were soon restored to health. Afterwards, two Britons, who were blind, had been conducted by a leper servant of theirs to the gate of that church, near which the saint dwelt. They asked her to heal them. She told them to enter the refectory and eat, while she should pray for their salvation. Then they indignantly said, "You heal the sick of your own family, but you neglect strangers, and attend only to prayer." She received this reproof, by meekly going out to them from the church, and taking with her blessed water. When she had sprinkled them with it, the leper was cleansed, and the blind men saw. They all praised God, and returned thanks for the benefits bestowed on them.

A woman came one day to St. Brigid, and the visitor drove a cow, with its calf, which had been intended as an offering for the abbess. But the calf strayed away in a very thick wood. Finding she could not drive the cow without it, the woman called out with a loud voice, that St. Brigid might assist her. Immediately the cow went gently with her conductor, and direct to the virgin's house. Brigid then told the woman not to feel concerned about the calf, which should follow in the traces of its dam.

Another day, when the octave of Easter had closed, Brigid said to her nuns, "Hath that beer, reserved for our Easter solemnity, been given out, for I am solicitous regarding Bishop Mel, and the guests of Christ?" The nuns replied that God would send them a sufficiency; when they brought on their shoulders a vessel filled with water to the saint, that she might bless it, according to her usual custom. Supposing it to be beer, their abbess said, "We give thanks to God, who hath reserved this for our bishop." On examination, it was found, water had been changed into that beverage mentioned by the saint.

On the morning of a certain day, as Baithen, his disciple, was going to sail on the wide sea, St. Columba of Iona told him about a monster of the deep. The holy abbot said, "Last night a great whale rose from the depths of the sea about midnight, and he will float this day on the surface of ocean, between Hy or Iona, and Ethica, or Tiree islands." Baithen, answering, replied, "I and that monster are under God's power." "Go, then," said the saint, "in peace, for thy faith in Christ shall defend thee from this danger." Baithen having received the saint's blessing, sailed accordingly from the port; and after crossing the sea a considerable distance, he and his companions saw the whale. While all others were much terrified, raising up both his hands, without any fear, Baithen blessed the ocean and the monster. At the same moment, this enormous brute, diving under the waves, never afterwards appeared to the navigators. Baithen sailed out to seek a desert in the great ocean, while he humbly asked St. Columbkille's blessing before engaging upon this perilous enterprise.

The following accounts are taken from still unpublished MSS. When St. Mochuda was in the habit of touching anything greasy with his hands, he usually rubbed them on his shoes. Having resolved on abandoning his monastery in Rathan, the saint wished to go on a foreign pilgrimage, lest he might become vain of that great character he had acquired at home. But first he went to St. Comgall, of Bangor, and told him regarding this design. After St. Mochuda sat down, and his shoes had been removed, St. Comgall said, " Come out of that shoe, thou demon." "It is not amiss that he has met you," said the devil; " because I should not have allowed him to remain two nights in any one place, for the partiality he has shown to his own shoes above those of his congregation." Thus was St. Mochuda reproved for this slight indication of vanity.

St. Brendan, son of Finnlogh, was at his church in Dubhdhoira—now supposed to be Doora, near Ennis— in Thomond. His nearest neighbour, living towards the north, was Dobharchu, from whom are descended the Ui Dobharchon—now the O'Liddys. Dobharchu had a grass field or meadow near Loch Lir. Brendan's oxen went thither to graze. Dobharchu killed these oxen, and this matter was told to St. Brendan. "If God permit," said Brendan, "may he be transformed into a real Dobharchu," —i. e., *an otter*. Some time afterwards, Dobharchu went to look at the meadow. A trout sprang up in the lake before him. Dobharchu caught it with a hook, struck a fire, and then roasted it. He next went to take a drink at the lake, into which he fell. Immediately he became transformed into an otter, owing to St. Brendan's imprecation. Dobharchu's son, Cuchuan, soon afterwards came on a fishing excursion to the lake, but his father cautioned him against this practice. Four Irish quatrains are extant which contain the metamorphosed chieftain's prohibitory admonition. The foregoing saint legends are only a few, selected from an exhaustless treasury of hagiographies and traditions.

CHAPTER XXXIV.

SPRITE FROLICS AND PECULIARITIES.

> "It seems to me these keys must ope
> The entrance to each secret cell,
> Or mossy knoll, in deep green dell,
> Wherein by day the fairies dwell,
> Awaiting till our Ladye Moon
> Hath reached in Heaven her highest noon,
> When forth they'll sally, gay and free,
> And till dawn comes, and they must flee,
> Dance their wild roundel merrily."
>
> MRS. ELLEN FITZ-SIMON.

WE are not prepared to lead our readers with us to witness the wonders of a spirit-world, nor to assure them, as Swedenborg has done his followers, that he both heard and saw all he has related and described. To deal lightly with some current popular fantasies is quite a different matter. With our lady friend, taking the fairies' key, we may unspring the lock for an instant, to have a short and passing glimpse of the midnight revellers. But trimming the magic lanthorn of fancy alone, we may hope to idealize such visions as they flit before our mental view.

With the popular Irish poet, Davis, who loved so much the history and traditions of his native land, it may be added,—

> "We'll look through the trees at the cliff and the eyrie,
> We'll tread round the rath on the track of the fairy."

Yet, while enjoying a rich prospect of scenes in our Green Island, and which must charm the eyes of every lover of the picturesque,—while lingering beside those venerable traces of antiquity, through raths, and duns, and lisses, which are thought referable to very remote times,—we should cautiously avoid inclosure within their enchanted recesses, unless as antiquaries, desiring to open some long-closed winding passage or subterranean chamber, for purposes of useful examination. Let us not disfigure, however, a single trace of former seeming or symmetry, as too many Vandal explorers' have done. For if the guardian spirits of those raths neglect to vindicate their prescriptive tenements from spoil and desecration, a sound public opinion must protect their fabled dwellings and fine landscape features from either wanton or utilitarian ravages.

Some slight variations of phrase and terminology will adapt the following old English song to the tricks of Irish fairies, who issue from their raths during the witching hours, and who disturb many a humble household with their pranks. The song is found in Poole's *English Parnassus*. It is almost unnecessary to observe, that this is the well-known ballad printed by Percy. A better copy is given from early MSS., in Halliwell's *Illustrations of Fairy Mythology*, published in 1845.

It may be observed, the sprites are represented as gregarious, when led by their celebrated Shakespearian queen. But it must be recollected, likewise, that the original of Mab may be looked for in our renowned Queen Meadbh or Meav, the heroine of Connaught. These are the opening stanzas of the "Fairy Song":—

"Come, follow, follow me,
Ye fairy elves that be
Lightly tripping o'er the green;
Come, follow Mab, your Queen;
Hand in hand we dance around,
For this place is fairy ground.

> "When mortals are at rest,
> And snoring in their nest,
> Unheard, and unespied,
> Thro' keyholes we do glide,
> Over tables, stools, and shelves,
> We trip it with our fairy elves."

If the house happened to be foul, or left in an untidy manner, with platters, dishes, or bowls scattered about, those frolicsome elves nimbly crept to the bedside where the servant maids were sleeping. Then were the unthrifty delinquents pinched on the arms and legs, while their tormentors, unheard, contrived likewise to be invisible. But if the house happened to be swept, and if its apartments were free from all uncleanness, Mab and her attendants praised and rewarded the household maid. As a token of remembrance, she was surely paid for her neatness and thrift. Every night, before those spirit revellers went, they dropped a shilling in the servant's shoe, and this the housemaid was certain to find in the morning.

On a mushroom's head, the fairies often laid their snowy tablecloth, in preparation for a banquet, spare and simple enough, if we are to believe that a grain of rye or wheat was considered a sufficiently substantial diet for the refreshment of such aerial beings. Pearly drops of dew they drank, and quaffed them from acorn cups, filled to the brim. Other viands consumed, however, do not give us an exalted idea of their delicacy of taste. Thus concludes their song:—

> "The grasshopper, gnat, and fly,
> Serve for our minstrelsy;
> Grace said, we dance awhile,
> And so we thus the time beguile;
> But if the moon doth hide her head,
> The glow-worm lights us home to bed.

> "O'er the tops of dewy grass
> So nimbly we do pass,
> The young and tender stalk
> Ne'er bends where we do walk;
> Yet in the morning may be seen,
> Where we the night before have been."

In Ireland, fairy men are more generally found to be disturbers of the household during midnight hours than fairy women. These latter appear to be better domesticated to the raths, in and around which they are usually seen. While the fairy hosts migrate, and often in military array, women richly dressed are observed among their troops. Rarely do the fairies intrude upon any Irish farm-stead or cottage, unless, indeed, it happen to lie on a direct line between two raths. Then it is said to be on their passage or route, and many peasants think it might prove dangerous to obstruct the fairies' entrance or egress. That their friendship must be secured, by civil language and decorous behaviour, is an opinion deeply grounded in the minds of our peasantry.

We have heard many strange stories regarding haunted houses. The inmates often become so alarmed, by fancying they hear unusual sounds, and see unaccountable lights or apparitions by night, that they desert such habitations. Last autumn, we recollect passing by a deserted but well-built house, two storied, and comfortably slated, while delightfully situated on one of the most romantic slopes of the Slieve Bloom Mountains, and near the Delour River. Not a living thing appeared within or without this farm-stead or its offices. On inquiry, we were informed that no family could live there, owing to ghost disturbances.

There are some Irish superstitions and customs which cannot be referred to any distinct heading, and the origin of which it might be equally difficult to define. Those fictions relating to ghosts are most numerous. The following are still prevalent in many districts of our island. A dog or horse, and more especially a mare, it is said, often sees a spirit, even when the ghost itself is invisible to a human eye. Again, it has been asserted that spirits cannot cross running water. Mortals who see them, faint away when they arrive at a house, and behold the light of a fire or candle. Ghosts are said often to give warning of approaching death to living persons.

Whoever can find fern seeds will be able to render himself invisible whenever he chooses. It is also supposed that if the root of fern be cut transversely, the initial letter of a chief's name will be found, and to him it is thought the land on which this plant grew formerly belonged. A native bard exultingly exclaims, while apostrophizing the mountain fern, in the following strain:—

"The fairy's tall palm-tree! the heath bird's fresh nest,
And the couch the red deer deems the sweetest and best,
With the free winds to fan it, and dew-drops to gem—
Oh! what can ye match with its beautiful stem?
* * * * * * * * *
"With a spell on each leaf, which no mortal can learn,
Oh, there never was plant like the Irish hill fern!"

According to a prevailing popular notion, black dogs are sometimes seen prowling about lonely places during the late hours of night. It is said, likewise, that witches are often found metamorphosed into rabbits or black cats, and chased by huntsmen under such disguises. Various hobgoblins assume very undefinable shapes in the imaginings of the peasantry; but their particular classification or functions must be reserved for elucidation by others, better versed in spirit lore than the present writer.

CHAPTER XXXV.

IRISH FORTUNE-TELLERS, AND PREDICTIONS.

"Gif Chanticleer's ta'en frae the roost whare he craw't,
Or horse, kye, or sheep, frae the pasture-fiel' ca't,
My head I'll bestow ye, if I dinna show ye
The leuks in a glass, o' the loun that's in faut:
Or else, if ye cleek up, an' toss my delft teacup,
If danger or death's near, the gruns plain will shaw't;
By cuttin' o' cartes, folk, an' no' by *black arts*, folk,
O' past, present, future, I'll read ye a claut."—JAMES ORR.

"To read the future, and if now my fire
   Is not as once it shone o'er thee, forgive!
I but foretell thy fortunes—then expire;
   Think not that I would look on them and live."—BYRON.

"For still he marks, with steady, fearless eye,
   The rising dawn, no mortal can defer;
Whose splendours shall relume the darkest sky,
   And guide the bondsman, from his prison drear,
To home, love, liberty,—to all his soul holds dear."
                                  JOHN D'ALTON.

FORTUNE-TELLING is too generally in vogue among young and credulous persons. Sometimes the future is predicted for them by ignorant or cunning deceivers, and by means of cup-tossing, card-cutting, or other similar absurd devices. Many fragments of prophecies, in prose and verse, attributed to Irish saints, are to be found written in our native tongue. These are yet recited, and they have attained wide-spread popular approval. The composition of several, however, may fairly be assigned to periods subsequent to special events, described with apparent historic accuracy. Numbers of these prophecies contain intrinsic evidences of having been prepared to serve some local, clan, or political purpose,

Pretended prophetic deductions from spells and divinations prevail among the humbler classes of our peasantry. However, they are fast waning into almost utter oblivion and contempt. In Vallancey's time, he tells us, that the Wise or Knowledgable Men in Ireland were called *Tamans*, and that he knew a farmer's wife, of Waterford county, who had lost a parcel of linen. She travelled three days' journey to one of those persons, who lived in the county of Tipperary. He consulted a black book, and assured his visitor that she should recover her linen. The robbery was proclaimed, and a reward was offered for the recovery of this stolen property. It returned into the owner's possession, not because of the reward offered, it was thought, but owing to the *taman's* efforts.

Englishmen and Scotchmen, as well as Irishmen, were entertained and duped by the issuing and publication of many strange predictions. In Queen Elizabeth's day, Ezekiel Grebner wrote a *Book of Visions and Prophecies concerning England, Scotland, and Ireland*. These are very curious, and they have been published in a small volume, so late as 1861. These prophecies, it is said, had been presented to the Queen. At a later period still, Elias Ashmole wrote the *Life, Times, and History of William Lilly, from the year 1602 to 1681*. It contains a portrait. Lilly wrote a work which was published in the latter year, and it is intituled, *Strange and Wonderful Prophecy; being a Relation of many Universal Accidents that will come to pass in this year, 1681, according to the Prognostication of the Celestial Bodies*. This formed a quarto tract, and it has a rude woodcut on the title-page. Various other similar productions were largely circulated; while at the present time, the gipsies, and even more fashionable pretenders to the gift of prophecy, have cheated credulous people in all the different ranks of social life.

Islain Ceallmhuin, the fortune-teller, or, literally, "the humble oracle," was a person to whose predictions much importance had been attached by the young and unmarried. This pretender to a foreknowledge of future events was generally a female, who led a sort of wandering life. She made occasional rounds, through a pretty considerable district, over which her reputation prevailed. Such, especially, was the case in the southern parts of Ireland. But in the northern province, men followed this vocation. We find in Charles Gavan Duffy's spirited ballad, entitled, "Innis-Eoghain," allusion made to these seers, supposed to have been gifted with the Highlander's prophetic "second sight." They are there designated "spaemen," tantamount to "diviners." The women fortune-tellers of the north are called "spaewives;" and these were usually consulted by foolish young people, on the probabilities or future contingencies of a married life. They were supposed to have had supernatural knowledge respecting family secrets, which they often acquired by very ordinary means; and thus they were enabled to direct or predict, as occasion served, for those credulous dupes that sought their counsel. To such practices, we find reference made by James Orr, in a little volume of poems, published at Belfast, in 1804. One of these compositions is entitled the "Spaewife," and set to a popular northern air. It is written in the Ulster or Scottish dialect. The concluding verse, already cited at the head of this chapter, gives us the prevailing notion of a spaewoman's peculiar profession. The author of these *Poems on Various Occasions* dates his dedication from Ballycarry, and intimates that he is an unschooled mechanic.

Towards the close of last century, and also in the beginning of the present, a certain roving character, called the prophecy-man, was often hospitably entertained in

Irish cottagers' and farmers' houses. He was supposed to be well versed in all ancient traditions of the country, and especially able to explain or unravel many of those prophecies referred to Saints Patrick, Brigid, and Columbkille, or to other Irish saints. Such effusions were generally versified in the native tongue, and evidently had their origin in times long subsequent to the English invasion. Many of these were also fabricated during the dark period of our penal days, when discontent and disaffection were deeply and widely spread among Irish Catholics. At this period of depression, although the liberation of Ireland from English domination was anxiously expected, yet the hero destined to achieve this result was thought to be some foreign general or potentate, then engaged at war with the ruling power. The revival of the Jacobite or Stuart cause was often the subject. Under some dark allegory or figure of speech, the late Emperor of France, Napoleon Bonaparte, was frequently regarded as Ireland's future deliverer, until the great defeat at Waterloo, and his subsequent captivity in St. Helena, completely destroyed such illusions.

The prophecy-man's usual predictions regarding Ireland were, that although her night of sorrow may have been long and dreary, a time of happiness and of liberty should come, before the last day. The stones shall cry out on the road side first; and, according to a gloss of the commentator, this has happened already, as our milestones speak of distance to the traveller. Fishes will be frightened from the strand and sea shore. Would the unproductiveness of our coast fisheries, and the arriving or departing steamers, account for the supposed fulfilment of this latter prophecy? A woman shall stand on the highest hill in Ireland, for three days, and shall not see a man. The cows will not be milked. The harvest shall not find reapers. The ghosts of murdered persons shall walk through the country by noonday. The last battle will be fought on the banks of Loughail, or the Lake of Sorrow, in Westmeath. For three long days, a mill in the neighbourhood shall be turned by a stream running with human gore. Then the Irish must drive their enemies into this lake, where all shall be drowned. Such a prophecy, however general in the main features, is referred for accomplishment to different localities in Ireland.

During late political ferments in this country, predictions of a nearly similar nature were industriously circulated among the people. Well-known names and localities were introduced, and circumstantial particulars were related; but so clumsily had these matters been concocted, that they were too ridiculous to obtain acceptance, even by the most credulous. The progress of education is already so far advanced, that popular taste and intelligence in Ireland require more rational, interesting, and creditable efforts, on the part of writers and publishers, to satisfy the growing demand for amusing themes and solid information.

THE END.

CPSIA information can be obtained at www.ICGtesting.com
Printed in the USA
243522LV00004B/39/P